Imagining Inclusive Society
in Nineteenth-Century Novels

Imagining Inclusive Society in Nineteenth-Century Novels

The Code of Sincerity in the Public Sphere

Pam Morris

The Johns Hopkins University Press
Baltimore and London

© 2004 The Johns Hopkins University Press
All rights reserved. Published 2004
Printed in the United States of America on acid-free paper
9 8 7 6 5 4 3 2 1

The Johns Hopkins University Press
2715 North Charles Street
Baltimore, Maryland 21218-4363
www.press.jhu.edu

Library of Congress Cataloging-in-Publication Data

Morris, Pam, 1940–
    Imagining inclusive society in nineteenth-century novels : the code
of sincerity in the public sphere / Pam Morris.
        p. cm.
    Includes bibliographical references (p.   ) and index.
    ISBN 0-8018-7911-6 (acid-free paper)
    1. English fiction — 19th century — History and criticism. 2. Social
classes in literature. 3. Literature and society — Great Britain —
History — 19th century. 4. Mass media — Great Britain — History —
19th century. 5. Great Britain — Social conditions — 19th century.
6. Social values in literature. 7. Sincerity in literature. I. Title.
PR878.S6M67 2004
823'.8093552 — dc22   2003018758

A catalog record for this book is available from the British Library.

To Tessa and Lilias, who make the sunshine

Contents

Acknowledgments

The final stages of research and writing for this book were funded by the Arts and Humanities Research Board (UK). I am most grateful for their support. An earlier version of chapter 3 appeared in *Nineteenth-Century Literature* 54, no 3 (© 1999 by the Regents of the University of California): 285–307; an earlier version of chapter 5 appeared in *ELH* 68 (2000): 679–98. I am grateful to the editors of those journals for permission to include some of the material. I am also indebted to the reader of my manuscript for the Johns Hopkins University Press, whose incisive comments helped me to bring a firmer shape and more rigorous articulation to my ideas. The invaluable expertise and undaunted patience of the staff at the National Library of Scotland make it always a pleasure to work in Edinburgh.

In the process of writing this book, I have been fortunate in benefiting from more support, friendship, advice, and critical feedback than I can possibly acknowledge. Special thanks are due to the generous and always stimulating group of colleagues I work with in the Research Centre for Literature and Cultural History at John Moores University: Timothy Bewes, Matt Jordan, Brian Gibbons, Berthold Schoene, and Tamsin Spargo. I have been most lucky, too, in the students I have taught at John Moores: their intellectual and political commitment ensures that academic work is never merely academic. In particular, I could not imagine this book being written without the unfailing enthusiasm and scholarly knowledge offered by my colleague and friend, historian Helen Rogers. As always, Liz Allen and Jeannette King have listened patiently and responded reassuringly to my thinking about this project from beginning to end; their confidence in its outcome was the gift of friendship that kept me going. It is a pleasure to acknowledge the kindness and support of Regenia Gagnier, Joseph Bristow, and Nancy Armstrong. Regenia's solidarity is unstinting and was offered when most needed. Joe's incisive response to various drafts encouraged me to find a more integrated approach for combining literary criticism with cultural history. Conversations with Nancy during the two years that she was visiting professor at the Research Centre for Literature and Cultural History inspired me with fresh perspectives and taught me to think in terms of a long nineteenth century. Deficiencies in the finished work are all my own.

Books are written in a space that traverses the always fictional boundary of public and domestic worlds. My family is my best space. Vicky and Adam and Audrey have made it a place of laughter, optimism, and joy, and, because they are the future, they make me take history seriously. Tessa's coming irradiated the beginning and intervening period of writing the book, and Lilias came in time to illuminate the final phase. Colin over long years has held both the space and me together with good humor and unfailing love. This book is his as much as mine.

Part I / Introduction

CHAPTER ONE

Imagining Inclusive Society, 1846–1867

Theoretical Perspectives

In 1834, John Stuart Mill observed of his fellow countrymen that "they revolve in their eternal circles of landlords, capitalists and labourers, until they think of the distinction of society into those three classes as if they were one of God's ordinances not man's" (*Monthly Repository* [1834], 320). Less than thirty years later, in 1859, he was struck by the opposite tendency: "Formerly, different ranks, different neighbourhoods, different trades and professions, lived in what might be called different worlds; at present, to a great degree in the same" (*Works*, 18:274). Mill's recognition of a radical shift in social relations conveniently encapsulates my fundamental claim that in the relatively short span of time encompassed between those two comments, a remarkable transformation of public consciousness, practices, and institutions occurred. From an almost unquestioned acceptance of social hierarchy as a natural order, there evolved, within just two decades, a general perception that in future, society would have to be ordered upon principles of inclusion.

Mill's response to the inevitability of an inclusive society was, like that of many of his contemporaries, ambivalent and complex. His rational ideals encompassed belief in democratic processes as both the means and the right of individual citizenship. Yet the prospect of what he envisioned as mass mediocrity filled him with dread. My use of the neutrally descriptive term *inclusive society* aims to allow conceptual space for the whole spectrum of Victorian people's imagining that brought about the transformed view of social relations. This ranged, on the one hand, from a utopian glimpse of egalitarian community to, at the opposite end of the scale, a sense of threat from an encroaching, amorphous mass culture. It is probably fair to say that for many the latter was the more prevailing response.

The importance of the Reform Bill of 1832 for this transformation in social imagining was symbolic rather than practical. It marked the formal recognition that birthright and landed property could not remain the exclusive prerogatives for national leadership and political citizenship. In the immediate term, however, there was little change in the substance and distribution of power. Indeed, the 1832 Reform Bill is now recognized by historians as an attempt "to repair and restore the systems of the past," and, certainly, the first post-1832 government, like all previous administrations, was composed largely of the nobility (Price, 13).[1] In real terms, it was in the 1840s, with the mass national platform of Chartism and with the modern politics of extraparliamentary campaigning developed during the struggles over the Corn Laws, that a new, inclusive social order began to be imagined as realizable, necessary, or inevitable. The repeal of the Corn Laws in 1846 marked the first political defeat of the landed ancien régime, and Chartism constituted the first nationally articulated claim to political citizenship made by the laboring population. For this reason, I locate the mid-1840s as the crucial initiating moment when inclusiveness changed from being an abstract political notion and became part of public consciousness as a practical problem of critical immediacy. Evolutionary theory, during the 1850s and 1860s, consolidated a general recognition of the inevitable movement of society toward complexity and massification, an acceptance formalized in the 1867 Reform Act and its extension of suffrage to a large part of the male working population. These two decades from 1846 to 1867 saw the emergence of the modern senses of the term *public* as both state provision, bureaucracy, and regulation and as a transformed public sphere dominated by modern mass media. During this period, too, the commodity culture of mass production began to transform notions of taste and social aspiration and to provide new disciplinary mechanisms of social ordering and exclusion.

I am far from suggesting that these two decades should be understood as constituting a new, self-contained epistemic regime. Rather, I see them as part of a long, uneven trajectory of historical imagining that begins (insofar as origins are ever more than convenient fictions) with the struggles against absolutism at the end of the seventeenth century and continues into the present. Yet I am claiming that the concentrated period from around 1846 to 1867 was characterized by a particular energized intensity that transformed perceptions of what constituted the social formation. By the end of the 1860s, most people had imaginatively come to comprehend a modern mass culture and to see themselves, necessarily, as participants within that proliferating aggregate.

I believe that nineteenth-century novels can provide unique insights into the collective act of imagination that produced a modern perception of social reality. In this sense, I share Mary Poovey's understanding of "history writing and textual analysis as facets of a single enterprise" (*Making a Social Body*, 1). My approach to this enterprise is much indebted to the rich and complex writing on nineteenth-century formations produced by cultural critics like Poovey, Catherine Gallagher, and Nancy Armstrong,[2] whose understanding of textual dynamics as processes of ideological fissure and consolidation, contestation and legitimation, is the insight underlying my discussion of the novels in this study. Like such critics, I read nineteenth-century fictional texts as part of a discursive continuum or network, while recognizing that literary forms and genres are distinctive signifying practices. My aim is to extend the scope of their cultural analyses by focusing upon the problem of social inclusiveness, rather than difference and division. It goes without saying, however, that the goal of social inclusion is predicated upon the problematic of what is perceived as other and alien; in particular, the working class and women, during the period under consideration, were excluded categories exerting pressure for a reformulation of the political nation. One advantage of approaching the fiction written during these two decades — major years of novelistic achievement — from the perspective of social inclusion is that it redresses a critical tendency to overidentify the nineteenth-century novel with domestic ideology.[3] As I show in later chapters, women writers like Charlotte Brontë, Elizabeth Gaskell, and George Eliot are concerned with women's agency in the public sphere as much as with women's private moral influence. Indeed, the novels I discuss need to be recognized as constituting a distinctive and ambitious political tradition of fiction, a tradition that consciously and responsibly participates in public debates and contention.

Strikingly, all of these novels figure, within their narrative structures, cultural transformations from one social and political order to another. Formally as well as thematically, they all plot a movement from one kind of social world to another that is quite differently organized. I argue that novels were active in generating new discursive modes that facilitated transformations of social relations from hierarchy to massification. Furthermore, they are undoubtedly complicit with the shaping and legitimizing of a perception of subjectivity that initiated new mechanisms of class distinction and repression that dovetail with capitalist consumption. Yet the novels also provide alternative and, at times, even utopian perceptions of inclusiveness as genuine community and democracy. In turn, this multifaceted dialogic participation in processes of imagining mass society produced intrinsic innovations to the formal structures and verbal codes of the novel as a genre. As John Plotz says, "One of the abiding merits of literary analysis is that it can uncover not simply a single pervasive ideology, but a buzz of discord within a single text" (12). Yet to render that buzz intelligible, it is necessary to recognize the other voices that make up the discursive web within which a text is responding. For this reason, I attempt to resituate each novel within as fully realized a discursive context as is feasible, reading it in close association with periodicals, political journalism, and essays. A further benefit of such an approach is to reveal just how interactive nineteenth-century novels were with newspaper and periodical publications.

Poovey's *Making a Social Body: British Cultural Formation, 1830–1864* focuses upon a similar although somewhat more extended time scale to that of my study. Her project in that book also has a close bearing upon mine. She describes her "task" as that of recovering "the process of forming" that eventually produced "the appearance of a single 'mass' culture" (1–2). She argues that the groundwork for this was laid in the three decades covered in her essays, pointing out that "this process of homogenization has not received as much attention recently as has the history of internal fragmentation" (2). The term *homogenization* stakes out the field of interest to Poovey and demarcates the different emphasis of my enquiry. Poovey is concerned with the technologies of aggregation and the protocols of knowing that derived from emergent and residual epistemological domains in the early nineteenth century. These technologies and protocols facilitate the process of abstraction whereby differences of class, gender, region, and race are homogenized into a mass consumer culture. By contrast, I am concerned with heterogeneity and inclusiveness — with the instabilities of difference within sameness. Even in modern mass societies, differences remain crucial, at once a means of political control and constitutive of individual identity. Yet diversity also exerts a constant threat of undoing both political- and self-cohesion. My aim, then, is to track the process of forming a collectivity of difference. I want to map the problematic and the politics of imagining social distinctions within aggregation. What is involved when self-identity or group identity is required to merge conceptually and materially with otherness? Rather than abstraction, I am interested in the embodied response of those living at the moment when this challenge was first felt.

The inclusive society that began to be realized, imaginatively and materially, in the mid-nineteenth century would most likely have been referred to as English by those living south of England's border with Scotland and as British by those to the north, but, as Linda Colley demonstrates, nationalism was not a crucial issue in English-Scottish relations at that time (129–40). Only the Catholic Irish were regarded as dangerously other and beyond the pale. I must emphasize, however, that the focus of my study is not the formation of either a British or an English national identity. I am concerned with the prior problem of what was actually involved in imagining social inclusiveness as an aggregated identity. This book's title, *Imagining Inclusive Society in Nineteenth-Century Novels*, acknowledges indebtedness to Benedict Anderson's groundbreaking account in *Imagined Communities: Reflections on the Origins and Spread of Nationalism* of the economic, productive, and cultural forces that underlie the modern conception and materialization of nationhood in general. Like Anderson, my aim is to analyze the problems, the discourses, practices, and institutions that brought into being a new way of understanding social collectivities. It is in society as an inclusive aggregate that I am interested, rather than in the making of any one specific national identity. This is not to deny the immensely powerful contribution of national rhetoric and rituals, and the conquest of an empire of "others," to the process of consolidating a sense of a unitary social formation.

Where I differ from Anderson is in preferring the phrase *imagining inclusive society* to *imagined communities* since the latter begs many of the questions I wish to ask. In the first place, Anderson's use of the past participle suggests a rather seamless and painlessly completed process of assimilation. I use the term *imagining* to stress the always-uncompleted process of collectivity. Any imagining of identity — individual or group — is fraught with difficulty. The perception of one and same is under constant pressure to unravel into many and other. Working against centripetal pressures for massification and conformity are equally powerful centrifugal mechanisms of division and distinction. Social exclusion, in the twenty-first century, remains an issue arousing intense, often destabilizing political and cultural responses. In Britain specifically, nationalism, regionalism, racism, and a growing underclass of the socially deprived foregrounds the precariousness of any achieved sense of social cohesion. The novels written during the middle decades of the nineteenth century can provide still fresh and valuable insights, unavailable elsewhere, into the moment when the issue of inclusiveness forced itself with new and urgent immediacy upon the collective imagination.

As already indicated, I prefer the term *inclusive society* to that of *community*. The former does not prejudge the kinds of social relations involved, whereas *community* carries with it ideological claims of a rather utopian nature. The nineteenth-century movement toward inclusiveness and away from formalized hierarchy was certainly threaded with emergent discourses of egalitarianism. Yet, crucially, there evolved new ways of understanding and ideologically managing continued massive inequalities of economic, social, and cultural capital. *Community* also elides issues of leadership and locations of power. Latterly, cultural studies, influenced by New Historicism, has tended to think of power as everywhere and nowhere, operating in capillary form through discursive disciplines. I have no wish to return to a "great persons" tradition of history, but it seems a bit too trusting of national leaders to allow them to slide so completely out of the frame. My study aims to rethink the relations of leaders to masses and to recognize more precisely the material interconnections between power and wealth, on the one hand, and, on the other, the social exclusion of those perceived as bodies, rather than persons.

In locating bodies as the focus of disciplinary regimes and mechanisms of exclusion, I am drawing upon Foucault's invaluable work in this area, especially his earlier, more empirically based texts, but also upon the later essay on governmentality. Where I disengage from his perspective is in its tendency to totalize a carceral regime, extending seamlessly across the boundaries of public and private, state and individual. I am also suspicious of the remythicizing of power, particularly in his studies of sexuality. Although I focus upon a short critical period of two decades, I locate this moment within the context of what historians like Richard Price see as the long nineteenth century, in the sense of recognizing an active continuity of Enlightenment concerns and discourses (1–16).[4] The shift from a religious and naturalized belief in inequality to an ideal of democratic inclusiveness is an unfinished project of eighteenth-century Enlightenment. Yet undeniably, that project carried within itself the specifications for new forms of distinction and control. Adorno and Horkheimer's analysis of the insoluble link between functional rationalism, consumer capitalism, and mass conformity remains the classic text for any account of the formation of inclusive society. Yet while accepting the main thrust of the Frankfurt school's critique of the Enlightenment, I wish cautiously to retain some of Habermas's political optimism as to the possibilities of community as consensual solidarity.[5]

One way of avoiding the closure of Foucauldian epistemic regimes and the pessimism and lack of futurity of the Frankfurt school is to utilize Cornelius Castoriadis's insistence upon the creative, contingent, and collective production of social reality. He writes, "The imaginary of which I am speaking is not an image *of* [anything already existing]. It is the unceasing and essentially *undeter-mined* (social, historical, and physical) creation of figures/forms/images, on the basis of which alone there can ever be a question *of* 'something.' What we call 'reality' and 'rationality' are its works" (3). The Athenians did not discover democracy, Castoriadis claims, they made something new — a social and political reality not previously existing. I would suggest that, in the same undetermined or rather overdetermined way, people in the nineteenth century brought into being the idea and the substance of a new social formation: they began to imagine and materialize the discursive modes, the social practices and institutions of an inclusive society. It was and is an immense collective undertaking. Certainly, the innovative discourses, practices, and institutions of inclusiveness refashioned mechanisms of class repression and exclusion, yet that should not blind us to what is at stake in this transformed way of imagining collective human existence.

Castoriadis argues that society transforms and produces itself imaginatively as it responds to perceived problems: "Society constitutes itself by producing *de facto* answers to these questions in its life, in its activity. It is in the *doing* of each collectivity that the answer to these questions appears as embodied meaning" (147). I identify three "problems" coming into general visibility in Britain during the middle decades of the nineteenth century that gave impetus to the process of imagining society as an inclusive collectivity. Although for methodological reasons of clarity and for empirical reasons I locate each "problem" within a separate decade, I should stress the overlapping, uneven, continuous, and contingent ordering of these issues. I am not tracing three orderly linear narratives of cause and effect: as I hope to show, the bundle of concerns that I identify with each one of these three "problems" and their corresponding three "answers" is inseparably entangled with and produced by the others. An anxiety over leadership and a relocation of legitimacy in relation to a new concept of "the people" came to the fore during the Chartist and Corn Law crises of the 1840s; during the 1850s there was pervasive concern over the limits and nature of "the public" both as a collective identity and as institutionalized state; and in the 1860s fears at the prospect of embodied mass culture surfaced sharply.

Following Castoriadis, these "problems" can be mapped onto associated "answers," or "emergences": the emergence of popular leadership as charismatic performance of "sincerity"; the emergence, within a transformed public sphere, of a public code of sincerity; and the emergence of a visualized hygienic body. I must insist again that although distinguishable in this way, these are not separate phenomena. All three problematics are interlinked by recourse to what I define as codes of sincerity, charisma, and visuality, although these codes are differently inflected, depending on whether they are considered in the context of leadership, the public, or the embodied mass. As I shall show, the novels in this study both contribute to the elaboration and imposition of these codes and bring a sharp critical focus to bear upon them.

Political Leadership for an Inclusive Society

From the 1840s to the 1860s, political leadership in Britain underwent a dramatic change. The visible trappings of power as charismatic endowment of sovereignty were refashioned into a form of domestic charisma with only indirect and underplayed linkage to power. The erosion of an unquestioned belief in the mystique of birthright due to the accumulating effects of eighteenth-century rationalism, growing sources of wealth other than land, and the American and French Revolutions brought a crisis of sovereignty. Legitimacy, no longer sanctioned by the absolutism of religion and tradition, had to be resituated on a secular basis that could sustain, at least formally, claims to universality: the collective generality of "the people." As Eric Hobsbawm comments, after the revolutionary era "whatever else a nation was, some element of citizenship and mass participation or choice was never absent from it" (18–19). Ideas of what constituted sovereignty relocated from a basis in a predominant sense of a territorial state composed of large, landed properties to a notion of the nation as people and population. However, these two terms — *people and population* — are by no means synonymous, and slippage between the two allowed governments and classes a fortuitous degree of ambiguity to underwrite their claim making.

Foucault argues that during the eighteenth century a new form of governance evolved that was "essentially defined no longer in terms of its territoriality, of its surface area, but in terms of the mass of its population and its volume and density" ("Governmentality," 104). This conceptual shift of legitimacy from land to population involved also a radical transformation of the spatial and visual imagination by means of which the nation is produced to consciousness as an existing location. The nation, thought of as a territory of land and landed properties, is visualized in terms of expansiveness, spaciousness, grandeur, and freedom.

The land itself in this perception is endowed with a kind of charismatic aura. The nation conceived as a territory of bodies, of population, is imagined in terms of density, closeness, and proximity. These opposing visual images of the nation are well exemplified in the contrast between a typical landscape painting of the eighteenth century, with its sense of extensive, classical vistas receding into a far distance, and a characteristic nineteenth-century painting like Frith's *Derby Day*, with its jostling crowds. This visualized, imaginative contrast between spacious-ness and closeness formed a pervasive ideological subtext throughout the nine-teenth century that was drawn upon in a wide variety of discursive contexts. Frequently it evoked a nostalgic desire for a gracious lost world of the nation in some more essential, purer incarnation. For example, in conservative patriotic rhetoric, throughout the nineteenth century a hale and mythic yeoman, sym-bolizing an old England of the shires, was opposed to the stunted, disease-spread-ing inhabitants of the crowded urban slums.

The shift of sovereignty from land to people entailed a revisioning of the imagined and actual relations of leaders to power. Leadership, understood pri-marily in terms of defending territorial sovereignty, is idealized in traditional celebrations of military force and conquest. Military heroes figure the might of the territorial nation and, as such, share in the charismatic visual grandeur of territorial imagining. In this case, the distance of the population from the mag-nificence of the leader is a measure of the greatness and power of the country in comparison with its external rivals or enemies. Leadership thought of in terms of population, however, must become twofold to overcome the inherent contradic-tion articulated in the slippage between population and people. The internal security of the state requires the imposition upon the population of power in regulatory forms, rather than the external use of force in military conquest. Paradoxically, though, leadership must also gain hegemonic consent and recog-nition as being in some way representative of the people. Leadership in an inclu-sive society must produce its own legitimacy. This entails a reorganization of the domain of power: leaders become more visible, but power is disassociated from specific persons and any specific class. Power melts from public visibility. When the nation is thought of in terms of territorial integrity, power is imagined pri-marily as military might and is identified with the military leadership of the nobility as great landowners. As I argue in the next chapter, the duke of Welling-ton was the last national leader to embody this unified patrician ideal.

When population becomes the focus of the imagined nation, the public domain of the state is much expanded, with the effect that power becomes less locatable and identifiable. The active power of the state flows increasingly through the impersonal bureaucracies and machinery of modern government. These dispersed routines of power are disassociated from any identifiable class or individual leader. Yet, despite this, actually existing power in terms of economic and cultural capital remained remarkably stable over the time when a ranked society was evolving into a class formation. The reification of the state and the mystification of power in mass societies serves a useful purpose, perhaps, in diverting attention from unaltered structural inequality. I argue in chapter 5 that Foucault is in danger at times of contributing to the mystique of impersonal and therefore unaccountable power, even though he suggests that the state may be "a mythicized abstraction, whose importance is a lot more limited than many of us think" ("Governmentality," 103).

While power slides out of view, visible leadership is resituated in the public sphere as the location of representation. Leadership, in an inclusive secular society, becomes a problem of representation. Divorced from the visualized grandeur of territorial sovereignty, how are leaders to refashion charisma? Edmund Burke recognized this default starkly: without the "decent drapery" of time-sanctioned reverence, "a king is but a man" (171). Burke's language acknowledges the strongly visual and physical aspect within all imagining of sovereignty. It is Hazlitt, however, as "the first great fame theorist of the modern age," who offers a more prescient understanding of the functioning of power in mass politics.[6] He uses his essay on *Coriolanus* as a way of speculating on the problems of power for an inclusive social order. At the center of the essay is a pessimistic perception that power visualized as conquest and might exerts a compelling charismatic force over the collective imagination. By contrast, he says, "the cause of the people is indeed but little calculated as a subject for poetry: . . . it presents no immediate or distinct images to the mind" (5:348). Hazlitt recognizes that the authority of leadership is dependent upon a strong element of visual identification on the part of the population. Yet he can find no charismatic figuring of power based in the concept of egalitarianism to oppose to traditional images of power as heroic conquest. The aura of "pride, pomp and circumstance," he admits, "has more attraction than abstract right." Hazlitt understands that a society that identifies itself in imaginary ideals of conquest is more likely to produce its social relations in terms of authority and obedience than in those of democratic consent. According to Linda Colley, Britain, as a nation, forged its identity largely by means of wars against France (1). It can be argued that myths of military prowess retain, to the present, a forceful hold on the national imagination of what constitutes

British citizenship that works against any identification with an egalitarian figuring of civic responsibilities and rights.

Hazlitt was speculating on the problems of imagining popular leadership before the event. At the other end of the nineteenth century, Max Weber (1864–1920) and Sigmund Freud (1856–1939), from their different epistemological positions, were also concerned to analyze the qualities that constituted a compelling authority over the masses. Despite the distance of their historical and ideological perspectives, all three writers understand charisma as a force of visual, physical presence that compels an immediate and total recognition in beholders. Hazlitt sees that "the cause of the people" is denied glamour by its basis in abstract rationality. Weber argues that charisma gains its power as the projection of an inexplicable plenitude and grace, exceeding the bounds of reason and utility. A charismatic leader, according to Weber, repudiates the exigencies of economics, personal danger, and habitual custom (Eisenstadt, 48). In this sense, the quality of charisma is closely associated with an ideology of "disinterestedness." A charismatic leader spurns individualistic self-interest and self-preservation. Equally, his or her followers identify self-forgetfully with the leader's values and aspirations. In projections of charismatic leadership, people gain an imaginary perception of their own ideal collective identity, for which they are prepared, ultimately, to sacrifice themselves.

In his essay "On Narcissism," Freud offers a way of understanding the psychic mechanisms underlying the compelling attraction of charisma as a quality of disinterestedness. In doing so, he foregrounds the key role of specular identification. He points to the fascination exerted by the visual presence of replete bodily grace as exemplified in the "charm of certain animals which seem not to concern themselves about us, such as cats and the large beasts of prey" (83). They "compel" us, Freud says, by providing a visual spectacle that projects a "narcissistic consistency . . . a blissful state of mind—an unassailable libidinal position which we ourselves have since abandoned" (83). Such self-consistency conveys a semblance of charismatic disinterestedness: there is nothing beyond libidinal plenitude to form an object of desire. Freud explains the general attraction to such visual spectacles by suggesting that they unconsciously recall the experience of primary narcissism: the infant's imaginary sense of omnipotence and plenitude and the autoeroticism of libidinal drives. To meet the reality principle, the child objectifies this narcissistic grace of self-completeness onto an external social ego-ideal. This ideal then becomes the displaced location of imaginary repleteness since, Freud argues, individuals never fully relinquish the early infantile phantasy of self-perfection: "What he projects before him as his ideal is the substitute for the lost narcissism of his childhood in which he was his own ideal" (88). The survival of that experience of imagined self-empowerment and plenitude depends upon the degree to which an identification is forged between self and ego-ideal. Freud describes a double mechanism at work here: loving an idealized other, insofar as it involves the experience of non-self-sufficiency, lowers the lover's own self-regard. In contradistinction, being loved by an other as an ideal raises the loved one's self-esteem (93). Thus the person who is able to identify their self wholly with a generally venerated social ideal increases their own self-esteem through a sanctioned self-love that regains the libidinal repleteness of primary narcissism.

Given the strong specular element in the functioning of narcissistic identification, this double mechanism works clearly to the advantage of those fortunate individuals who are endowed with elements of physical grace. They have the means of identifying themselves with social ideals of beauty, while their grace and bodily repleteness irresistibly charms from all beholders the tribute of admiration and love. In contrast, those who, for whatever reason, have failed to objectify their primary narcissism in an object in which they can reencounter an esteemed self are in search of an ideal to love. For them, an other's narcissistic self-sufficiency and self-empowerment represents an irresistible attraction. In this way, "unassailable" narcissism charismatically attracts ever more devotion and submission to itself simply by the force of blissful, apparently effortless consistency with an ideal. Such self-repleteness constitutes the semblance of "disinterestedness"; apparently lacking nothing, the self has no self-interest to pursue. In contrast, those who submit to the charisma of a powerful plenitude, loving it as an unattainable ego-ideal, continually diminish their already depleted self-regard. This perpetual sense of lack can easily be construed as the semblance of self-interest. Such individuals are driven by a continuous sense of their own insufficiency. Freud notes the dangers of "a crippling dependence" in those whose self-depletion compels the awed submission that creates charismatic power. He argues that insight into this mechanism of narcissistic identification offers "an important avenue for the understanding of group psychology," whether that be of family, class or nation (96).

This understanding of charismatic attraction as visual presence, able to convey the semblance of a replete disinterestedness, goes some way to explaining the aristocratic class's continued hold upon power long after the formal rejection of birthright as the prerogative for rule. Those born into self-sufficient privilege could claim to offer a leadership above self-interest. Furthermore, the appearance of distinctive physical grace is largely a matter of good health, deriving from diet and exercise, clothing that is stylish and sumptuous, and a confident public bearing. Such physical repleteness, for most of the nineteenth century and argu-ably well beyond, was primarily the endowment of aristocratic birth. In addition, the nobility had the advantage of a long assumption of identity in terms of a quality that Habermas calls "publicness." By this he means that the dignity and authority of rank were staged visually as presence in terms of grandeur of de-meanor, sonority of tone, formality of language, and ease in the performance of ceremony. Habermas claims that this theatrical "publicness" seems to make "something invisible visible" (*Structural Transformation*, 7). Outward material signs are taken as utterly reliable indicators of an inner grace: "The noble man was authority inasmuch as he made it present" (13). Indeed, within the logic of publicness, physical embodiment is the only way in which charismatic grace can be signified. To make any verbal claims to such authority is already to admit the lack of such repleteness: hence to be "self-interested."

Habermas argues that in the transformation of the public sphere in the nine-teenth century, there occurred a "refeudalization," in that visibility and public-ness were again foregrounded in the context of the movement toward a more heterogeneous, inclusive social formation (*Structural Transformation*, 195). The theatrical elements that the nobility brought to public leadership gave them headway in the stakes of popular leadership.[7] The expanding commodity culture of industrial capitalism was quick to invest in the increasing visuality of public life. Yet although, by the middle decades of the nineteenth century, these two forces had combined to consolidate the importance of the stylistic representation of leadership in the public sphere, something further was required. Commodified style and publicness needed to find a new ideal to that of military conquest around which to crystallize: an ideal that incorporated the ordinariness of the people with the charismatic. Popular leadership ideally projects some commonly recognized human attribute but irradiates it with compelling, larger-than-life charm. This quality was found in a performance of "sincerity" as a public inter-pellative code based upon an assumption of common human interiority. Having entered the public sphere, the concept of leadership was remade in the transfor-mations to that sphere. Nineteenth-century fiction participated in that public refashioning of leadership in a variety of ways. All of the novels I discuss articu-late a recurrent concern with the qualities of leadership required of both men and women. Novelistic representation, more than any other discursive form, explores the compelling qualities of visual attraction. In *Shirley*, *Henry Esmond*, and *North and South*, a code of sincerity is considered as a discursive style capable of transcending the contesting interests of exclusionary public spheres.

The Transformation of the Public Sphere and the Code of Sincerity

During the 1850s, the term *public* recurred within an expanding range of discourses. Then, as now, the different meanings of this word in different contexts were not always distinguished. What was seen by some as the tyrannous encroachment of the state into the properly private domains of housing, health, employers' responsibilities to workers, and education was demanded by many reformers as the requirement of public health, public order, and public provision. In these arguments, the opinion of "the public" was authoritatively claimed for all perspectives. What this indicates is the difficulty of making any categorical distinction between the public and private domains; the boundaries between the two are permeable and shifting. What can be claimed more confidently is that the expansion of the public domain of the state into the domestic and everyday lives of increasing numbers of the population was instrumental in materializing a sense of belonging to a collectivity. Furthermore, a new articulate class of professional state officials — statisticians, medical men, public health experts, lawyers, and teachers — were prominent in asserting claims of authority based on a disinterested ethic of public service. This points to another complexity involved in the term *public* in its actual usage. Habermas distinguishes his ideal public sphere of enlightened opinion from the sphere of state power. Yet, with the professionalization of the state from the middle of the nineteenth century, some of the most powerful and adept voices shaping public opinion were those of public officials. Moreover, as Harry Boyte claims, too much emphasis on the purely discursive nature of the public sphere neglects the agency, action, and skills that citizens, women as well as men, bring to public life (340–55).

The many commentators on *The Structural Transformation of the Public Sphere* recognize that Habermas does not always distinguish rigorously enough between his sense of the ideal potential of an informed rational forum of all private citizens and the actually existing public sphere that developed in conjunction with capitalist production and bourgeois wealth and confidence in the eighteenth century. Habermas's brief and rather unsatisfactory comments on the omission of women and popular politics from his account have led to productive work by other scholars. The extent of women's exclusion from and participation in the public sphere has been the subject of detailed empirical research. Recent studies have also stressed the contested nature of the public sphere from below, from regionalism, as well as from women.[8]

While accepting this sense of the greater complexity of the constitution of the public sphere, I want to reconfigure Habermas's account further by arguing that there were two major transformations of the public sphere during the nineteenth century, rather than one. I recognize the first as taking place around the 1840s and into the 1850s and the second as initiated around the late 1860s. The first comprised a struggle to bring into practical reality the universalism that was only an abstract ideal of the eighteenth-century sphere: the inclusiveness of all voices in the population. The second transformation constituted a rejection of that ideal of inclusiveness and effected the permanent division of the public sphere into the popular sphere and a sphere of cultural distinction. Two closely related processes, part of the long nineteenth century's continuity with eighteenth-century Enlightenment, structure these transformations: the establishment of a new discursive code of sincerity to facilitate collective sociability, and a new way of understanding human nature as individual interiority.

Habermas's eighteenth-century "blueprint" of the public sphere is that of a free forum of informed communication in which private people come together as a public to engage in debate over moral, legal, civic, financial, and aesthetic matters of general concern, making public use of their reason (*Structural Transformation*, 27). Essential to this ideal of "the public" was the bracketing of actual differences of status, wealth, and power in formal deference to the notion of a universal human nature. Habermas concedes that "the public sphere of civil society stood or fell with the principle of universal access" (85). The enabling medium for this universalism was the elaboration of a public discursive code of civility that replaced the deferential discourse of the court. Habermas sees this code of tact as stemming from the interpersonal relations of the private sphere that fostered a concern with what was "purely human" (48). Yet, since the discourse within the private, domestic realm was interpersonal, speech was always orientated to an audience. Richard Sennett's idealizing description of the public culture of the period in *The Fall of the Public Man* (1974) shares many similarities with Habermas's account of the eighteenth-century public sphere. Sennett's "fall" constitutes the postlapsarian decline of an Enlightenment public ethic of civility and a consequent loss of balance between public and private life. Sennett argues that civility as a public performative code drew its efficacy from an integration of the public and private, yet it was based upon a very different understanding of human nature to that of modern individualism. Sennett claims that a perception of identity as publicly formed and based on performative civility gave way during the nineteenth century to what he calls the intimate vision of identity as distinctive interiorities. He aligns this shriveling of the public with Lionel Trilling's suggestion, in *Sincerity and Authenticity* (1972) that modern culture has moved from the more public value of sincerity to the self-concerned, internalized value of authenticity (29).

In contrast to the modern individualistic understanding of identity that focuses upon the distinctive qualities of a unique or authentic sensibility, both Habermas and Sennett recognize that the eighteenth century saw human nature as transpersonal and nonindividualized. Sennett argues that "before the nineteenth century, the realm close to the self was not thought to be the realm for the expression of unique or distinctive personality; . . . The peculiarities of individual feeling has as yet no social form because, instead, the realm close to the self was ordered by natural, universal human sympathies" (89). Neither Habermas nor Sennett pay much attention to that central eighteenth-century concern with "sympathy," but a brief consideration of some of its vicissitudes throws light on the ultimate inadequacy of the public code of civility once it came under pressure to transform the abstract notion of universal access to the public sphere into a material reality of divergent voices.

For philosophers like David Hume and Adam Smith, as well as for readers and writers of sentimental novels and the periodical press, the natural human sympathies constituted the basis of sociability. They were the universal force that produced social cohesion and underwrote interpersonal moral relationships and public civility. As such, "sympathy" was not construed in any individualistic sense. Adela Pinch notes that in the writing on sentiments or passions from Hume to Austen, there is a general tendency in all authors to characterize feeling as transpersonal (3). Typical of this view is Hume's claim in his earliest work, *Treatise on Human Nature*, that "the passions are so contagious, that they pass with the greatest facility from one person to another, and produce correspondent movements in all breasts" (605). It was this belief in a harmonious alignment of human sympathies that made possible the bracketing of social differences within the public code of civility. Adam Smith gives perhaps the most optimistic description of this ideal of sociable civility in his *Theory of Moral Sentiments*. He writes: "The great pleasure of conversation and society, besides, arises from a certain correspondence of sentiments and opinion, from a certain harmony of minds, which like so many musical instruments coincide and keep time with one another" (337).

The references in this passage to harmony and instruments keeping time with one another seem to point to a grand impersonal scheme of human order. It was probably such sonorous phrases that led one eighteenth-century reader to claim that Smith projected sympathy as "a general principle, like that of gravity in the natural world" (quoted in Mullan, 43–44). Despite this, the passage from Smith quoted above reads much more like an empirical description of the specific cultured sociability shared by a like-educated, polite social class enjoying the leisure and benefits of private wealth. Recognition of this cultural specificity underlying universal claims accounts for a vein of unease and ambiguity that runs through eighteenth-century thinking on civility and sympathy. A further problem was the anxiety aroused by the notion of the "contagious" nature of sympathy. When understood as the medium of an urbane harmony of sentiment, as described by Smith, above, natural sympathies were believed to be the necessary underpinning of the social fabric. Yet contagious sympathies could equally be understood as the divisive passions of factionalism and the collective turbulence of the mob. John Mullan claims that any eighteenth-century description of how sentiment, sympathy, or articulacy of feeling "hold the promise of unfettered communication must refer also to how this prospect . . . is often remote, oppositional, and even despairing" (25–26).

The point of fracture in eighteenth-century accounts of sympathy is always that at which the rules underwriting the public code of civility have to be extended to incorporate a more inclusive and heterogeneous model of sociability. The logic of Lockean empiricism, with its sensationalist understanding of consciousness, moved inevitably toward a perception of psychological individualism. Roy Porter argues that for his followers, like David Hume, Adam Smith, and the third earl of Shaftesbury, the further implication of Locke's thinking was the prioritizing of interiority: "Heretofore profoundly suspect, subjectivity was now being tentatively validated" (163). It is significant that Hume's early optimistic notion of sympathy as contagious was abandoned in his later writing and replaced by the concept of utility. It is no longer sympathy that holds society in harmony, but rules that are for the benefit of all. What this implies is that social order ultimately requires the disciplining of divergent interests that cannot be harmonized by any flow of shared sensibilities. Adam Smith's *The Theory of Moral Sentiments* was influenced by Hume's work, but Smith's analysis of natural sympathies is more complex and more skeptical as to their harmonizing function. Smith places the inevitability of divergent points of view and interests at the center of his account of sympathy. It is not the spectacle of sentiments per se—as, for example, the sight of someone in tears — that produces instant contagious compatibility of sentiment, Smith argues, but the belief that the feeling expressed is justified by the cause. If we discover that the feelings exhibited stem from a cause that would evoke the same response in ourselves, then we experience sympathy: "To approve of the passions of another, therefore, as suitable to their objects, is the same thing as to observe that we entirely sympathise with them" (16).

Smith's analysis of sympathy moves a considerable distance from that of Hume's "contagion." In Smith's account, a universal, impersonal human nature has become a more static, residual element; what is foregrounded is the question of the reasonableness and genuineness of the underlying individual motivation. Smith has moved much closer to making sympathy, fellow feeling, dependent upon recognition of what we might call sincerity. He writes, "Frankness and openness conciliate confidence. We trust the man who seems willingly to trust us. . . . The man who . . . invites us into his heart . . . seems to exercise a species of hospitality more delightful than any other" (337). During the eighteenth century, the term *sincerity* retained strong intonations of its seventeenth-century religious meaning to denote inner conviction of faith.[9] It was not until the nineteenth century that the usage became predominantly secular. Even then, it continued to evoke implications of inwardness that are less apparent in the more eighteenth-century term *frankness*, which tends rather to describe outward manner.

The first usage of the modern conventional term *Yours sincerely* for concluding a letter is given in *The Oxford English Dictionary* as 1817. The convention came into being to demarcate a newly perceived social space within the public sphere midway between formality and familiarity, or intimacy. As such, it indicates a changing perception and a changing actuality of public relationships. Discursively, it implies a formal egalitarian recognition of mutual interpersonal regard and confidence, making no reference to relations of hierarchy or subordination. Practically, the need for the new form suggests a growing area of social interaction that was structured neither deferentially nor upon purely familial or private contexts. By the end of the eighteenth century, the public discursive code of civility, based in actuality upon a restricted class identity, was under increasing strain due to the expanding, more socially diverse nature of the public sphere. In the novels of Jane Austen, the proper meaning and demarcation of "civility" constitutes a major theme and a location of ideological struggle, whereas "sincerity" is not a central issue in her work. From the 1840s onward, however, "sincerity" as a mode of public discourse can be seen as a predominant novelistic theme frequently figured in oppositional terms to a discursive code of civility.

As studies like those of Charles Tilly, Nicholas Rogers, John Plotz, and Geoff Eley have shown, the 1840s marked the point where the public sphere was transformed by the explosive pressure upon it of heterogeneous social voices: those of the organized working class, those of self-made industrial entrepreneurs, and, by the end of the decade, by the writing and claims of women. In this context, a public performative code of sincerity came into being to mediate the discursive struggles of public debate. Whereas the code of civility bracketed difference by means of an abstract ideology of universal human nature, the code of sincerity rests upon and sustains an ideology of individual interiority. It posits the inevitability of divergent interests and perspectives, but implies a formal consensus that differences can be transcended by mutual trust and respect for another's motivation. This is the assumption underlying the convention of "a frank exchange of views" to describe tough political bargaining. Rather than universal human nature as the grounding of sociability, the concept of sincerity propagates an ideology of human interiority that is mutual to all but individual to each.

By this means, the code of sincerity facilitates an interpellative mode that is both grammatically plural and yet operates at an intersubjective person-to-person level. As such it is able to interpellate the collectivity of "the people" as simultaneously one and same and different and many. There is an egalitarian potential within this discursive mode that came to the fore within the public sphere in response to the transformative pressures of the 1840s. Both Brontë and Thackeray recognize, in *Shirley* and *Henry Esmond*, respectively, that the code of sincerity is an enabling transpersonal medium of community and sociability. Yet, importantly, they also show that the ideological functioning of the code is likely to be far less utopian. In practice, the code facilitates the operation of "manipulative sincerity" to exploit the egalitarian promise of selfhood held out by the ideology of individualism.

In the first place, the discursive performance of sincerity was popularized by political leaders who fashioned themselves within the public sphere upon this new egalitarian ideal. The charismatic projection of sincerity has become the dominant mode of modern mass politics. The social efficacy of a performative code of sincerity, for those who seek power by means of a popular mandate, lies less in its capacity to *actually* mediate divergent conflicts of interest than in the flattering and insinuating interpellative gesture it offers of mutual confidence and shared regard. For those within the population who are effectively marginalized by lack of economic and cultural capital, the proffered invitation into community, into a relationship of egalitarian trust, is powerfully compelling, glossing over as immaterial continued divisions and inequalities. In that sense, the code of sincerity, as practiced, is frequently manipulative, and even duplicitous.

In addition, the expansion of speculative capitalism in the second half of the nineteenth century required the elaboration of a persuasive public rhetoric of confidence. The code of sincerity was tailor-made to meet this new ideological need of maturing capitalist finance and production. For these reasons it is absolutely essential to recognize that the code of sincerity I am proposing here as coming to dominate the public sphere from the 1840s onward was always public and performative. It is a discursive mode that is formally egalitarian, nothing more. Just as the code of civility could provide for speech and behavior that was actually very uncivil, so, too, the code of sincerity could be utilized, and doubtless often was, to utter great insincerities: that indeed was part of its manipulative political and commercial utility.

More fundamentally, the utopian potential for community implicit in a public code of sincerity was always undermined by the notion of disembodied interiority upon which it is formally based. The universalism implicit in the code of civility allowed for the abstraction of humanity from any corporeal actuality. The open access that formally underwrote the public sphere was based upon the impersonality of print as medium of communication. Yet, as Michael Warner claims, "the rhetorical strategy of personal abstraction is both the utopian moment of the public sphere and a major source of domination" (377–401). Warner argues that while the bourgeois public sphere discursively declines any recognition of embodiment or corporeal presence, this negativity actually privileges a "universal" subject that is white, male, educated, and propertied. Warner goes on to note the contradiction between the construction of disembodied subjects within the rhetorical mode of the public sphere and the public visuality of consumer capitalism that puts bodies on display everywhere and seeks endlessly to differentiate them.

If we consider this insight from the perspective of the transformation of the code of civility into the code of sincerity around the middle of the nineteenth century, just as mass consumption gets under way, then that contradiction becomes endlessly productive. The code of sincerity foregrounds human interiority as transcending corporeal differences and inequalities. Yet although this interiority is universal to human kind, it is far from homogeneous; instead, it is based upon and privileges the notion of inevitable differences and individual distinctions. Mass production, paradoxically, offers the means of displaying this inward distinctiveness in the form of individualized personal taste. Bodily needs are elaborated into desires that display "personality." Taste within this ideological perception is neutered of overt political content. The code of sincerity articulates an ideology of egalitarian sameness (interiority) founded upon unique differences, while mass consumerism offers the notions of "choice" and "taste" based upon the same dualism of a coexisting one and many. Together, these two forces of performative, often manipulative, sincerity and consumerism bring about the second transformation of the public sphere and an ideology that excludes some people as distasteful bodies.

Before turning to this second change, it will be useful to indicate the various ways in which nineteenth-century novels actively participated in the transformations of the public sphere. The complex psychological representations of the protagonists of nineteenth-century novels have long been recognized as making a major contribution to Victorian liberal individualism, with its moral regard for unique and complex subjectivities. For this reason, it needs to be stressed that the novels I discuss are more thematically concerned with sincerity as a public mode of discourse than as a personal attribute of interiority. In addition, by means of narrative voice they contribute to the elaboration and popularization of a code of sincerity within the public sphere. Yet the later novels, *Romola* and *Our Mutual Friend*, also show a prescient insight into the way diverging ideologies of sincerity would function to divide the public sphere by the end of the century.

Plotz has argued forcefully that novel writers were fully aware of the contested nature of the public sphere, their works supplying "evidence of a previously undescribed tussle for the right to define public speech and action" (3). Plotz maps the way in which literature contested the discursive force of the crowd. Ultimately, he sees this as a defensive strategy to reinforce the boundaries of sanctioned bourgeois private space as the site of personal inwardness. In contrast, I attempt to demonstrate the creative interaction of novels with other media like journalism and political essays. The fiction I discuss responds positively as well as defensively to the shifting status of novels within the expanding territory of public debate and the increasing commodification of cultural life. What is more, in the writing of Brontë, Gaskell, and Eliot, novels form part of the transformative pressure to admit different perspectives and voices. Far from supporting any defining distinction between a "feminine," private, domestic realm and a "masculine," public sphere, these writers challenge the gender-specific boundaries of public discourse and public agency. I shall claim that novels provide imaginative insights into the utopian potential of genuine community based on a public code of sincerity, while, at the same time, they foreground its manipulative force.

Furthermore, as Peter Brooks has pointed out, nineteenth-century realist fiction is characterized by an unprecedented focus upon the visual, and in particular upon the visual representation of the body (28, 29). From this perspective, novels are deeply implicated in the second transformation of the public sphere in the latter decades of the nineteenth century and with the refiguring of the body as site of class distinction and exclusion. In this aspect of its imaginative work, the novel, as Plotz suggests, is closely involved in reconstituting a spacious inwardness or sensibility as an individualized territory distinctively set apart from the embodied plebeian crowd (190). Commodity culture brought about an increasing uniformity of appearance in terms of clothing. Fashionable gowns were quickly copied and reproduced for a mass market. A paradoxical response to this growing uniformity of appearances was the elaboration of a new ideology of human nature: instead of being a universal attribute of humanity, interiority was reformulated as occupying a highly differentiated scale of evolved cultivation. A person's position on this evaluative spectrum was indicated by particularities of appearance, ever more finely detailed, read as utterly reliable signifiers of individual taste, refinement, and sensibility. Novels, in the way that characters were visually represented, played a particularly influential role in identifying the physical attributes of the body with the sensibility or lack of sensibility of the soul. Carlyle's *Sartor Resartus* (1833–34) proposes itself as a theory of clothes as "emblems of the soul" (56). Most nineteenth-century novels subscribed to this belief.

Embodied Masses and the Second Transformation of the Public Sphere

By the 1860s, the inevitability of some form of mass society was becoming generally accepted. Evolutionary theories consolidated a resigned or fearful belief that the social organism, just as much as the individual biological creature, was caught up in processes of change that could not be resisted. Herbert Spencer argued that "Progress, therefore, is not an accident, but a necessity. Instead of civilization being artificial, it is a part of nature; all of a piece with the development of the embryo or the unfolding of a flower" (*Essays*, 1:58). Evolutionary discourse also exerted a major influence upon the way in which an impending mass order was imagined. At the center of this imagination was the corporeal physicality of actual bodies, and especially the bodies of the working-class poor. Mass society was imagined above all else as an embodied mass. The dominance of corporality in the imagining of mass culture was a decisive factor in the further transformation of the public sphere and in the consolidation of a new visual classifying (class-ifying) code of human nature and social reality. Bodies, within this process of imagining, constituted a complex system of signification ranging from experientially encountered bodies to various degrees of abstraction and figuration: signifying bodies, engulfing bodies, brutish bodies, class-ified bodies.

Increasing urbanization brought a qualitatively as well as quantitatively new apprehension of massification to nineteenth-century city dwellers. The population of London topped one million around 1800 and, as Plotz notes, its inhabitants mingled more frequently upon the streets than those of most other European cities (1). Chance encounters with quite diverse kinds and classes of people were commonplace, as was the experience of self amid a crowd of unknown others. As the century progressed, railway stations, exhibitions like the Crystal Palace, concert halls, and department stores greatly increased the opportunities for encountering others as proximate bodily presences. Plotz shows graphically the ways in which early-nineteenth-century literary texts register both the pleasures and the terrors of the experience of anonymity in the urban crowd. Significantly, pleasure is more associated with a crowd that is clearly demarcated from the self, as in Wordsworth's friendly intercourse with crowds during his time in revolutionary France. Such encounters serve to strengthen a perception of self-identity through difference. In contrast, the experience of crowds in London, where there is no easily rationalized recognition of otherness, is more likely to cause a radical anxiety at threatened loss of self-identity. The boundaries of self seem to give way before the unfixed, orderless chaos of sheer agglomeration.

Nevertheless, signifying crowds could prove to be as disquieting as those whose anonymity was randomly encountered. The mass platform of the Chartists during the 1840s articulated a very clear political demand on the part of the collective laboring population for inclusion within the body politic. The "repertoire of gestures" developed within this new form of mass contention articulated a dual message. The organization of a large, numerical movement on a national scale, the deployment of mass marches, and huge meetings at which bodily discipline was carefully maintained were all intended to express the rational and determined readiness of working people for active and equal participation in national life. On the other hand, the massification of such numbers of bodies always entailed, as an underlying subtext, the potential threat of the sheer physical power of that corporate strength. Plotz's brilliant analysis of Carlyle's *Chartism* demonstrates the way Carlyle refashions those two elements of political articulation and the power of numbers within Chartism's mass platform to conjure up discursively a completely revisioned laboring population as poor, dumb, physical brutes, their "clamoring" but an inarticulate cry for strong government.

Although Carlyle was bitterly opposed to the "dismal sciences" of utilitarianism and political economy, the emphasis upon the poor as physical bodies was initiated within the discourses advocating first the new poor laws of 1834 and, during the following decades, the public health measures required by urban sanitation and housing in response to the mortality and devastation of cholera and other contagious diseases. It was within this discursive formation that a figuring of the body, particularly the massed body of the poor, as uncontainable and engulfing came to dominate the imagination. Gallagher has noted how "the body came to occupy the centre of a social discourse obsessed with sanitation, with minimizing bodily contact and preventing the now alarmingly traversible boundaries of individual bodies from being penetrated by a host of foreign elements, above all by the products of other bodies" ("Body versus Social Body," 90). It was particularly the bodily excesses of the poor that were graphically conjured up before the visual imagination of the well-to-do by advocates of reform. What was constantly reiterated was the gross fleshliness of the poor in terms of disease, parasites, vermin, filth, waste, and sexuality. The prevailing perception deriving from all of these visualized aspects was of spillage, proliferation, swarming, and swamping numbers. The physical appearance of the poor during the nineteenth century was necessarily devoid of specular charm: undernourished, underwashed, deformed by accidents, stunted by chronic disease, the laboring poor could easily seem to the delicately cultivated so grossly physical as to lack a fully human sensibility. Throughout much of this discursive formation on urban slums and spawning pauperism, there is a figurative spatial or territorial subtext that opposes population, as crowding proximity and proliferating, engulfing sameness, to distinctiveness, spaciousness, and distance as cultivated sensibility.

In *Oliver Twist* (1837), the young Oliver compares the nightmare image of the starving inhabitants of slum tenements to the dead rats lying in the gutter. Public health discourse initiated the visualized imagining of the laboring poor as brute-like in their physical, bodily existence. Carlyle refashioned and further disseminated the dumb-brute analogy. Evolutionary theory gave it the respectability and authority of science. Indeed, evolutionary theory went a step further: it denied the poor, along with other races and women, the capacity for a fully human nature, now understood as the interiority of sensibility. Focus upon the physical body as a signifying presence was intensified in the heated debates as to the possible animal origins of humanity and by speculations as to the relative positioning of different classes and races upon an evolutionary scale that ranged from brutes to cultured civilization. Popular journalism invariably contained illustrations depicting physical attributes like facial features, shape of skull, posture, and bone structure. Just as societies were seen as evolving from the most simple and primitive collectives to the complexity of European, industrial mass cultures, so individuals could be ranked from dull, insensate physical organisms to highly complex, cultivated, spiritual sensibilities. Spencer accounted for the divisions of wealth, employment, and status in society purely in terms of gradations of the different social classes upon a biological evolutionary scale. On this imaginary scale, bodily manifestations became signs of proximity to brutish origins, while bodily refinement was a measure of cultured distance from such debasement.

In this context, the code of sincerity underwent ideological modification. In the first transformation of the public sphere during the first half of the nineteenth century, a code of sincerity was opposed to that of civility as undercutting the exclusionary, class-based formality of cultivated "tact." The code of sincerity promised a more direct and immediate expression of opinion, point of view, and interest in the egalitarian assurance of an intersubjective recognition of and respect for the other's mutual but different interiority. From around the middle of the century, however, the notion of sincerity began to be separated out from that of interiority. Sennett has traced the way public performances in the new concert halls and theaters of the nineteenth century disciplined spontaneous expression of feeling. "To sneer at people who showed their emotions at a play or concert became *de rigueur* by the mid-nineteenth century," he claims (206). He quotes a French writer's cultivated amusement that "right here in the 19th Century, there still exist primitive creatures who are pushed to the incontinence of tears by the unhappiness of some stage heroine" (206). Direct, "sincere" expression of feelings is here linked to uncontrolled bodily excess and the absence of cultivation or sensibility. This negative association of immediacy of emotional response with lack of cultivation was reinforced by Darwin's claim in *The Expression of the Emotions in Man and Animals* (1872) that man shared with other animals a system of involuntary muscle action that revealed feelings. Interiority, as measure of the evolved cultivation of a full humanity, therefore, had necessarily to be distanced from direct emotional expression and from any bodily gestures that indicated impassioned feeling. Sensibility increasingly became identified with disinterested distance, dispassionate judgment, and refined outward manner; the discourse of "I feel" was replaced by the discourse of "one feels." From within this discriminating perspective, the only acceptable form of sincerity became that of a detached, modernist skepticism and irony.

The cultural effect of this rejection of a code of sincerity, with its formal recognition of a common human interiority, was the radical division of the public sphere into a popular realm and a realm of distinction. The predominant discursive mode of the latter became that of irony and "disinterestedness." The interpellative efficacy of this performative code is the invitation it proffers of entry into an imagined distinctive community that defines itself against the constituting otherness of a popular mass culture. Within that popular realm, the code of sincerity continues as the communicative medium of the mass media, politics, and interpersonal relations. The social effect of this division is to literalize Carlyle's reimagining of the laboring population as dumb creatures. The disciplinary mechanism operating here is the reverse of Foucault's confessional subject. What is produced are subjects perceived as lacking, and self-perceived as lacking, the interiority of a fully cultivated humanity. The division of the public sphere produces an evaluative separation out of two discursive registers: the code of sincerity and the code of cultivation — the former involved and personal, the latter distanced and impersonal. Both are the means by which people express opinions and judgments and make claims, but, by the end of the nineteenth century, only the latter mode was accorded prestige and legitimacy in the national public sphere.

Cultural norms especially dominate those who have no access to their acquisition. People whose speech operates only within the personal register are, as Pierre Bourdieu shows, frequently silent or at a loss when asked to express opinions or judgments in a public or formal context (398, 414). Sincerity no longer implies the basis of a common interiority as a shared attribute of human nature. Interiority now strives to be recognized as uncommon, an index of cultivated distance from corporeal origins. The most poignant aspect of Dickens's representation of Bradley Headstone in *Our Mutual Friend* is Headstone's deadly sense of the damaging social worthlessness of the impassioned speech in which he tries to assert his personal worth (387–88). Speech in this sense had become a treacherous medium that could reveal an uncultivated lack of distance between sentiment and corporeal existence. As Darwin had claimed, even brutes express emotions.

The expanded commodity culture of the late nineteenth century was the final factor in consolidating bodies within a new classifying system, establishing a complex code of visual protocols for placing people in their place. The ideology of personal taste and choice facilitated an identification of outward appearance with an inner sensibility or with lack of this fully cultivated humanity. The multiplying possibilities of consumer preferences brought into being an ever more finely nuanced system for coding and classifying bodily appearance and style. Regenia Gagnier, in *The Insatiability of Human Wants: Economics and Aesthetics in the Market Place*, shows how the shift within economics from the focus on labor and productivity in the first half of the nineteenth century to a focus on consumption in the last decades led to an aesthetic perception of culture and individuals. To use *Our Mutual Friend* again as fictional illustration, Dickens shows in that novel how sweat, the respected signifier of honest labor in the early part of the century, has become the shameful stigma of Headstone's irremediable closeness to brutish origins. That fear of bodily manifestations as indicative of a classifying lack of distance from corporeal existence has become the ever more productive driving force of commodity marketing. The charismatic body has become that which signifies its gift of grace and plenitude by disavowing all taint of the body. The disciplined hygienic body, purchased with commodities, leisure, and an education not available to all, has become the price of full inclusion in the social collective. The visual classification of bodies within an ideology that erases corporeal necessity—the commonness of hunger, fatigue, labor—has become the most powerful mechanism of exclusion within modern "inclusive" social orders.

As I have indicated briefly throughout this chapter, novels are implicated in multiple ways in the transformations that brought about a repositioning of class inequality from birthright to bodies. The naturalizing of social status in familial lineage was reinscribed for a formally egalitarian political collective within the inherent inequalities of sensibility as measured by distance from the corporal. Nineteenth-century realist novels foregrounded the visual and helped to consolidate a belief in the identity between a person's bodily appearance and their individual interiority. Yet fiction offers a discourse more consciously aware of the power of physical attraction and repulsion in social relations than can be found in any other discursive form. Novels are shameless about admitting the irresistible force of charismatic appeal and the disgust aroused by what is perceived as other and threatening. The condensations and displacements of narrative prose convey, often in a unique way, insight into the structures of feeling embodied in social relationships as they are imagined in terms of desired proximity and identification and in a shrinking horror of contact. In this context, novels provide a previously unrecognized exploration of the charismatic power required of leadership and the necessary contradictions of charisma within a popular order.

Novels, especially those authored by women, form part of the pressure toward heterogeneity that transformed the public sphere in the 1840s and 1850s. They also consciously engage with the debates and struggles that were shaping public opinion as to the impending prospect of an inclusive society. There are striking and illuminating points of contact between novelistic and journalistic discourse and political essays. The code of sincerity is thematized and practically elaborated by the novelists in this study. The novels I discuss also function in the realist manner described by Benedict Anderson to provide "confirmation" of imagined social reality. In the six novels published from 1849 to 1864, the fictional worlds of the stories are represented as increasingly inclusive national societies. The characters who inhabit these worlds are represented as perceiving their reality in terms that move from a predominant consciousness of social exclusions to an acceptance of heterogeneity. The fictions are fully implicated in the formation and legitimation of new rules of social exclusion and inequality put in place in the process of this transformation. Yet they do also articulate utopian perceptions and aspirations of genuine community. In summary, these six works provide dramatic insights into the forces, discourses, aspirations, and fears that constituted a radical new mode of perceiving human existence — not only the inception of mass commodity culture but also the goal of egalitarian inclusiveness.

CHAPTER TWO

Producing Inclusive Society, 1846–1867

Empirical Histories

People living through the middle decades of the nineteenth century would not of course have thought of themselves or their times in the abstract terms of the three problematics outlined in the preceding chapter. Yet British citizens did apprehend, debate, and participate in events, processes, and discourses that shaped the coming into being of an inclusive society. People at the time articulated a shifting but ever-present concern with the condition and proper position within society of the laboring population, and most people were involved, in some way, in the search for new forms of political leadership. Many shared a keen anxiety about the implications for self and cultural identity posed by the prospect of a mass society. By tracing the extended development of these interconnected discursive and empirical histories of class relations, popular leadership, and massification of culture, this chapter aims to provide other viewpoints to that of current theoretical perspectives. These narratives take us closer to the context of ideas and happenings as Victorians themselves, including the major novelists, experienced them. Undoubtedly, this is largely history told from above. The literary works, the periodical press, and the political essayists I discuss are all securely removed from the precarious existence of working-class life. Yet this does not constitute a total absence of any perspective from below. As subaltern studies have shown, the impress of the demands and the consciousness of those excluded from decision making exerts a shaping pressure upon the discourse and the actions of those seeking to retain hegemonic control. Thus, Charles Tilly, for example, argues that after 1833, while the authorities by no means began to do the people's bidding, they did strive "increasingly to anticipate popular reactions, to co-opt or repress popular leaders . . . and even to bargain with carriers — authentic or otherwise — of popular demands" (14). As Plotz has shown, the impact of the popular crowd constituted a powerful influence upon the imagination of literary writers in the first half of the nineteenth century and thereby had a formative effect on novels and other literary writing.

Reimagining the Laboring Class

The sense of accommodation, even if grudgingly conceded, described by Tilly above as characterizing post-1830 attitudes to the claims of labor, indicates a dramatic shift from the general view set out by Hazlitt only ten years earlier: "We are accustomed to hear the poor, the uninformed, the friendless, put, by tacit consent out of the pale of society . . . they are familiarly spoken of as a sort of vermin" (*Works*, 19:219). Historians like E. P. Thompson and Nicholas Rogers have argued that eighteenth-century authorities were largely tolerant of the sporadic, somewhat ritualized expressions of popular discontent that typified the century; crowd interventions, Rogers says, "were a constituent element in the rich and ramified demotic political culture of the Georgian era" (17). The shock of the French Revolution and the catastrophe theories of population and pauperism emanating from Malthus and political economists imaginatively reconstituted the laboring poor, at the beginning of the nineteenth century, as a feared other, threateningly in the midst of the nation, but not of it. In coming to imagine an inclusive society, people had to rethink this perceived vermin-like mass, not simply as a problem to be managed but to be assimilated as like fellow beings. This demanded an immense process of reconceptualization, involving deeply lodged visceral impulses of disgust and shrinking flesh. As historians Corrigan and Sayer suggest, " 'Society' in discovering society tried to find a place for *les autres*, labour, to conceptualize them as more than objects of pity and mercy, or terror and punishment, or, importantly, as simply unknown" (117).

This reconceptualization of the laboring population is the focus of two largely separate historiographical traditions: one concerned primarily with poverty and the other with class and conflict. Within the epistemology of nineteenth-century political economy, poverty was not construed as a social problem. Rather it was understood as the original state of human existence, providentially designed by divine and natural laws to provide the necessary impetus to those individualistic, wealth-creating virtues of exertion, diligence, frugality, and self-discipline. Patrick Colquhoun argued in 1806 that poverty is "a most necessary component of society" without which there could be no wealth "since riches are the offspring of labour, while labour can only result from a state of poverty" (7). From this basic proposition, political economy elaborated an insistent logic, held to be irrefutable, that individual morality was part of an impersonal system of biological and economic laws sanctioned by God and Nature. As Mitchell Dean demonstrates, this rationale imposed upon the poor the responsibility for self-government as the unavoidable requirement for continued physical existence. Advocates of this moral logic preached to the working class—frequently from the pulpit—its unavoidable and irrevocable truth for most of the nineteenth century. In 1828, the *Westminster Review* urged,

> It is not enough that the language addressed to the labouring population is that of general exhortation. . . . Everyone may think that his marriage taken singly will not overstock the labour-market, why, therefore, should *he* abstain? Rather let the admonitions be personal, and point directly to the views and plans of each individual in domestic life. . . . Prove to each labourer, that, poor as he is already, there is yet a lower depth of wretchedness to which improvidence may force him to descend.[1]

Yet embedded within this harsh rationality was a wholly new perception of the working class as potential citizens. Able-bodied men were interpellated as responsible moral agents whose labor supported their families and contributed to national wealth. In 1850, the *Westminster Review* was still repeating the same mixed message, half threat at the destitution inevitably following improvidence, aligned with the demand for responsible and intelligent financial management: "The labourer who would secure future as well as present well-being must not neglect to ascertain, as nearly as possible, what out of his fluctuating wages are the average real wages on which he can rely. Out of these he must feel that he has to make provision for sickness and old age."[2] The worker who met this moral and financial challenge clearly deserved the respect of his fellow citizens. If working people demonstrated the responsible choice of industry and independence, on what rational grounds could they be denied the full rights of political citizenship? Yet the economic basis of this claim extended only to laboring *men*. Within the discourse of political economy, women were cast entirely as dependents. The quotations above are typical in concerning themselves solely with the role of the male worker. It was the male breadwinner who was perceived and who could therefore understand himself as a self-governing, independent agent. Indeed, the dependency of wives and children constituted the most powerful signifier of that masculine responsibility. Ironically, the claim of laboring men to a voice within the widening public sphere in the 1840s and 1850s was founded upon the exclusion of working-class women from the domain of popular politics and the workplace. As has been noted, this removal of laboring women occurred just as middle-class women were demanding a public space and role for themselves.[3]

The other negative aspect of the discursive constitution of working-class men as responsible moral citizens was the necessary defining opposition: in stark contrast to the positively imagined individual breadwinner, there was the amorphous pauper mass. The lurid terms in which these were imagined remained largely unchanged from the conception of the poor that Hazlitt had deplored. Edwin Chadwick's *Report on the Sanitary Conditions of the Labouring Population* (1842) projected urban pauperism as "characterised by a ferocious indocility that makes them prompt to wrongs and violences, destroys their social nature and transforms them into something little better than wild beasts" (199). A review in *Blackwood's Magazine* in 1851 conveys a nightmare image of the labyrinthine space of the urban slum, inhabited by a teeming form of existence that bears little resemblance to human life: "Amidst the dark, noisome, narrow streets and interminable courts and alleys . . . each house — each sty — swarms with life. And oh heaven! What life it is! They are heaped like vermin. They prey upon each other."[4] This visceral sense of horror was exacerbated by aspects of evolutionary theory that emphasized the bestial qualities of more primitive races and classes. In the same edition as its review of Robert Knox's *Lectures on the Races of Men* (1849), the *Westminster Review* noted the large "number of savages and semi-savages that form a permanent portion of society."[5]

Despite the fact that evidence abounded to demonstrate that the division of the laboring population into deserving individual citizens and a mass of demonic savages was entirely mythic, the dualistic representation was persistently reiterated. Depending on the exigency of the moment, journalists and other writers drew readily and without sense of contradiction upon these two images. Significantly, in the chorus of approval at the respectable demeanor of the large numbers of working people who visited the Great Exhibition in 1851, the mass was perceived almost invariably as *families* of working people. In reality, the conditions of laboring life for the vast majority of working-class people were always precarious, with accidents, illness, childbirth, and old age, as well as endemic unemployment, likely to plunge even the most frugal and diligent family into extreme poverty. Yet laboring people themselves, and especially their own political leaders, tended to accept the imagined division between respectable laboring people, thought of as individuals, and disreputable numbers, perceived as aggregate. Social-problem novelists in the 1840s also repeated this dualistic perception of working people: sympathetically represented, individualized working-class characters were contrasted to the unthinking, easily-led mass, who lack the individual's moral responsibility and integrity. Some variation of this pattern forms the structure of *Mary Barton, Shirley, Hard Times,* and *Felix Holt.* By contrast, in *Romola* and *Our Mutual Friend,* both written in the 1860s when mass society was seen as inevitable and imminent, it is the individualized character of lowly origins who is represented in such a way as to suggest the absence of a fully human moral sensibility.

The historiographical tradition concerned with class conflict and contention divides over the issue of whether the popular disturbances of the first half of the nineteenth century should be understood as expressions of a working-class consciousness newly acquired by laboring people or whether the mobilizations were part of an older tradition of protest in which Enlightenment notions of "the people" were more significant than any class identity as such. Thus Patrick Joyce supports the latter view, arguing that " 'popularism' points to a set of discourses and identities which are extra-economic in character, and inclusive and universalizing in their social remit in contrast to the exclusive categories of class. As intimated earlier, extraproletarian identifications such as those of 'people' and 'nation' are involved" (11). Gareth Stedman Jones and James Vernon, adopting similar discursive approaches, also conclude that popular contention in the nineteenth century gained much of its identity from political rhetoric with strong roots in eighteenth-century libertarianism.

These linguistically orientated historians question the underlying assumption of E. P. Thompson's hugely influential *The Making of the English Working Class* (1963). Thompson marshals a massive detail of evidence to suggest that the material conditions and experiences of working people in the early decades of the century produced a shared class consciousness. Tilly's work somewhat brings together both approaches, in that Tilly is very concerned with the shaping force of what he terms "repertoires of contention" — the expressive language wrought by a tradition of collective protest and demand — but he equally accepts the impact of material existence upon people's consciousness and identity (38–39). Thompson claimed that the intolerant reactionary domestic politics in Britain after the French Revolution and the imposed mass drudgery of factory and mill regimes combined to transform an inherited popular tradition into a class consciousness. To these experiences, Tilly adds the impact of the long war with France, which led to increasing centralization of state administration and greatly strengthened the power of Parliament over the Crown (267). The effect of this was that politics generally became national, rather than local.

In one sense, it might seem to make relatively little difference to the imagining of an inclusive society whether the laboring population demanded assimilation into the political collective as part of the people or as a class. Indeed, Patrick Joyce is surely mistaken in thinking of these identities as mutually exclusive; it seems reasonable to assume that the large numbers of ordinary people involved in mass movements positioned themselves politically across a range of identifying affiliations: familial, local, class, national, and universal. Nevertheless, the central claim that Tilly makes has an important bearing on the histories I am concerned with. Tilly argues that out of the popular struggles with power holders, a new relationship between constituents and national leaders was created, which in turn "laid the basis for most people's participation in national politics some time after 1832" (23). The most important force determining this new relationship was the constitution of the mass platform.

Tilly demonstrates that by the 1830s the apparatus of mass public assembly was firmly in place, involving widely advertised meetings open to all, election of chairmen, the presentation of speakers, resolutions, votes, acclamations, and petitions. Not only did this apparatus formally imitate parliamentary structure and procedure, the great themes of the public meetings, Tilly claims, were essentially the same issues that Parliament was debating (13). Participation in these events gave to ordinary people a dramatized sense that they were performers within the theater of national politics. Involvement also connected working-class participants to people and events well beyond traditional and hierarchical local worlds. As Nicholas Rogers says, "the mass platform . . . represented the sovereignty of the People assembled" (280). As such, it is true to say that the excluded numbers of the laboring population came to exert a force via their mass platform that changed the nature of political leadership.

The Styling of Popular Leadership

A continuous concern with national leaders has been much less noticed by historians of the nineteenth century than the preoccupation of the age with class relations. Writing about Carlyle, Eric Bentley sees the century as engaged in a quest for heroes following the loss of the traditional aura and mystique of kingship (5). Certainly, not only Hazlitt and Burke confronted the problem of legitimizing rulers in a popular political order. Coleridge, Disraeli, Carlyle, Kingsley, and Bagehot, as well as the writers discussed in the following chapters, all explored the qualities needed by leaders to achieve authority within an inclusive mass society. P. D. Marshall connects this century-long concern with leaders to the emerging use of the term *celebrity* in the nineteenth and twentieth centuries. He sees the notion of celebrity as deriving from the twinned discourses of capitalism and democracy (4). On the one hand, celebrity, from the nineteenth century onward, has worked closely with those modern forms of mass media that Adorno and Horkheimer labeled the culture industries. Public personality, by the twentieth century, had become a form of commodity to be projected to mass audiences as representative in an idealized sense of their own identities and lives. On the other hand, the ideal representation of celebrity, Marshall argues, is the triumph of the masses, in that celebrity status springs from popular recognition in the public sphere, rather than any traditional sources of inherited status and veneration. He connects this democratic sense of the term with the Latin *celebrem*, which includes the connotation of thronged, as well as famous: "The celebrity, in this sense, is not distant but attainable — touchable by the multitude" (6).

Nineteenth-century writers on political leadership were intuitively aware that when sovereignty was formally invested in the people, rulers could no longer rely upon distance to maintain awe. Embodying the mystique of an expansive territorial might was no longer enough. A felt connection and closeness to ordinary life had to be dramatized. Yet political essayists also recognized that power or charisma in some form had to be reattached to leaders in order to attract the mass acceptance in which authority was now vested. The problem in a secular political order is how to combine power with leaders who seem to be in touch.

As Catherine Gallagher notes, Coleridge provides one of the earliest nineteenth-century articulations of "a complicated tradition of political thought" (1985, 187). Coleridge's thinking on the "Idea" of the state and the constitution forms part of a long-extended and troubled response to the secularization of sovereignty by Hobbes and Locke. For Hobbes (1588–1679), the brutal anarchy of a state of nature required the concentration of power in some form of sovereign authority. Only the enforced obedience of the governed to the ruler would guarantee the necessary security for civil society. Locke (1632–1704) transformed submission into a contract freely entered into by subjects with their rulers. Authority was universally accepted to prevent the competitive interest of all against each jeopardizing the natural rights protected by contractual civil society.

This Hobbesian-Lockean legacy denied sovereignty any transcendental justification: in effect, the authority of rulers rested on nothing more than the pragmatic self-interest of the governed. For those who were unwilling to resort to calls for the restoration of divine right yet who wanted to locate social bonds in an ideal larger than that of individual self-interest, some form of argument had to be made for the disinterested identification of the self with the organic whole of the state or nation. In an inclusive society composed of great inequalities of wealth and status, this need to appeal beyond self-interest to a source of disinterested attachment to the whole becomes particularly critical for social stability.

Coleridge, despite his romantic conservatism, recognized that in modern times the nation had in some sense to comprehend the whole people. He was also radically at odds with the ethic of individualism and self-interest that he believed was coming to dominate national life. Yet he was far from proposing a democratic, inclusive order. Rather, the people were to be united by an identifying attachment to the organic ideal of the state. In his *Notebooks*, he writes, "The State is the disembodied yet not bodiless Soul *(amina unifica et integrans)* of the nation — each Generation of the individual citizens being the Body" (quoted in Calleo, 78). Coleridge realized that for most people this abstract idea of the nation as "soul" would be ineffective in producing any firm sense of personal identification. What was required was a ruler in whom the people could find an identifying image of themselves within the sovereignty of the state. He provides a strikingly complex figure of the interpellative identification of people with national leadership: "The Subject who kneels in homage before a rightful king, as the Symbol and acknowledged Representative of the Unity of the nation . . . [recognizes] in the Symbol of the Nation simultaneously an image-of his *very Self*" (quoted in Calleo, 80–81). Coleridge recognizes here, in the simultaneity of act of homage with act of self-identification, the complex interplay of power in the narcissistic, interpellative function of modern leadership.

Walter Bagehot was a more cynical political observer than Coleridge, but he, too, realized that, in an inclusive secular social order, there had to be some form of identification between rulers and ruled so that "we do not need bayonets to disperse crowds" (*Works*, 5:82). He also recognized that for those without a self-interested stake in the preservation of property and wealth, this attachment had to be achieved not by Lockean rational consent but through some imagined ideal that leaders could project. "The ruder sort of men," he argued, require "some vague dream of glory, or empire, or nationality" (5:209). Hence, the necessity for "theatrical elements" in the manifestations of state power. Rituals of power need to be visualized for the populace; "that which is brilliant to the eye" produces a willing public admiration (5:209). Yet Bagehot shrewdly identified the contradictory duality at the center of popular leadership: on the one hand, it must impose itself upon the general imagination by visual spectacles of glamour, mystical repleteness, and power, but, on the other hand, for those ordinary citizens who are largely without influence or agency, it must seem representative of the common life and experiences of the people. Only in this way can those who are interpellated into loyal obedience seem vicariously to share the power that their collective recognition confers on those who lead. For Bagehot, this duality of glamour and ordinariness was the great utility of a royal family over a republic: "A princely marriage is the brilliant edition of a universal fact, and as such, it rivets mankind" (5:229). With the expansion of empire, military heroism, the traditional idealized image of disinterested power, could be combined with domestic intimacy in the figure of the queen. Typically, Victoria was projected sentimentally as mother and glorified as empress.[6]

Compared with either Coleridge or Bagehot, Carlyle, in his hugely influential lectures entitled *On Heroes and Hero-Worship* starts from a much clearer perception of the irrevocable loss, within a secular world, of the traditional belief in the sovereignty of kings. In his essay "The Hero as King," no kings are named; instead, he writes, "In rebellious ages, when Kingship itself seems dead and abolished, Cromwell and Napoleon step forth again as kings." (*On Heroes*, 204). Yet what constituted their ineffable claim to leadership and their right to the obedience of their fellow beings? What was the source of their compelling charismatic power that sanctified it as other than the brutal right of might? This is the problem that Carlyle wrestles with in all of his writing on heroes. In so doing, he articulates more forcefully than any other writer the contradictions at the heart of modern mass leadership.

Like Bagehot, Carlyle recognized that in the modern social world, the willing and disinterested identification of the masses with an embodied ideal is the necessary means of preserving collective order without resort to bayonets. Hero-worship produces in ordinary men and women "a heartfelt prostrate admiration, submission, burning boundless, for the noblest godlike Form of Man" (11). The near oxymoron "god-like Form of Man" encapsulates the contradictory duality: the hero must simultaneous express the common touch of humanity and charismatic power. Carlyle meets his own first requirement in that most of his heroes are drawn from humble life, yet the only means he can find to dramatize their power over other men are images of conflict, struggle, and conquest. His writing everywhere testifies to the imaginative fascination with power as the ability to subdue and conquer that Hazlitt also recognized, but deplored. Carlyle has been criticized for the inspiration he gave to later twentieth-century authoritarian concepts of leadership. Yet there is also a genuinely democratic impulse in his rejection of inherited wealth, rank, and status as a basis for influence. From this perspective, his writing testifies to the real difficulty of imagining leadership within an inclusive society in which population, rather than territorial security, is the basis of legitimacy. It is small wonder that military ideals of heroism are still resorted to by domestic political leaders.

Despite Carlyle's imaginative allegiance to heroism visualized in terms of conquest and might, he brilliantly foresaw the ways in which leadership would be transformed and domesticated by the mass media of an inclusive society. Once print-capitalism becomes fully established, Carlyle insisted, "Democracy is inevitable. . . . Whoever can speak, speaking now to the whole nation, becomes a power" (164). Although he is writing about the expansion of popular print publication, the word Carlyle seizes upon here in his perception of democratic power is *speaking*. The sense of physical in touchness conveyed by the direct speaking voice was to become the supreme vehicle for establishing an identifying contact between leaders and led. In constructing the public platform, the radical popular movements of the first half of the century had prepared the apparatus that could be appropriated by those aspiring to democratic power. Carlyle also offered them the necessary style with which to forge a charismatic hold upon a mass audience. It is the only quality distinctively set apart from those of struggle and conflict with which he endows all his heroes: "I should say *sincerity*, a deep, great genuine sincerity is the first great characteristic of all men in any way heroic" (45).

Wellington, Palmerston, and Gladstone were all highly popular political leaders during the nineteenth century, but the basis of their appeal was immensely different. A consideration of this in relation to their performative style provides an almost paradigmatic model of the transformation of leadership to meet the new demands of a mass order conceived in terms of population, rather than territory. Although Wellington held prime ministerial office only from 1828 to 1830, he occupied high government positions for much longer. Above all, he embodied the traditional landed aristocratic military hero. In his obituary, the *Times* noted that he was "attached by birth, by character, and by opinion to the order and the cause of the British aristocracy."[7] His funeral was watched by an estimated million and a half people. Yet even in the midst of its obituary praises, the *Times* admitted that Wellington's sense of aristocratic hauteur meant that he possessed neither ability nor desire to command popularity in any personal sense: "In those qualities which conciliate personal affection he was naturally deficient."[8] This inbred aloofness was immaterial to the kind of traditional national leader he represented in that for the general population he functioned as a distant, mythic figure, an epic national hero defending Britain against an external foe of like epic proportions — Napoleon. In that sense, Wellington's efficacy as a national leader depended upon the general invisibility of the private domestic man.

Palmerston, who held office almost continuously from 1855 to 1865, was also aristocratic, almost to the point of caricature, in personal style of speaking and in demeanor. But, by the middle of the century, great landowners were no longer necessarily active military leaders. Palmerston fought no military campaigns, but, within the public sphere rather than in the theater of war, he very successfully projected himself upon public imagination as a heroic defender of Britain against the unwarranted territorial ambitions of other nations. He utilized the rhetoric of conquest to construct a charismatic national might with which ordinary people were eager to identify themselves. One of his biographers, Denis Judd, writes, "Palmerston became prime minister not for what he really was but for what people thought he was. . . . In the 1850s newspapers did not even carry photographs; the word picture of Palmerston could diverge considerably from reality" (120). Palmerston, like Wellington, remained unknown personally to the general public. He gained their consent, not for himself, but for a John Bull image of national territorial belligerency — a larger-than-life, heroic figure with which to identify. While Wellington could afford to disdain attempts at popularity, Palmerston, at the middle of the century, had to grasp the contradictory duality of leadership in a mass society: the need to embody some form of charismatic power fused with a sense of in touchness with ordinary life. While remaining largely invisible within the public sphere, he commanded its space by speaking. His bellicose speeches were aimed at wide distribution in the national press as much as at his fellow peers in the government. He perfected this technique of "speaking" so well that even the radical newspaper *Reynold's Weekly* called him "the people's darling" — an epithet it would have been unthinkable to associate with the duke of Wellington (Judd, 97).

Gladstone did not become prime minister until 1868, and thereafter he dominated British politics and public life until almost the end of the century. He achieved this leadership without associating himself either with heroic militarism or territorial might. Whereas both Wellington and Palmerston remained largely invisible and personally unknown to the public, embodying an abstract ideal of the nation as territory, Gladstone's popularity was based upon the sense of a personally known identity that he projected orally and visibly to the nation. He became the first leader to gain popular consent by engaging directly with the people en masse. His charismatic presence derived its force from the overwhelming response he drew from mass meetings; in a collective act of identification, the crowd shared in the power their acclamation conferred upon him. The technique of direct personal appeal to large numbers of people was a performative style that Gladstone acquired before he came to power. He learned to speak from the platform of mass meetings as an oppositional location of power to that of a Parliament that, in the 1850s and 1860s, was still largely dominated by aristocrats.

In his classic account *The Platform* (1892), Henry Jephson traces the increasing importance and changing function of public political meetings in the course of the nineteenth century. In the early decades of the century, mass meetings were regarded by governments with intense hostility and suspicion. Whenever possible, they were prohibited or obstructed. Their platform was regarded solely as providing a space for dissension and troublemaking. No minister of the Crown would have thought of addressing a mass meeting. Gradually, in the course of about half a century, the attitude of established politicians and administrations swung full circle until public meetings were thought of as offering positive opportunities for enabling more interpersonal relations between leaders and people. Even at midcentury, Lord Palmerston would have regarded it an act of vulgarity to speak at a mass meeting, but by the 1870s mass meetings addressed by leading political figures had become an institutionalized part of national life. Jephson attributed the attraction of this new form of political communication to "the personal acquaintance which it enables the people to make with their leaders"; it was the means by which they gained a sense of "personal contact with them" (2:602). Gladstone founded his political career upon this form of mass, but directly personal, communication, beginning with his first major public speech, in Manchester in 1852, to an audience largely composed of working men.

It is probably significant that Gladstone developed his capacity to move large audiences while he was out of office and ambitious for power. It helped him to recognize the force that resided in popular consent made articulate. After a speaking tour of Lancashire in 1864, he describes it as an "exhausting, flattering, I hope not intoxicating circuit. God knows I have not courted them: I hope I do not rely on them: I pray I may turn them to account for good. It is however impossible not to love the people from whom such manifestations come, as met me in every quarter" (quoted in Shannon, 1:523). Even the disavowals here make evident the capacity Gladstone developed, as a public man, to win, absorb, and reflect back the power he attained from collective assent in an interactive, doubled-mirror action. All of Gladstone's biographers remark upon his completely innovative form of political communication. The above quotation of Gladstone's words suggests the quality that made his hearers feel that they were each being directly addressed: he speaks the language of almost confessional sincerity. Gladstone's political addresses articulate an impassioned interiority, and as such his words seem to appeal from one human consciousness directly to a like being, quite regardless of any material outward differences of wealth or status. After his defeat in the general election of 1865, he told the crowded meeting in the Manchester Free Trade Hall, to shouts of applause, "At last, my friends, I am come amongst you. And I am come...unmuzzled." Going on to Liverpool, he was confessionally explicit on the exchange of power between himself and his mass audience, "If I came here a wounded man, you have healed my wound" (quoted in Magnus, 172).

It is important to see this as a performance of sincerity without in any way implying that Gladstone personally was insincere. The public projection becomes clear if we compare it to praise of Wellington's sincerity as a politician. A popular collection of essays, largely reprinted from *Fraser's Magazine*, entitled *Orators of the Age* (1847), notes that an impression of a speaker's sincerity is more persuasive than rhetorical flourishes. Wellington's strength in the House of Lords is imputed to this quality in his speech. This sincerity, however, is manifested as an "indifference whether what he has delivered has pleased or displeased his audience." This patrician belief that whatever he says "will be held of value" can sometimes, the essayist admits, "degenerate into an abruptness almost rude."[9] Nothing could be further from this aristocratic disdain than Gladstone's mode of confessional sincerity when speaking directly to the people. His biographer H. C. G. Matthew connects this dramatic projection of his own political persona to his lifelong interest in the theater and an intuitive sense of performance (277–78). Richard Shannon remarks of Gladstone: "Without being strictly handsome . . . there was no doubt as to the winningness of effect," especially the impact of his "brilliant flashing eyes" (92). While the queen and the court found fault with his nonaristocratic manner and his residual, slightly provincial accent, these aspects became strengths for a politician set on gaining legitimacy from the people.

Gladstone's capacity to initiate an innovative public political code of sincerity undoubtedly drew credibility from his own habit of confessional heart searching, his sense of his own interiority. Nevertheless, he combined this with an astute sense of the political efficacy of performed sincerity. His retention of power to the end of the century derived in no small degree from his capacity to exploit every new mass means of speaking to the people. To that extent, he made his public personality and his performance of sincerity into political commodities. He was the first party leader to address an annual conference, and he was the first European politician whose voice, through the medium of the phonograph, was heard across the English-speaking world. Recordings of his voice were relayed at fairgrounds around Britain. Yet the shift he had been instrumental in accomplishing to a highly individualized, visual, mode of public political leadership is perhaps best illustrated by his capacity in his eighties to address huge meetings without any means of amplification. They were, Matthew, says, "extraordinary occasions," projecting a charismatic figure who drew his power from a two-way relationship with his admirers articulated as a performed code of sincerity (298).

Gladstone was undoubtedly of singular importance in establishing a performative code of sincerity as the preeminent mode of modern political communication. Yet his was certainly not the only voice that popularized the code more generally across a widening public sphere. Carlyle exerted an enormous influence, not only by his passionate advocacy of sincerity in *On Heroes and Hero-Worship*, but also by his own distinctive and foregrounded style of sincerity in speaking and writing. In reviewing his second edition of *Oliver Cromwell's Letters and Speeches*, a writer in the *Westminster Review* recognized that Carlyle had deliberately rejected the formal universalism of the code of civility in favor of a highly direct and personalized style: "He has chosen to abandon the moderated and regulated tone of a universal mode of address."[10] Novelists like Dickens and Thackeray not only thematized sincerity in their novels, they also projected the code performatively in their narrative voices and in public lectures, speeches, and journalism. The rapid expansion of letter writing as a form of communication after the middle of the century, as a result of Rowland Hill's reform of the postal services, must have encouraged the espousal of a code of sincerity as the appropriate mode of correspondence between those whose relations were neither intimate nor hierarchical. From 1838 to 1864, there was a rise in the number of chargeable letters from 76 millions to 642 millions. The first recorded uses, in

The Oxford Dictionary, of colloquial expressions like *really, honestly, personally, I myself* as emphasized denotations of sincerity begin to occur around the turn of the nineteenth into the twentieth century, as do phrases signifying egalitarian interpersonal regard like *seeing eye to eye, shake hands, on the level*, and *man to man*.

Culture and the Masses

By the 1860s the code of sincerity was itself about to undergo a process of transformation and division. A rhetoric of public sincerity, I have suggested, came to replace the eighteenth-century notion of sympathy as the basis of sociability or social coherence. Whereas sympathy and its code of civility was predicated upon the Enlightenment belief in a universal human nature, the code of sincerity projected its interpellative offer on the presumption of mutual but differently interested human interiorities. It was the ideology of interiority, as a common defining quality of humanness, that was undermined in the second half of the century as the reality of a mass society moved into closer imaginative focus. As the traditional distinctions of birth and rank lost their hold, a class-based prescription of culture became the site of a new apparatus of social exclusion.

The utility of culture as a measure of social distinction was stated with particular clarity by the 1868 Taunton Commission, an inquiry into the curriculum of the public school system. The commission defended the exclusive teaching of classics and mathematics, rather than the more relevant modern sciences, on the grounds that the poorer gentry "had nothing to look to but education to keep their sons on a high social level. And they would not wish to have what might be more readily converted into money, if in any degree it tended to let their children sink in the social scale."[11] This perception of classical culture as a marker of social distinction came just at the moment in the century when, Harold Perkin tells us, "for the first time in history, non-landed incomes and wealth had begun to overtake land alone as the main source of economic power" (64).

Yet cultural distinction was not sought only as a means of separation from the nouveau riche. Since 1846, government funding had been available for the teacher-training of working-class children, and as such it provided one of the few routes of upward mobility for able children of the poor. Even when the idea was being considered in 1842, the *Christian Observer* noted that while it would be necessary to raise the students morally and intellectually, it would be equally important to "inure them to the duties of a humble and laborious office."[12] By the 1860s, there was a general feeling among the well-to-do that this humble aspect of the job had been lost from view; a new generation of teachers of lowly origins were presuming to the status of gentlemen and ladies. It was objected that the present system "raised up a class of overtaught and self-conceited masters and mistresses, who are not content with doing the humble work of a teacher of poor children."[13] The Revised Code of 1862 cut funding to teacher colleges and imposed a much more utilitarian, less intellectual and less cultural syllabus.

Yet the ideology of culture functioned as a much deeper, more internalized apparatus of distinction and exclusion than the rather mechanistic routines of certificates and syllabi, as Dickens makes very plain in his opposition of Wrayburn and Headstone in *Our Mutual Friend.* A class-defined understanding of culture was integral to the long tradition of political philosophy that moved in the nineteenth century through Burke, Coleridge, and Arnold and that had evolved in the preceding century as a patrician response to Hobbes and Locke. In *The Vulgarization of Art: Victorians and Aesthetic Democracy,* Linda Dowling traces the origin of this philosophy that fused moral, aesthetic, and political perspectives to the third earl of Shaftesbury, whose tutor had been John Locke. In the wake of the political settlement of 1703 that instituted a limited monarchy and established an aristocratic Whig oligarchy, Shaftesbury felt impelled to justify and legitimize his own social position and that of his party on surer moral grounds than those of Hobbesian opportunism and the ruthless operation of power. If the political and social order had henceforth to be understood as unsanctioned by divine will, what was there to check the anarchy of individualist political ambitions?

Shaftesbury found the answer to this anxiety by combining a perception of aesthetic sensibility with that of moral sensibility, both understood by him as common human attributes. He argued on Lockean lines that the human mind is receptive to moral sensations in the same way as to aesthetic stimuli. The mind "feels the soft and harsh, the agreeable and the disagreeable in the affections" just as it responds to what is "foul and fair" or "harmonious and . . . dissonant" in music or visual forms (1:251, quoted in Dowling, 11). The moral sense here becomes one with an aesthetic sensibility, and both are perceived as common to human nature. More importantly, this aestheticizing of moral sensibilities implies, against Hobbes, that virtue can be pursued disinterestedly as its own reward, just as human beings seek out what is beautiful and harmonious for its own sake. Yet, just as Adam Smith, in describing a harmony of minds in concord like musical instruments, was actually projecting a specific class ideal as a universal law of sympathy, so, too, Shaftesbury's moral-aesthetic sensibility is a projection of his own aristocratic culture onto a notion of humanity as a whole. In this way, a concept of what defines "humanity" or "humanness" gets entangled in an elite perception of sensibility as culture and taste. For Shaftesbury, as Roy Porter comments, "virtue stemmed from a benign disposition, which was of a piece with good-breeding. Exercise of taste and virtue were thus comparable activities" (164).

Shaftesbury was immensely influential in his own time, and his ideas were taken up and developed by German idealist philosophers like Kant and Schiller, whence they returned somewhat unacknowledged to Britain through the mediation of Coleridge, Carlyle, and Arnold. Significantly, *Fraser's Magazine*, in 1873, introduced readers to Shaftesbury as the "Matthew Arnold of Queen Anne's reign" (quoted in Dowling, 2). In response to anxieties about the democratizing spirit of the century, both Coleridge and Arnold sought comfort in an ideology of culture that was inherently contradictory and ultimately elitist. On the one hand, they associate it with the quality of humanness, while, on the other hand, they define it in terms that are actually aristocratic and exclusive. Coleridge, in his most political publication, *On the Constitution of Church and State*, argues that civilization understood simply as progress can exert a corrupting influence unless it is grounded in *"cultivation."* He glosses cultivation as "the harmonious development of those qualities and faculties that characterise our *humanity*. We must be men in order to be citizens" (34). Humanity here, which grounds the right to political citizenship, is far from being the common shared nature of the species so denominated: humanness is being defined as a quality of cultivated sensibility. Matthew Arnold's thinking owes much to Coleridge, as the language of harmonious development of faculties suggests.

In *Culture and Anarchy*, Arnold struggles to define culture as a universal quality of goodness attainable by and essential to all human kind. In contrast to unchecked individualism that threatens sociability, culture aims at the universalism of "perfection as a *general* expansion of the human family . . . as a *harmonious* expansion of human nature" (49). Far from being restricted to aesthetics, culture, for Arnold as for Shaftesbury, is of a "moral, social, and beneficent character" (46). Yet Arnold's account of culture remains full of contradictions. Although its goal is the harmonious development of "all sides of our humanity . . . [and] all parts of our society," it turns out that the generous scope of "all sides" and "all parts" is limited in its application to the "growth and preponderance of our humanity proper, as distinguished from our animality" (11, 47). Not infrequently, the function of culture shrinks to even narrower remit, becoming the arbiter of a refined class taste against "hideousness and rawness" (62). "Culture says, 'Consider these people, then, their way of life, their habits, their manners, the very tones of their voice'" (52) — so much for sweetness and light! Throughout his social and political writing, the word that Arnold instinctively turns to to oppose culture is *raw*, indicative of the physical immediacy with which he registered vulgarity, in true Lockean fashion, upon his pulses.

Arnold wrote *Culture and Anarchy* in personal response to the Hyde Park riots of July 1866: he had watched the crowd stone the windows of his neighbor, the commissioner of police. However most of the ideas developed in *Culture and Anarchy* had already been set out in his earlier essay entitled "Democracy," which appeared in 1861 as introduction to *The Popular Education of France*. Arnold described "Democracy" as "one of the things I have taken most pains with" (*Complete Prose Works*, 2:331). R. H. Super, editor of *The Complete Works*, describes it as "in many ways ... the keystone of his thinking about politics" (2:330). In Arnold's essay, there is a more ready acceptance of democracy as "something natural and inevitable"; it is an impulse "identical with the ceaseless vital effort of human nature itself" (2:8). Yet democracy requires, Arnold argues, a noble and disinterested ideal that will provide "a true bond of union," transcending the "pushing, excited and presumptuous" individualistic nature of a wholly popular order (2:19, 2:10). Arnold locates this unifying ideal in culture, as opposed to the "rawness of the masses" (2:14), but in "Democracy" the ideal of culture that is to lift the mass into enlightened, unraw humanness is quite explicitly associated with an aristocratic order (2:6). For Arnold, this nobility, constitutive of full humanity, is crystallized *"in the grand style"* of classical writers like Homer (2:5). The phrase *grand style* is a reference to three earlier, somewhat controversial essays that Arnold had written in 1860 and 1861 on modern translations of Homer. In these essays, Arnold defines the nobility of a grand style as a quality he calls "simplicity" — the word *simplicity* having the same root as *sincerity* and similarly suggesting a lack of embellishment (1:206). However, the sensibility required to recognize this quality of simplicity is, Arnold says, like faith: "'One must feel it in order to know what it is.' But, as of faith, so too one may say of nobleness, of the grand style: 'Woe to those who know it not!'" (1:188). On further expansion, the sensibility that Arnold advocates as having the capacity to appreciate "simplicity" turns out to be almost the opposite of Carlyle's passionate sincerity. It is much closer to the form of sincerity attributed to Wellington — disinterested hauteur. It is a sensibility constituted as aloof distance, a replete disinterestedness that is never embroiled in "ignoble personal passions" (1:215). Although signifying a humanity separated from "animality," it is visually embodied in "a pose so perfect" and "the most free flexible and elastic spirit imaginable" (1:174). In contrast to this aristocratic ideal projected as the perfection of humanness, Arnold, in "My Countrymen," describes the common people of British cities as "more raw . . . less enviable-looking, further removed from civilized and human life, than the common people almost anywhere" (5:18).

The exclusionary identification of full humanness with a class-defined sensibility or interiority (that nevertheless manifests itself visually and physically in a privileged-class manner, speech, and outward appearance) remains less than fully articulated in Arnold's writing due to his contradictory invocations of culture. Not so in the writing of Herbert Spencer. In his essay "Personal Beauty," published in the *Leader* in 1854, Spencer comments that he has never been reconciled to the common opinion that beauty of character and beauty of visible appearance are unrelated. He proceeds to a demonstration of the interactive influence of sensibility upon physical appearance and bone structure. He does this by singling out, as "universally" acknowledged, ugliness — features that can then be associated with "the lower human races" and their uncultivated conditions of existence: "If, then, recession of the forehead, protuberance of the jaws, and largeness of the cheekbones, three leading elements of ugliness, are demonstrably indicative of mental inferiority . . . and disappear . . . as intelligence increases, both in the race and in the individual; is it not a fair inference that all such faulty traits of feature signify deficiencies of mind?" (*Essays*, 2:392). The conclusion irresistibly forced upon us, Spencer argues, is that "the aspects which please us are the outward correlatives of inward perfections, while the aspects which displease us are the outward correlatives of inward imperfections" (2:393).

The class dimension of this identification of interior cultivation with external appearance is made explicit in Spencer's other writings. In "Progress: Its Law and Cause," published in the *Westminster Review* in 1857, he gives as illustration of the natural law of increasing evolution toward ever greater complexity and differentiation the process by which simple societies progress into complexly segregated "distinct orders and classes of workers" (*Essays*, 1:21). The word *segregated* is Spencer's, and he uses it in an organic, rather than a social, sense, in that the separation between different classes and races of men is understood to be physically embodied: "We may infer that the civilised man has also a more complex or heterogeneous nervous system than the uncivilised man" (*Essays*, 1:18).

Spencer also applies the law of increasing complexity to the evolution of human language. The more primitive the mind, he argues, the more directly emotional is the language expressed, while at higher levels of civilization, emotions are modified into an idealized language of poetry and vocal inflections and verbal forms to adequately convey "the multiplied and complicated ideas of civilized life" (*Essays*, 2:422). Sincerity, from an evolutionary perspective of complex cultivation, would have to be far removed from any direct utterance of feelings. Interiority, or sensibility, has become the measure of the distance traveled from raw emotion. In addition to Spencer's popularization of evolutionary notions that equated an upper-class manner and education with the highest form of human development, the eighteenth-century ideas of phrenology or physiognomy were still pervasive in nineteenth-century writing and thinking. Johann Casper Lavater's *Essays on Physiognomy*, first translated in 1804, was continuously reissued throughout the nineteenth century, purveying Lavater's equation of external appearance with inner worth: "The beauty and deformity of the countenance is in just and determinate proportion to the moral beauty and deformity of the man. The morally best, the most beautiful. The morally worst, the most deformed" (99).

This location of the body as the classificatory site of physical signifiers of a deformed animality or a fully human sensibility was caught up in the increasing visuality of everyday life, associated with the extension and consolidation of commodity capitalism. There has been little study as to the impact this new visual order had upon the self-imaging of ordinary working-class people as that section of the population previously least exposed to visual representations of themselves. The process of silver deposition that made possible the cheap mass production of mirrors was introduced in the 1840s. The 1860s saw the beginning of mass pictorial advertising and the opening of large department stores, with their large, plate-glass windows. Simultaneously, with offering models of ideal fashion and clothing, the windows also acted as reflective looking-glasses to those passing by. To the poor, the contrast between self and ideal must surely have been striking. Yet, Henry Mayhew noted, in 1861 in working-class districts of London like Bermondsey, the New-cut, and Whitechapel Road, one could not "walk fifty yards without passing some photographic establishment" (3:204). In *The Printed Image and the Transformation of Popular Culture*, Patricia Anderson notes that the increasingly pictorial character of popular publications from 1830 to 1860 brought about an "unprecedented expansion of the cultural experience of working people" (1).

More generally, cultural critics and historians have emphasized the way visual signification gained dominance over the written word as authorizing what was held to be true and real. As, Susan Horton argues, the sheer inundation of Victorian culture with a mass of optical gadgetry and amusements must have helped condition a new cultural consciousness as to the visualness of acts of looking (3). This act of looking as a means of gaining knowledge about the world and about people was immensely encouraged by the Great Exhibition of 1851, which was largely composed of spectacular displays for public visual consumption. For the first time, people could learn about exotic parts of the world by looking, rather than reading. Thomas Richards argues that the exhibition "inaugurated a way of seeing that marked indelibly the cultural and commercial life of Victorian England" (18). Jennifer Green-Lewis suggests that the concern with corporeal "testimony" to interiority was intensified by "the explosion into the representational world of photographic portraiture" (159). Nancy Armstrong has developed this idea in a complex and detailed study of the impact of photography upon Victorian realism, arguing that a pictorial order of reality was established that organized perceptions of racial and class identities around physical indexes of "interiority" and set up urban space in oppositional evolutionary terms of vigorous economic circulation versus stagnant slum district. Those writers who wanted their fiction to be convincing, Armstrong says, had to conform to this pictorial "archive" (26–27).

As a way of bringing together the three interconnecting histories outlined in this chapter and of turning the focus to literary writing, I will briefly discuss two fictional narratives that imaginatively rework these concerns central to people at the time as they contemplated the evolution toward an inclusive society. In 1863, Charles Kingsley published *The Water-Babies* and George Eliot published *Romola*. Although it would be difficult to find two stories more divergent in form and apparent content, both relate the tale of a child of humble, unknown origins who moves from an outcast, brutalized position in society to the central eminence of a great man and leader. In both cases, this transformation of a self begins with acts of looking. Tom's journey toward a new identity begins when, as a child chimney sweep, he comes down the wrong chimney into an exquisitely snow-white bedroom to behold the most beautiful little girl he has ever seen, of delicate skin and golden hair. The next instant, he is confronted by the nightmare reverse of this image of untainted purity. Standing close beside him is an ugly, black, ragged figure. "He turned on it angrily. What did such a little black ape want in that sweet young lady's room? And behold, it was himself reflected in a great mirror" (22). Self-recognition for the little chimney sweep is simultaneously an act of self-repudiation and shame. Kingsley's language invokes class, racial, species, and gender stereotypes in the field of force of this remarkably primal scene. Tom excludes himself even before the hue and cry is set up to chase him off like a wild animal. He rushes headlong away, barely stopping until he plunges or falls exhausted into a purifying mountain stream, murmuring continually, "I must be clean, I must be clean" (37).

In the water, Tom undergoes a reverse evolutionary process, growing gills and becoming a smooth-skinned "water-baby." The fairies who watch over him are told not to make their presence known since "he is but a savage now, and like the beasts which perish; and from the beasts which perish he must learn" (38). Tom must learn to become fully human by developing a soul, or sensibility, which, the narrative makes clear, involves a sensitivity to suffering in others, honesty, and courage, but also a refinement of taste. One of the creatures who teaches Tom the lessons of evolution is the aristocratic salmon, who deplores the downfall of trout, his near relations, who have sadly declined due to low company and low manners. "A great many years ago," the salmon tells Tom, "they were just like us; but they were so lazy, and cowardly, and greedy, . . . they chose to stay and poke about in the little streams and eat worms and grubs; and they are very properly punished for it; for they have grown ugly and brown and spotted and small; and are actually so degraded in their tastes, that they will eat our children" (73). This linkage of external appearance to inner sensibility is reinforced later by the narrator, who says, "in solemn, serious, earnest," that people's souls make their bodies just as surely as a snail makes its shell (126).

As Tom undergoes the adventures that will transform him from a beast devoid of interiority into a man of intelligent sensibility, the language in which his regeneration is couched fuses notions of class with those of race and imperialism. His final testing involves diving under a "great white gate" into the unknown of "black darkness." Yet by this stage, Tom is unafraid: "He was a brave English lad, whose business is to go out and see all the world" (155). Tom emerges from the water that has remade him as a sensible being, a tall man, fit for the company of Ellie, first seen in the white bedroom and now become a beautiful lady. He rises to be "a great man of science," able to take a lead in the most important and progressive undertakings of the day, "plan railroads, and steam-engines, and electric telegraphs" (189). Nevertheless, Kingsley does not let him marry Ellie; that would be to admit that full humanity retains much that links us to the beasts.

In *Romola*, Tito Melema has also escaped from brutal physical origins, but in this case by means of the cultured, classical teaching of his adoptive father, Baldassare. After shipwreck and near drowning, Tito arrives in Florence with his life to remake. He is fortunate in being taken in hand by Nello, a barber, who tells him that the encroachment of hair upon the face effects a "certain grossness of apprehension" (36). Using delicately scented lather, Nello shaves away Tito's abundant, curling hair and beard before giving him a mirror to contemplate his face in which the "human outline" is now made distinct from that of an ape (36). As Tito gazes narcissistically in the mirror, Nello projects for him a path to eminence as a cultured man in Florence. Accordingly, Tito becomes a leading player in Florence's heterogeneous and contentious public sphere by capitalizing, literally, on the classical education he gained from Baldassare. He fashions himself into an acclaimed popular leader who can speak to the masses, yet he also gains the trust of the most aristocratic and cultured classes in the city.

Initiated in that act of looking at his reformed self in the barber's mirror, Tito's rise to influence and power are shown by Eliot to be a skilled performance of what Habermas calls a refeudalized "publicness." In his person, he seems to substantiate people's ideals and desires. Tito assumes the image of all things to all people: he commodifies a suave "sincerity." He can do this because he has no inherent self as interiority, no sensibility as the full measure of humanness. Throughout the text, animal imagery is linked to Tito, but unlike Tom the chimney sweep, neither water nor the razor can regenerate him. When the savagery of the mob threatens his life, he leaps into the river, hoping to swim to safety as before and remake a new self for a second time. But there is no baptismal rebirth: Tito's life is throttled from him by the cultured man, Baldassare, whom he had pushed down into a degenerate savagery. Eliot's imagination can more easily comprehend the loss of human cultivation in engulfing brutishness than the evolutionary progress of the masses, those of lowly origin, into a full human sensibility. For that reason, she remains suspicious and skeptical of all claims to popular leadership in a public sphere, like that of Florence, open to the voices and demands of all. Writing earlier in the century, Brontë and Thackeray consider more optimistically what kind of new leadership would be able to speak across the social divisions of a contentious public sphere.

Part II /Inclusive Leadership

Heroes of Domesticity

CHAPTER THREE

Shirley

Charisma or Sincerity?

To speak of any particular time as a moment of historical transition is to impose an interpretation or a narrative pattern upon the contingency of temporal continuity. Yet a survey of journalism during the last years of the 1840s conveys a sense that people at the time felt themselves to be living through such a moment, when the old, exclusive political regime came under immense pressure for change to a more inclusive, heterogeneous order. In addition to recurrent references to "crisis" and "end of an era," there were many comparative allusions that explicitly linked the early-nineteenth-century moments of political transition with a much longer perspective of constitutional contention. In these accounts, the Reform Bill of 1832 and the Corn Law conflicts of the 1840s were represented as part of a continuing political struggle originating in the seventeenth-century Civil War and Cromwell's republic, the rejection of Stuart claims for the divine right of kings, and the constitutional settlement of 1714, which secured a limited Protestant monarchy and aristocratic control of parliamentary government.[1] Despite the bitterness of this struggle that rested power from the Crown to vest it in Parliament, it was essentially interclass factionalism. The governing landed interest fought within itself, but its members, whether Whigs or Tories, shared a common perception of their political and social reality. From the eighteenth century onward, those with property in land formed the core of civil society, set its tone, and dominated the public sphere. In its immediate aftermath, the 1832 Reform Act appeared to have had little effect upon the monopoly of political and social power that the landed nobility had enjoyed since the Act of Settlement (1701). Britain seemed a society as securely structured as ever upon the traditional and naturalized exclusions and divisions of rank. Even in 1848, a writer in the *Westminster Review* could still complain that "the majority of the House of Commons continues to be returned, not by the people, but by the nobility. The patronage of every office in the state, of every high station or emolument, is seized upon, as before, as the birthright of the same privileged class."[2] The reviewer estimated that at that time the House of Commons contained six marquesses, eight earls, twenty-seven viscounts, and thirty-two lords.

Yet, as commentators at the time appreciated, by 1848 fundamental changes had occurred to the underlying disposition of power. The struggles over Chartism and the Corn Laws initiated a process of erosion at the foundations of the old order of exclusion. The repeal of the Corn Laws in 1846 marked the end of the unquestioned privileges of birthright and land. Within the periodical press, the struggle over the Corn Laws was accorded almost greater significance than the campaigns of the Chartists. Conservative opinion, as expressed in numerous essays in *Blackwood's Magazine*, saw, in a somewhat overlurid light, the repeal of the Corn Laws as marking the final destruction of the traditional principles of nobility, hereditary order, reverence for authority, and loyalty to crown and church "upon which our national greatness was achieved."[3] In similar hyperbolic mode, progressive opinion, as voiced in the *Westminster Review*, recognized that "the commencement of a new era" began with the downfall of the Corn Laws.[4] The Corn Law struggle precipitated a calamitous leadership crisis for the Conservative interest when Sir Robert Peel voted in favor of repeal, thereby splitting the party into two hostile factions and ensuring the parliamentary dominance of the Whigs for the next twenty-eight years.

The successful challenge, in the form of the repeal of the Corn Laws, to aristocratic prerogatives initiated a pervasive concern with national leadership that spread well beyond party. If noble birth did not confer an inherent right to rule, what was the legitimating basis of power? And if landed nobility in itself did not authorize national leadership in times of crisis and in peacetime, what style was to replace aristocratic grandeur as commanding general consent and obedience? It was in this context that Carlyle's timely *Heroes and Hero-Worship* lectures made such a stir. The *Westminster Review* commented wryly on the loss of political authority at the end of the 1840s: "A remarkable feature in political aspects is the number of vacant leaderships. . . . The headless bodies of parties may be seen floating everywhere."[5] The reviewer ascribed the problem of leadership to "the general uprooting of old authorities." In this sense, Charlotte Brontë is imaginatively astute in using Shakespeare's *Coriolanus* to raise, in *Shirley*, questions about qualities of leadership. The problem coming into general visibility by the late 1840s was the need to invent or evolve a new style of leadership — one able to bring into being a new kind of political and social order. The article in the *Westminster Review* heralding the new era inaugurated by the downfall of the Corn Laws concluded on a hopefully prophetic note: "The man may be amongst us, but unknown, who is to be the architect of the new Downing-Street — the weaver of the new red tape."[6] Such a man, the writer argues, would need to discover "principles of affinity" upon which to form a government.

The crisis of Chartism in 1848 was responded to in the immediate term with a resort to old-style leadership based upon the principle of force, not affinity. The duke of Wellington, heroic defender of the nation against the old enemy France, came out of retirement to take charge personally of preparations to safeguard the capital against insurrection and to subdue any show of violence or disorder. As the *Times* noted in his obituary in 1852, no person was more qualified than the duke, by virtue of his attachment by birth and by opinion to the cause of the British aristocracy, to be the champion of resistance to popular turbulence. Yet, with the benefit of retrospect in 1852, the *Times* also noted his "honest recognition of popular rights" and his forbearance once the authority of the state had been secured.[7] As this implies, when the moment of perceived danger was over there was a general recognition that it had also been, in some sense, a moment of transition. Even conservative opinion allowed that the main body of Chartist support was composed of peaceful subjects whose discontent was caused by real privation and suffering.[8] For conservatives, the main culprits were laissez-faire and the new poor laws, which had disaffected loyal working people who were then preyed upon by demagogues and republicans. Liberal opinion looked to the revival of trade and the lowering of food prices, following the repeal of the Corn Laws, as a means of lessening unrest. Nevertheless, across the spectrum of opinion within the governing classes, there was a sense that a more conciliatory and more mediating form of relationship between the different social orders must be evolved.

This was by no means a general recognition of the need for democratic social inclusiveness or for democratic institutions, but it was an acceptance that communication and understanding within society should be more open. By use of the platform, the Chartists had claimed for themselves a right to discursive space in the public sphere. Thereafter, it was tacitly accepted that some form of dialogue between classes was preferable to the resort to coercion and force on either side. Again there is a clear parallel with the political challenge posed in *Coriolanus* of the need to find a new style of domestic politics. An article printed in the *Westminster Review* in 1848 concisely brings together the two connected issues of leadership and a more inclusive style of social intercourse. The writer draws the attention of "all earnest reformers," including the "moral force section of the Chartists," to an important distinction: "the distinction between *ruling* a nation, and *representing* a nation. To *rule*, is a question of force; . . . but to *represent*, is a question of discussion." The article goes on to suggest that "a national *Council*" should be established in the "exact image of the nation itself, *in petto*, with all its multifarious shades of opinion."[9] In effect, the journal is advocating recognition of a heterogeneous national public sphere. The *Westminster Review* is silent on whether this exact image of the nation would involve women's participation in a national council. Women, in the 1840s, lacked the political means of forcefully entering the public sphere, as had the Chartists, to articulate demands for greater recognition and inclusion in the body politic.

Both *Shirley* (1849) and *Henry Esmond* (1851) are historical novels in the literal sense of setting their stories back in a time prior to the time of writing. More importantly, they are illuminated by a fully historicized imagination that constructs a transitional narrative perspective encompassing an earlier social world that reaches forward to the evolution of a new order. This dual perspective may well account for some of the confusion of their critical reception. *Henry Esmond* has been praised for its rendition of an eighteenth-century world, but also condemned for being wholly Victorian.[10] A contemporary reviewer of *Shirley* found in the story a "hankering" for "Toryism and High Church," even while these were regretted as things of the past. Another reviewer enjoyed the novel's "moral freedom, the spirit of insubordination, the impulse of revolt."[11] What has not been noted, either in nineteenth-century commentary or in twentieth-century studies to date, is that both Brontë and Thackeray are responding imaginatively to the general debates on constitutional leadership in the public sphere of the 1840s and, more specifically, to Carlyle's influential ideas on heroes and hero worship. Both fictions represent traditional types of territorial national leaders in terms of high-born charismatic military heroes, and each explores the dangers that these pose to the common weal. Yet both Brontë and Thackeray recognize that narcissistic identification with glamour and erotic attraction to power are probably inseparable from effective projections of charismatic authority.

In different ways, the narratives of *Shirley* and *Henry Esmond* both start from societies structured upon principles of exclusion and attempt to imagine more inclusive principles of social affinity, as the *Westminster* reviewer terms it. Brontë and Thackeray associate this social affinity with a national identity that is in contrast to class exclusivity and in opposition to what is not British. For both writers, the need to discover principles of affinity is understood as a problem of public language; a new kind of inclusive social communicative code is required within the public sphere to bring into being a newly evolving form of domestic national order.

In this sense, Brontë is extremely conscious that as a woman writer attempting to deal, albeit in a novel, with political issues, she is entering a contested public sphere. It might seem somewhat surprising, therefore, that *Shirley* (1849) opens with the narrator picking a quarrel with the reader, who is accused of misreading the introductory promise that the story will evade the present years as too "hot" and "arid" and return to earlier times "and dream of dawn" (5). This assumption that the reader is probably making erroneous assumptions characterizes almost every address to the reader by the narrator throughout the fiction. "If you expect to be treated to Perfection, reader, . . . you are mistaken," declares the narrator, on introducing Mr. Yorke (46). This plain speaking and rejection of the forms of civil compliance probably contributed to one contemporary reviewer's sense of the book as pervaded by "a sort of ingrained rudeness," while another declared that the first chapter would be enough to deter most readers.[12] The contrast with the narrative tone in novels by Jane Austen could not be more striking: the precision and security of Austen's voice derives from her sense of addressing the known community of civil society, whose perspective, values, and cultural assumptions she largely shares. Brontë speaks to no such known community. She determinedly positions her work within the critical debates of the public sphere, but it is a public sphere that has become much more heterogeneous than that of Austen's day. Brontë has to make guesses as to her readers' perspectives, and she expects that miscommunication, misunderstanding, and misrepresentation will result. Raymond Williams diagnoses this loss of known community as "a problem of language" (*Country and City*, 209), and Brontë's uncertainty of tone, especially in *Shirley*, foregrounds this problem. The narrator's opening assumption that she will probably be misunderstood is borne out by the quite opposing political perspectives that critics ascribe to the text.[13]

The promised "dream of dawn" in which the story is to be set would thus appear to be sometime after Babel and the resulting confusion of tongues. Yet the opening image of dawn does hint at the utopian possibility of a new world. Nevertheless, it is babel that reigns in the masterly first chapter, with its trio of curates who associate not for "friendship . . . for whenever they meet they quarrel" (7). In this opening episode, Brontë swiftly illustrates the narrative's thematic conflicts of gender, class, and region by means of the curates' incivility to Malone's landlady "just because she doesn't keep a servant, but does the work of the house herself, as her mother did afore her" and their offensive propensity to be "always speaking against Yorkshire ways and Yorkshire folk" (8). In the curates' drunken dissent among themselves, the further conflicts of race, religion, and nationality form the basis of shouted insults, so that the Reverend Helstone, who commands their silence, likens the din to "the confusion of tongues," rather than the "miracle of Pentecost" (12). The narrator describes Helstone as having "more of the air of a veteran officer chiding his subalterns than of a venerable priest" (13). Shortly on, the visions of Mike Hartley, an Antinomian, violent Jacobin, and leveller, are related. Mike has seen thousands and tens of thousands of disciplined soldiers commanded by "a man clothed in scarlet [who] stood in the centre and directed them" (17). It would seem that both levellers like Mike Hartley and clerical upholders of the Establishment dream of leadership in military images.

This first chapter, then, foregrounds a problem of language and initiates the ideological agenda of the text: the transformation of babel into the gift of tongues — the resolution of social contention and misrepresentation into open communication and understanding. It suggests the further question of whether a military ethos of leadership, a Coriolanus figure shaped by conflict, is best suited to achieve such a cultural transformation. Visions and dreams are implicated in this chapter, both with the traditional romanticism of conquest and glory and with utopian hopes for a new order.

The story is set, with careful accuracy of historical detail, at the time of the Luddite disturbances, but the dissonance of language and violence of opposing viewpoints, encompassing every sector of national life, situates the text discursively within a "hot" and "arid," post-1832 perspective.[14] Shirley's dismissive comment that those who insist that charitable relief should not be offered to the poor during times of exceptional hardship are "great fools" echoes conservative responses, not to Luddism, but to Chartism, imputing blame for the unrest to the harshness of liberal political economy. The bitterness of debate between Helstone and Robert Moore — the former an upholder of the traditional sanctities of noble birthright, primogeniture, and the Establishment, the latter a proponent of laissez faire and liberal individualism — belongs to the era of the Corn Law struggles of the 1840s. During that struggle, both conservatives and liberals sought to ground the legitimacy of their cause in claims to patriotism and national interest. This discursive interpellation of "the nation" and "the people" helped to produce, imaginatively, the sense of the national collectivity that it was, simultaneously, invoking. Yet two quite different forms of leadership and patriotism were envisaged: on the one hand, the traditional, highborn heroic defender of the ancient land and territorial honor against external foes, and on the other, a progressive leader of the new world of industry enhancing British interests by means of trade and commerce.

In *Shirley*, these two types and two worlds are figured as the two heroes — the older Reverend Helstone and the young Robert Moore. An article in the *Westminster Review*, in 1848, typically propounds the "progressive" case, contrasting the more rapid progress of manufacturing, since 1801, to the slow pace of agricultural change; this unanswerably establishes "the wisdom and patriotism" of those who released trade from the "fetters" of the antiprogressive agricultural interest. The writer goes on to invoke a heroic tradition of patriots, all "born in Great Britain": Arkwright, Hargreaves, Crompton, Kaye, and Cartwright. The article concludes, "In our humble opinion, the steam engine alone, were it our one only achievement in mechanical skill, would place us at the head of nations."[15] In *Shirley*, the mechanic Joe Scott puts forward similar claims for the active intelligence of a northern mentality: "I reckon 'at us manufacturing lads i' th' north is a deal more intelligent, and knaws a deal more nor th' farming folk i' th' south. Trade sharpens wer wits; and them that's mechanics, like me, is forced to think" (59). Joe reckons there are thousands like himself in Yorkshire.

The form of patriotic leadership offered by the adherents of aristocratic rule was more closely aligned to the use of force than to progressive invention. Rather than mental vigor, as in claims for the preeminence of trade and industry, aristocratic leadership was figured in terms of masculine virility. In 1849, *Blackwood's Magazine* devoted a long article, "Feudalism in the Nineteenth Century," to asserting the claims of aristocratic leadership as primarily a military order, a nobility "of the sword," entrusted with the honor and security of the nation. The nobly born leader, the writer enthuses, is "the representative, the *beau ideal*, of the virility of the whole nation: he is the active principle of its force — the leader, the chief agent, in building up the fortunes of his country."[16] Other articles in *Black-wood's* embellished the idea of a nobility "of the sword" with a purported inherent territorial characteristic of the English to be a warlike people destined, under proper leadership, to overseas conquest and expansion. A reviewer, in 1847, wrote, in an article extolling the heroic virtues of Wellington, that "the North [of Europe] brings forth a bolder race of men than the south"; it is the vigor and resolution of the English people combined with "an ardent and aspiring disposition" that has constituted them a race "to whom was destined the dominion of half the globe."[17] *Shirley's* topical concern with national leadership is early expressed in the conflicting claims made for Wellington and Napoleon by Helstone and Moore. The arch Tory, Helstone, affirms a widely held conservative view when he asserts, "Wellington is the soul of England . . . the fit representative of a powerful, a resolute, a sensible, and an honest nation" (38).

The society that Brontë imagines as the fictional world of *Shirley* may well seem in need of a form of leadership capable of resolving its multiple social conflicts and divisions. Brontë represents it as a society that imagines its social reality almost wholly in terms of naturalized exclusions. The society — it can't be called a community — of *Shirley*, as a whole, is riven by divisions. The public sphere of the fictional world is an extremely restricted one, and the automatic response of most characters to dissent from their views is to exclude the dissenter. The narrative is punctuated by injunctions to silence.

Despite this exclusionary social order, there is a striking difference between the fictional worlds imagined by Austen, on the one hand, and by Brontë, on the other. For Austen, the restricted world of her fiction *is* the social world that matters, whereas for Brontë, the limitations have become a problem to be addressed. Brontë is imagining a divided heterogeneous national society, rather than a homogeneous cultured class community: in *Shirley*, the words *England, English* and *Britain* are conspicuous in their frequent recurrence. The nature of the conflicts and divisions dramatized in the narrative are also national in scale, rather than individual, deriving from structural social and economic inequalities. But this is not yet the representation of a whole national society in the sense that Dickens conveys it in *Bleak House* and even more so in *Our Mutual Friend*, or even as Thackeray represents it in *Henry Esmond*. The world of *Shirley* is a local one that, in its social and political heterogeneity, is a microcosm of national society. Although larger historical events impinge somewhat upon the plot, they happen elsewhere. What is more, existing alongside the text's ambitious and percipient engagement with the discursive struggles for political hegemony that were part of its moment of production, there is a strange sense that the story is located in dream time and dream space. The narrative enacts a shuttling duality between the historicized time of realism and the ancient timelessness of romance. This slide between realism and romance marks a pervasive political ambivalence in the text between an impulse for reverence and an impulse for egalitarianism.

Brontë's handling of the attack under cover of darkness on Moore's mill has been criticized by Terry Eagleton and others for its failure to represent the working-class attackers, who remain invisible and anonymous (45–49).[18] Yet the whole episode needs to be read as a precise symbolic figuring of the complex and multiple fissure lines and compelled absences of a society structured upon exclusions. Inside the mill, fortified like a garrison and protected by troops, Tories and Liberals have, in the "solemn league and covenant" of propertied interest, pragmatically buried their mutual hostility to repel the demands of the massed working-class attackers outside. These outsiders are unseen, their voices unlistened to, wholly excluded from the public sphere and never even imagined as potential participants of the national collective by those inside the mill. Beyond that conflict of two male worlds, even further to the margins, women observe, in the dark, wanting to be involved, but also unnoticed and excluded. The framing narrative context of the attack upon the mill, however, offers voices to those silenced in the symbolic event. Shirley Keeldar, finding herself alone with Caroline Helstone, says that in the absence of men "we may speak what we think" (320). Responding in a visionary way to the grandeur of the encompassing hills in the evening light, she goes on to "dream of dawn," imagining Eve, not as misrepresented by Milton but as a rebel against a long history of oppression: "The first woman's breast that heaved with life on this world yielded the daring which could contend with omnipotence: the strength which could bear a thousand years of bondage" (320).

Shirley's meditation on Eve as symbol of oppressed womanhood is followed immediately by a conversation with the workman William Farren in which he asserts that working-class discontent is caused by real distress: "starving folk cannot be satisfied or settled folk" (325). The potential for alliance here between women and working people as like victims of "years of bondage" is cut through by the intervention of the mechanic Joe Scott, who articulates a misogynist biblical injunction that women should be silent and in subjection (328). The exclusion of women from all fields of activity but the domestic allied the interests of working-class men with those of the middle class. During the attack upon the mill, the middle-class heroines forget all sympathy for the working people in their class solidarity with those defending the property. In its entirety, what Brontë's representation of this episode calls attention to is the self-interested, pragmatic, shifting nature of social and political alliances; but all alliances function to maintain the structural exclusions and silences that constitute the social world and public sphere of the story.

The narrative of *Shirley* is punctuated with incidents and accounts of exclusion: intraclass, interclass, and gender divisions. The Reverend Helstone breaks off all relations with Moore because of his "unpatriotic" opposition to the war with France and excludes his niece Caroline Helstone from visits to Hollow's Cottage. At an earlier confrontation at the mill, Moore has held at gunpoint a group of working men who come to put their grievances to him, refusing to accept their arguments and brusquely excluding the reasonable complaint of William Farren from consideration. Much later, Mrs. Pryor is represented also as feeling a great gulf between herself and Farren — a gulf it would degrade her to cross (445). Mrs. Pryor herself has experienced class exclusion as governess to an aristocratic family who intimated that she must "live alone, and never transgress the invisible but rigid line which established the difference between me and my employers" (376). In this situation, she suffered the "dreadful crushing of the animal spirits, the ever prevailing sense of friendlessness and homelessness consequent on this state of things" (376). Mrs. Pryor's speech here articulates two central insights of the text: repression or crushing of the self leads to lack of vitality and physical decline, and a society that is structured upon exclusions constitutes the experience of most of its citizens as a state of homelessness and unbelonging. Louis Moore, Robert's brother, is represented as undergoing a similar process of alienation to that of Mrs. Pryor. As tutor to the Sympson family, he is treated with "austere civility," connected to the house "yet apart; ever attendant — ever distant" (455). To some extent, the tables are turned by Shirley when she excludes Mr. Donne almost physically from her home on account of his snobbish southern affectation and vilification of Yorkshire.

Exclusions of women also pervade the narrative, most obviously so in the case of Shirley's and Caroline's exclusion from all knowledge and discussion of the plans to defend the mill against the expected attack. However, more subtly, the story shows women to be friendless and "homeless" even within the so-called haven of the home — excluded from esteem, fellowship, or sympathy. Mary Cave's experience after her marriage to Helstone strikingly resembles that of Louis Moore as a despised tutor. She was "ever attendant — ever distant," dying in silence without experiencing any sense of shared community or sympathy with her husband. Caroline Helstone admits to Shirley that although her uncle has brought her up from childhood, she "would rather be out of his presence than in it," and she wonders if all men resemble him in their domestic relations (216). Her mother's experience of the domestic hearth reveals that they can be far worse. At the opposite political extreme from the Reverend Helstone, even the republican Mrs. Yorke preaches the duty of women's silence to her daughters (155).

The social exclusions of class and gender were commented on by many contemporary writers during the nineteenth century and are central to twentieth-century critical and cultural analysis. But Brontë foregrounds yet another basis of exclusion, albeit entangled in perceptions of class and gender, that modern theory and commentary still overlooks or looks away from: social exclusion based upon physical appearance. When Mr. Yorke asks Robert Moore if he would ever marry an ugly woman, he responds, "Bah! I hate ugliness and delight in beauty" (164). He goes on to say that his eye and heart take pleasure in what is fair and are repelled by what is grim and harsh. Narrative commentary suggests that this is a pervasively general attitude and one based upon a deeply naturalized visual response. When the narrator describes the picturesque architecture of Fieldhead, with its surrounding lawns and trees, she concludes that it satisfies "the very desire of the eye," as if there is an inherent human yearning for what presents itself as graceful to the sight (188). Shirley Keeldar is described as "no ugly heiress: she was agreeable to the eye" (198). The narrator describes Shirley's appearance as exercising a kind of charismatic attraction upon beholders: her face possesses "a charm as well described by the word grace as any other" (198). Jessy Yorke possesses a similar physical charisma, "the gift of fascination, the power to charm when, where, and whom she would" (156). In contrast to this capacity to meet the "desire of the eye" for beauty, the narrator implies that plainness is perceived as a "defect" that deters the impulse toward confidence and affection (94). Caroline Helstone suffers from no such deficiency of grace, but, although she comes to recognize "how wrong it is to neglect people because they are not pretty," she, too, has joined Robert Moore in mockery of those who are shrivelled, old, and ugly (176–77).

Clearly women, without other means of social authority and esteem, are more vulnerable to exclusion from community on account of their appearance than men. The representation of Miss Mann is used by Brontë to highlight the pain of being thus outcast on account of appearance, and she indicates its similar effect to all other forms of social exclusion. The old, plain, and humble, the narrator insists, still "have a longing for" appreciation and affection, still hunger for a sense of belonging in terms of "a Home, a Friend, a Refuge" (180). Yet although subjected to the "desire of the eye," women are also represented in the text as equally vulnerable to the power of visual attraction. Joe Scott says sarcastically that "women judge men by their faces," and this is borne out when Shirley admits the charismatic attraction of manly grace: "There is a charm in beauty for itself, Caroline; when it is blent with goodness, there is a powerful charm. . . . Indisputably, a great, good, handsome man is the first of created things" (219).

In a regime that orders social acceptability in terms of physical grace, the poor are inevitably disadvantaged — dis-graced by ugly clothing, poor posture, disfigurement, and deformity. Shirley scoffs at Caroline for mistaking a soldier for Robert: "How could you imagine it? It is a shabby little figure of a private soldier" (342). Mrs. Pryor is quite unable to believe that William Farren, a "rough-handed, rough-headed, fustian-clad clown," could have any feelings in common with the educated and cultivated (446). Yet despite Brontë's foregrounding of appearance as a mechanism of exclusion, she, too, naturalizes disfigurement as allied to defective personal worth by representing the radical Methodist, Moses Barraclough, as minus a leg.

In the narrative, all forms of social exclusion are manifested as problems of language. The world of the novel is post-babel. Not only is there confusion of tongues, there is also a silencing of the excluded in both public and private spheres. Caroline Helstone is represented as coming to recognize that prosperous society stops its ears to the suffering and complaints of women and the poor: "Such grievances as society cannot readily cure, it usually forbids utterance, . . . Old maids, like the houseless and unemployed poor, should not ask for a place and an occupation in the world" (391). She has reached this insight as a result of Moore's overnight withdrawal of a lover-like affection toward her. The narrator comments: "A lover masculine so disappointed can speak and urge explanation; a lover feminine can say nothing" (105). The working-class men who urge Moore for speech and explanation are also met with scorn, and when, later in the story, they attack the mill, Shirley is represented as saying with unwitting irony, "Moore speaks at last! . . . and he seems to have the gift of tongues," as he opens fire on the men outside (344).

Exclusion and silence have the opposite effect to the gift of tongues: misreadings and misunderstandings of the different languages of men and women, classes and regions, abound, babel-like, in the story. Shirley depicts Donne's southern accent as "lisping cockney," while Mrs. Pryor confesses that she cannot under-stand a word of Mr. Hall's "broad, northern tongue" (289, 449). More seriously, Shirley argues that men "fancy women's minds something like those of children" and consequently "they do not read them in a true light" (352). Toward the end of the story, her words are borne out as Robert Moore confesses how he misin-terpreted the frank kindness she has shown toward him as "a complicated, a bold, and an immodest manoeuvre to ensnare a husband" (536). The novel hints at the utopian possibility of a Pentecostal gift of tongues by means of the many charac-ters who are bilingual or bi-dialectical and in the episodes in which characters read or translate from one language into another.

Underlying the exclusions that structure the narrative, there is a subtext of yearning for union and community. The word most frequently used to evoke this is *longing*—there is a longing to belong. This desire is most romantically or regressively expressed in the adolescent story of origins purportedly written by Shirley. In it, an orphaned child, Eva, "bereaved of both parents," wanders "for-saken, lost" through a landscape that is primal but suggestive of Britain, with its "island oak-woods" and temperate climate, propitious of harmony rather than violent extremes of coloring and heat (486, 485). The story culminates when the indefinite but anguished yearning of Eva is fulfilled in union with an invisible Bridegroom who gathers "her in like a lamb to the fold," promising "to sustain, to cherish, mine own" (489). Although the Bridegroom is referred to by mas-culine pronouns, this ending to Shirley's adolescent romance is remarkably simi-lar to Caroline Helstone's long-sought reunion with her lost mother.

When Caroline begins to fall into depression, she "longed to leave Briarfield, to go to some very distant place." The next sentence seems to associate this idea of place with her mother: "She longed for something else: the deep, secret, anxious yearning to discover and know her mother strengthened daily" (186). Imme-diately following on from this passage, Caroline is described almost as an excluded or homeless ghost, haunting the picturesque vicinity of Fieldhead and Hollow's mill, where she suddenly sees, close by her, Robert Moore with Mr. Yorke. Unable to speak out, she feels more totally bereft than ever — overwhelmed by "the utter sickness of longing" (189). During the course of this sickness, while she is being nursed by her as-yet-unknown mother, she tells Mrs. Pryor, "I have a longing wish for something" and asks her to sing the hymn in which the first verse concludes: "Our shelter from the stormy blast; Our refuge, haven, home!" Shortly on, the mother and daughter are properly reunited, and Mrs. Pryor promises Caroline, "I return now to cherish you again," holding Caroline to her bosom while "the offspring nestled to the parent" (434). This language of belonging and cherishing is echoed in Miss Mann's longing for "a Home, a Friend, a Refuge" and in Shirley's myth of origins; it is also strikingly similar to Louis Moore's sense of a natural right to "sustain" Shirley and "nestle her to my heart" (522). In contrast to this, Robert Moore later admits that he and Shirley "never *could* be at *home* with each other" (538).

Early on in the story, a passage describing Caroline's sense of loss of community brings together the textual linkage of dreams of mythic origins, place, longing, home, and an associated slippage between maternal enclosure and sexual union. Caroline's uncle has prohibited her visits to Hollow's cottage, "her earthly paradise; how she longed to return to it, as much almost as the First Woman, in her exile, must have longed to revisit Eden" (250). The name *Hollow's cottage* and the building's deeply embanked position are also suggestive of a womb-like space. The narrator introduces Caroline Helstone into the story at that liminal point in life when she is about to leave the enclosure of childhood and enter the world of reality. The world of childhood is imaginary; it is "a marvellous fiction," says the narrator, "almost always unreal" (97). The world of reality, on the other hand, contains knowledge and experience of sorrow, death, and loss. It is a world that frequently "humbles" and "crushes" the emerging self, as well as often refusing it a place or home (98). We might associate a liminal position at the junction of these two worlds with an ambivalent perspective that oscillates from imaginative reverence and visionary romance to skepticism and rational realism.

Within the narrative, these two ways of "reading" the world are represented separately in the characters of republican Mr. Yorke, utterly bereft of the organ of veneration, and Shirley, with her visionary trances that "make earth an Eden" (47, 387). The ambivalent perspective belongs not only to the narrative as a whole but perhaps also to Caroline, the more skeptical and disillusioned character. The imaginary world of childhood that Caroline is on the verge of leaving is described by the narrator as constituted by two aspects of romance: it is land-scaped by "dream-scenes" and peopled by heroes (97). The places of childhood have an imagined intensity never again experienced; they are, says the narrator, stranger, sweeter, brighter, more dangerous, or of unutterable beauty. The inhabitants of this world are "half-divine or semi-demon," moving between the extremes of good and evil, love and hate, beauty and ugliness (97). Unconscious memory of this imaginary space may well persist as an undefined longing to identify with power, beauty, and place as home or refuge.

Shirley is full of references to heroes and epic national leaders: Coriolanus, Luther, Moses, Napoleon, Nelson, and Wellington. While writing the novel, Brontë was responding consciously to Thomas Carlyle, who was described in the *Westminster Review* in 1847 as "the great heroic biographer, the reviver of hero-worship in the present generation."[19] This comment was part of a review of Carlyle's second edition of *Oliver Cromwell's Letters and Speeches,* published that year, but in *Shirley,* Brontë is engaging pervasively with Carlyle's very influential published lectures *On Heroes, Hero-Worship, and the Heroic in History* (1841). Carlyle's lectures passionately articulated his belief that the eighteenth-century legacy of rationalism and skepticism, especially as materialized in the new poor laws, had contributed largely to the class unrest that marked the late 1830s and early 1840s and to the upsurge of support for Chartism. His solution to social division and the political ambitions of the working class was a return to traditional imaginative reverence for heroes. For Carlyle, the hero, the great man, is endowed with charismatic force as by divine grace. "The great man," he writes in a typical passage, "with his free force direct out of God's hand, is the lightening. His word is the wise healing word that all can believe" (5:13). Not only *can* he be believed, the hero is he who *impels* belief and who has the charismatic power and authority within himself to attract willing submission to his command: "There is no act more moral between men than that of rule and obedience" (5:199). Only obtain heroic leaders, Carlyle insists, and social unrest and unlawful class ambitions will give way to a willing, reverent docility. For Carlyle, divisions and exclusions are to be imaginatively dissolved within the encompassing folds of hero worship. Self both finds a home and loses itself in an identifying union with greatness.

Brontë was clearly thinking of Carlyle during the time she was writing *Shirley.* She mentions his name in several letters during 1848, and in April 1849 she wrote, "I like Carlyle better and better. . . . [I do not] always concur in his opinions, nor quite fall in with his hero-worship; but there is a manly love of truth, an honest recognition and fearless vindication of intrinsic greatness, of intellectual and moral worth, considered apart from birth, rank, or wealth, which commands my sincere admiration" (*Correspondence,* 2:326). Brontë's reservations about hero worship derive from a suspicion she shares with Hazlitt as expressed in his essay "*Coriolanus.*" On the one hand, the need to belong, the desire for a social space, a home, may be assuaged in a willing submission of self to a greater other, but, on the other hand, that imaginative investment in admiration for and submission to the figure of the hero may involve an unhealthy desire to identify with power. Brontë's class, gender, and regional position offers her a liminal vantage point in which her concern with the hero oscillates ambivalently between reverence and skepticism.

The most explicit discussion of heroes in *Shirley* occurs in the conversation between Caroline Helstone and Robert Moore in response to his reading of *Coriolanus*. Although Caroline has earlier insisted to Robert that he is "made to be great," the moral she wants him to take from Shakespeare's play is that he must not be contemptuous toward his workpeople but must learn to make those beneath him love him, or, as Carlyle would phrase it, revere him as a leader (85, 93). Yet *Coriolanus* might be read more appropriately as warning of the difficulties of transposing a traditional form of leadership — a leadership of the sword against external enemies — into a new changed social context of domestic peace. This is a situation demanding very different skills to those of the hero shaped in the conflict of battle or in violent oppositions. Yet again, Hazlitt read the language of the play as an expression of the dangerous, charismatic glamour of power upon the general imagination. The problem for Hazlitt was how to prevent hero worship.

On the face of it, Robert Moore would seem to be representative of a suitable kind of hero and leader for a modern manufacturing nation: he is a self-made industrialist, rational, enterprising, and of European outlook. When Caroline wants to rush impetuously to his aid during the attack upon his mill, Shirley responds scornfully, "How? By inspiring him with heroism? Pooh! These are not the days of chivalry: it is not a tilt at a tournament we are going to behold, but a struggle about money, and food, and life" (342). Yet Moore is not subsequently shown struggling to make money, throwing all his energies into the competitive battle to succeed in business. Although, during the reading of *Coriolanus*, he dismisses war as "out of date," he is represented as feeling a "warlike excitement" in his consciousness of the hostility and hatred he has provoked in the working people of the area (91, 31). Subsequently, he is represented in heroic opposition to working-class threats, striding into his mill yard, in his eyes a "deep dancing ray of scorn," to hold at bay twelve angry men and arrest the ringleaders of those who broke his new machinery (133). In the attack upon the mill by a working-class army, Moore enthusiastically seizes the role of commanding officer, disciplining his troops not to open fire until the attackers have fired the first shot. After the mill has been saved, far from settling down to the prosaic business of profits and cloth production, Moore is still represented in dashing military action. Hunting down the leaders of the riot offered an "excitement . . . pleasant to his nature," while the danger of assassination acted as a "spur in his high-mettled temper's flank" (383, 384).

In a letter to her friend, Margaret Wooler, in March 1848, while she was engaged upon *Shirley*, Brontë wrote that she had outgrown her youthful sense of war as romantic and glamorous: " 'the pomp and circumstance' of war have quite lost in my eyes their factitious glitter" (*Correspondence*, 2:202). Yet despite this rejection of the charisma of military glory, the representation of Robert Moore seems to suggest that Brontë finds it very difficult to imagine a hero in terms other than those of the physical and mental energies aroused in combat and conquest. Indeed, in the character of Robert Moore, heroic strife is undoubtedly connected to sexuality. To Margaret Wooler, Brontë had admitted that even to think of the romance of war "makes my pulse beat fast" (*Correspondence*, 2:202).

The need to constitute Moore as hero by means of an oppositional other to battle against causes something of a problem for the narrative. The working class must remain unrepresented or must appear like Moses Barraclough as lame and ridiculous figures. Rebel leaders represented as powerful might themselves become heroic and glamorous. The unlawful but charismatic ambitions of Napoleon haunt the text. The effect of this is that Moore is always fighting with shadows; he can hardly be represented as heroic in opposing unseen men, himself safely hidden within the mill. The only alternative means available to the text, apart from subordinating the unruly but absent working class, is the representation of Moore's relations with women. His appearance is shown to exert a strong physical attraction for women. Caroline is dazzled by his handsomeness: "his image struck on her vision with painful brightness" (308). Shirley recognizes him explicitly as a leader: "Prince is on his brow, and ruler in his bearing" (556). It is particularly in his relationship to Shirley, his social superior, creditor, and landlord, that his capacity for command is foregrounded. Instead of the deference and respect that might be due, almost every representation, throughout the narrative, of an encounter between Shirley and Moore underlines his inherent authority: "He contrived, not withstanding, to command a little; because of [his] . . . deeper voice, however mildly modulated, [and] the somewhat harder mind" (251). At the School-Feast, "you would not have thought, to look at him, that he was a poor, struggling man seated beside a rich woman; . . . you would have fancied his station towered above hers" (310). After the attack upon his mill, he rides up to Fieldhead and quietly countermands Shirley's orders to take an excessive quantity of provisions down to the victims of the fight. In the absence of a rebellious class "other" to subdue, heroic qualities in Moore are signified as the power to command and control any potentially rebellious woman, ambitious for equality of regard with men.

The story ends as Moore is about to become an unheroically contented husband and a concerned, large-scale employer with nothing further to fight for or against except increased profits and commercial competitors. Before this happy culmination, he makes a double confession to his friend Yorke: he admits to arrogance in his cavalier treatment of Caroline and Shirley and to error in his dismissive attitude to the working class. It seems poetically logical that, at this confessional moment, Moore, who has gained vitality and excitement from his scorn of the assassin, is shot down. It is as if in renouncing his claim to the heroic charisma of conquest, the narrative underlines his prosaic mortality. Heroism and leadership within an inclusive, domestic national context seems to evade Brontë's imagination. As in Carlyle's lectures on the subject, while the revival of hero worship is advocated to dissolve class ambitions and conflict in reverence, it is struggle and opposition that continues to excite and energize the writer's vision.

The Tory, the Reverend Helstone, provides *Shirley* with a traditional conservative hero. Like Moore, Helstone is prone to "war-like excitement" and rides out to meet the machine breakers "elate with the knowledge" he may be shot at. Helstone resembles Carlyle's "warfaring and battling priest" (5:116), but Helstone's own hero is the duke of Wellington, whose dispatches he reads in his morning newspaper (102). Despite his age, and in stark contrast to "old maids," Helstone is represented as being sexually attractive to his female parishioners: the romantic heroine, Shirley, quickly becomes a willing admirer. In representing Helstone, the novel points explicitly to the distinction between a public romantic reverence for heroes and the skeptical viewpoint associated with domestic familiarity. While Mrs. Sykes and her three daughters are willing adorers, responding eagerly to Helstone's flirtatious manner toward them, the narrator insists that "he neither respected nor liked the sex, and such of them as circumstances had brought into intimate relation with him had ever feared rather than loved him" (115). Those like Mary Cave, whom he married, and his niece Caroline see the Coriolanus-like domestic tyranny behind the charismatic public persona.

Hannah Sykes, whose silly vanity singles her out for his attentions, would have willingly married him despite his age, but had she done so, comments the narrator, she "would have fluttered through the honeymoon a bright, admired butterfly, and crawled the rest of her days a sordid, trampled worm" (117). Women like Hannah are necessary to Helstone because they confirm his belief that women are inherently inferior. In allowing themselves to be trampled upon, they justify the submission and humiliation he requires to constitute his sense of masculine authority and right to command. The double representation of Helstone as public figure and private man makes explicit the danger to women of their willingness to endow men with heroic charisma. Women's adoration confirms Helstone's sense of himself as godlike, and this energizing self-plenitude and certainty is the source of his glamour. The logic that the narrative persistently reveals and then denies is that heroic leadership requires for its existence a subordinate other so that power may be materialized as the force to command or crush. Textual discourses oscillate between the romantic longing to believe that "they are the lords of creation. . . . a great, good, handsome man is the first of created things," and the skeptical realism that "undue humility makes tyranny" (219, 174).

Helstone's views of leadership are modeled upon the aristocratic ideal of a military nobility of the sword. He responds to class discontent with patrician contempt: "In this case my duty is a thorough pleasure. To hunt down vermin is a noble occupation" (43). Helstone is represented as totally devoid of any Pentecostal vision of himself as a priestly leader who could speak what Carlyle calls "a healing word," bringing discordant classes into harmony through reverence for his authority. His public qualities of leadership are most clearly and ironically shown in his marshaling of the School-Feast, described in the narrative in comically military language (301). This is the occasion when the rival band of Dissenters are confronted and routed. This is a musical rather an armed combat, one that links the established church to national identity, resolution, and military discipline, as Helstone orders his brass bands to play "Rule Britannia" while he strides out at the head of his force with "a determined and deliberate gait . . . well-seconded by his scholars and teachers — who did exactly as he told them . . . marching with cool solid impetus" (304). Since the Dissenters are elsewhere identified with working-class protest, this incident constructs a reassuring image of social inclusiveness, a vigorous national solidarity, embracing women as well as children of the laboring class, rallied effectively by firm leadership under the banners of nation and church against ill-led, rebellious ambition.

Yet a wholly conservative reading of the passage is too simple; Brontë's handling of the episode in its entirety is much more ambivalent. It begins with Shirley's response to the music of the brass band, which arouses in her "if not a martial, yet a longing spirit" (302). Helstone can identify a kindled imagination only with ideas of territorial glory and conquest: "There's no battle in prospect,

. . . our country does not want us to fight for it: no foe or tyrant is questioning or threatening our liberty" (302). Shirley replies that she will "borrow of imagination what reality will not give me." Lacking the heroic in actuality, she satisfies her unnameable "longing" by envisioning herself heroically as a covenanter holding meetings in the hills, "out of reach of persecuting troopers . . . ready and willing to redden the peat moss with our blood" (302). What Helstone's interpretation of "longing" and Shirley's fantasy both suggest is that heroic dreams or imaginary ideals require for their constitution some oppositional other as a force to be overcome or defied. The imaginative investment in this opposition as absolute good and evil—a regression to the childhood dreamworld of gods and heroes—underpins the impulse for both martyrdom and conquest. It is significant that while the male Helstone thinks of battle, Shirley imagines sacrifice.

Shirley's description of the covenanters "following [their] captain up into the hills to hold a meeting out of the reach of persecuting troopers" and ready if necessary to redden the moss with blood for their beliefs inevitably invokes a heroic analogy with the secret meetings that the Luddites held in the hills of northern England to organize for their demands. This analogy is pressed home as Shirley is roused from her imaginative identification with the covenanters by the sight of "a line of red" (303). This is the troop of cavalry soldiers coming to defend Robert Moore's property against working-class protest—a conflict that will redden the mill yard with blood. The ambivalence of that representation of violent combat expresses most clearly the tensions that Brontë explores between the romantic allure of the heroic and the skeptical perception of its price, the oscillating transposition between the glamour endowed by distance and the oppression revealed by closer familiarity. Unable in the darkness of the night to see the actual fight in the mill yard, but able to "guess that the fighting animal was roused in every one of those men there struggling together, . . . Both the girls felt their faces glow and their pulses throb" (345). The physicality of the language accentuates the sexual implications in fantasies of heroic male struggle. That such fantasies belong entirely to the imaginary is made equally clear by the pathetically unheroic scene revealed as darkness lifts and the realistic light of day shows only "desolation" and the bodies of wounded men who "writhed and moaned in the bloody dust" (346). Nevertheless, physically roused to such conflict, men are willing to kill and be killed, and women to hero worship the combatants.

In February 1848, Brontë linked Carlyle's name to thoughts on intellectual leadership and to a more inclusive democratic constitution for Britain. Writing to her publisher, Williams, about the new popular political order in France, she comments, "How strange it appears to see literary and scientific names figuring in the list of members of a Provisional Government! How would it sound if Carlyle and Sir John Herschel and Tennyson and Mr. Thackeray and Douglas Jerrold were selected to manufacture a new constitution for England?" (*Correspondence*, 2:194). In *Heroes and Hero-Worship*, Carlyle himself had no doubts as to the importance of intellectual leaders: "The man of intellect at the top of affairs: this is the aim of all constitutions and revolutions. . . . Get *him* for governor, all is got" (5:169). In *Shirley*, Brontë figures Louis Moore as such a type of hero and leader, as is indicated when Robert Moore tells Caroline that his brother has an "intellect of his own of no trifling calibre. . . . ere he had been master of Fieldhead a year, all the district will feel his quiet influence, and acknowledge his unassuming superiority: a magistrate is wanted — they will, in time, invest him with the office voluntarily and unreluctantly" (634).

Yet the narrative fails imaginatively to substantiate Louis Moore's heroic stature. Louis is never represented in the public domain exercising leadership or charisma. He is only ever perceived within the domestic sphere of the home, where his mastery consists of subduing the independence of the heroine. Shirley confesses to her uncle that the idol of her soul is Lord Wellington and that her husband must be "one in whose presence I shall feel obliged and disposed to be good. . . . A man I shall feel it impossible not to love, and very possible to fear" (552). Few readers have been impressed or convinced by this part of the story, in which Shirley's own heroic qualities are diminished to elevate her future husband.[20] Yet this conclusion has been trailed from early on in the narrative. The character of Shirley — independent, ambitious, demanding inclusion within men's sphere of power and action — is the means by which Brontë seeks to demonstrate the force of reverence to compel willing obedience and submission to authority. As the two heroines begin to confide in each other, Shirley tells Caroline, "Nothing ever charms me more than when I meet my superior — one who makes me sincerely feel he is my superior" (219). Shortly after this, the reader is informed that "to admire the great, reverence the good, . . . was very much the bent of Shirley's soul" (224). To Louis Moore, himself, Shirley speaks a Carlylean language: "Gratitude is a divine emotion" (514). Yet Louis remains ungodlike: his opposition to Mr. Sympson seems only a petty family quarrel. There is no action, no conquest, and no distance to confer glamour. The language of the narrative fails to endow him even with the physical sexual charisma of Robert Moore, whose brightness dazzles Caroline Helstone's desiring eyes. Perceived always within a domestic context, Louis seems an unlikely substitute to fulfil Shirley's romantic "longing" for the heroic in the form of Lord Wellington.

There is a sense in which all three heroes — Robert and Louis Moore and Helstone — form a series of substitutions for originary ideals of greatness: Wellington and Napoleon. The narrator describes the world of epic military battles in which thousands on both sides are slain as that of a "Titan-boy" playing like a god in a distanced imaginary Europe, "uproot[ing] mountains in his game, and hurl[ing] rocks in his wild sport" (635). The term *Titan-boy* is revealing; the dream of heroes belongs to the fictional world of childhood and perhaps to the regressive desire for an imaginary maternal enclosure. In the fantasy of origins, represented as Shirley's adolescent writing, the orphaned child is gathered up by an enclosing invisible might. This embrace is imagined as a fusion of timeless territorial grandeur with an erotically attractive force: "the power of sovereign seas, . . . the rooted endurance of hills wide-based, and, above all, . . . the lustre of heroic beauty" (489). The revival of hero worship, the subtext of the novel suggests, can be understood as a longing to return to an imaginary, unnameable world constituted of an intense, preverbal sensory experience of an enclosing place, power, and beauty. As such, it is always a regressive dream, and a potentially dangerous one. The eroticization of feminine powerlessness, as a means of shedding "the lustre of heroic beauty" on men, entangles women's "longings" with fantasies of submission and suffering. Deprived of a place in the political and social world, their vitality and ambitions crushed, women are tempted to invest in martyrdom. The text suggests, also, that an unconscious yearning for an ideal of beauty leads to the naturalized exclusion of those, like the poor, who lack the charisma of physical grace. In the opposing nighttime and daylight perspectives of the representation of the battle at the mill, in the double presentation of Helstone as charismatic public persona and domestic tyrant, in allusions that slide from European war to mythic epic scenes, the text also suggests that the desire for heroes can involve a collective blindness. The lustre of heroic beauty can dazzle a nation; reverence for greatness may produce general blindness as to its close familiarity with the force to subdue and silence. Brontë's complex exploration of the darker counterside of leaders as heroes is profoundly more modern and skeptical that Carlyle's glorification of conquest.

To be fair to Carlyle, he does also stress that one of the main distinguishing traits of the hero is his sincerity: "Such *sincerity*, . . . has in very truth something of divine" (5:54). While the majority of people are content with formulas and hearsay, the hero is a "spontaneous, passionate, . . . true-meaning man!" (5:53).

Carlyle argues that insincerity makes meaningful social association impossible, but "a whole World of Heroes" could come into being: "If Hero mean *sincere man*, why may not every one of us be a Hero?" (5:127). He does not explain how a world of passionate truth speakers is to be made compatible with the qualities of reverence and submission he set out as the ideal response on the part of the majority of men to heroic leadership. The *Westminster Review*, was much clearer in its distinction between "representation as a matter of discussion" and "rule as a matter of force." The ideal of a representative public sphere as forum for discussion put forward by the *Westminster* was "the exact image of the nation itself, *in petto*, with all its multifarious shades of opinion."

The narrative of *Shirley* foregrounds both sincerity and discussion as the necessary basis of community in opposition to silencing and exclusion. In challenging the conventional assumptions and formulaic expectations of the reader, the narrator is effectively staking out a claim to sincerity. Civility and complaisance must give way to the demands of truth: "Yet I must speak the truth" insists the narrator, thus affirming a pervasive narrative ethos (184). Sincerity is a quality that the narrator shares with all the main and many of the minor characters; the word *sincere* punctuates the narrative and is most frequently used of Caroline and Shirley, but it is also applied to Robert and Louis Moore, Miss Mann, Miss Ainsley, Mr. Hall, and Mr. Yorke. Sincerity, in the novel, is forcefully associated with communication, with facilitating interpersonal relationships, especially friendship, rather than with individualized sensibility. Robert Moore says to Caroline of Shirley, "If she professes friendship, be certain she is sincere: she cannot feign; she scorns hypocrisy" (253). Earlier, he has asked Caroline to assure him that "my kinswoman is my sincere friend," to which she replies, "Just so; I am your sincere friend, Robert" (86). After she has spoken hastily to Mrs. Pryor, Shirley says to Caroline, "I regret my error most sincerely: tell her so, and ask if she will forgive me" (364).

The code of civility that functions to sustain hierarchy, authority, and social convention is shown throughout the narrative to impede sincerity and hence block understanding and sympathy between different classes, genders, generations, and interests. Caroline admits to herself that "sometimes I am afraid to speak to [Robert], lest I should be too frank . . . he would disapprove of what he might deem my indiscretion" (99). Shirley also complains of the difficulty of holding completely equal and open discussions with Moore (314). Mrs. Pryor is represented as maintaining a distance in her relations with everyone but the two heroines by means of a "strict civility," which freezes any approach to the familiarity of sincerity. Similarly, the genteel Sympson family, who practice "austere civility," have a horror of any "fresh, vigorous style" or "unhackneyed, pure, expressive language" (454). When Caroline has to offer the expected hospitality of the rectory to Mrs. and the Misses Sykes, who are the standard of what is proper, it costs her a struggle to "perform this piece of civility" (111). In complete contrast to "civility" thus perceived is the egalitarian community of Caroline, Mr. Hall, Louis Moore, Harry Sympson, and Shirley, gathered round the little schoolroom fire, sharing a communal feast of Yorkshire oatcake and scorning the "proper luncheon" set out for "proper people" in the dining room (465–66).

Unlike the code of civility that maintains distance, a code of sincerity is represented throughout the story as productive of community and fellowship. In this sense, it can be understood as a utopian principle of affinity, or a Pentecostal gift of tongues able to bridge across different perspectives and social worlds by means of sympathetic, interpersonal respect and trust. When Caroline makes friends with Miss Mann and Miss Ainsley, the intercourse between them is described as candid and sincere. This allows both reclusive women to speak with unaccustomed freedom of their interests and feelings. The narrator warns, "Let those who cannot nicely and with certainty, discern the difference between the tones of hypocrisy and those of sincerity, never presume to laugh" at those they might, from prejudice and lack of familiarity, deem objects of ridicule (182). Mrs. Pryor, normally diffident and reserved, is similarly drawn into a sense of confidential community by Caroline's sympathetic tone: "in ten minutes they would have been friends," but for the abrasive presence of the Reverend Helstone (196). Mr. Hall relates how he and Caroline have "been friends ever since" he shared her duties of tea making at the School-Feast and she expressed her thanks "with an earnest sincerity" (284). The friendship between Shirley and Caroline is cemented as Shirley declares, "If you really are what at present to me you seem — you and I will suit. I have never in my whole life been able to talk to a young lady as I have talked to you this morning" (220). As a result of this discursive sincerity, Caroline feels none of the humiliation and dependency that might have been expected from their different social positions, but instead experiences "a safe sense of equality" unknown in her interaction with the other neighboring gentry. In addition to a community of feeling based upon mutual esteem and trust, the ability to speak freely and sincerely is linked throughout the narrative with vigorous mental and physical health, whereas repression of personal opinion and needs is associated with decline and sickness.

With the exception of Robert and Louis Moore, all those characters in the story whose sincerity is emphasized as being at the core of their personality and value system are also strongly associated with Yorkshire. This vigorous and fearless northern sincerity is opposed to the affectation and conventional civility represented as typifying the southern agricultural shires of Britain. Joe Scott makes a clear distinction between civility as a discursive code, located in the south, and sincerity as a northern form of speech. "We allus speak our minds i' this country; and then young parsons and grand folk fro' London is shocked at wer *incivility*" (59). Yorkshire identity is thus understood as embodied in a discursive sincerity that produces community. As such, this gift of tongues certainly does not preclude dissent. Those characters who are represented as proud of a Yorkshire identity scorn hypocrisy and false compliance and openly relish debate and the vigorous clash of opinion. Mr. Yorke offers Helstone hospitality, rather than civility, declaring that he still held himself "free to oppose you at every turn" (43). The narrator comments upon the working people's contempt for flattery and their enjoyment of good-humored abuse, "calling it plain speaking, and tak[ing] a sincere delight in being the objects thereof" (355). Within this discursive community, dissent is not perceived as a reason for excluding the dissenter; public sincerity offers the basis for open, unrepressed discussion of the multifarious shades of opinion that constitute a heterogeneous community. The Yorke family offers an image, in little, of fearless free speaking and freethinking. Mr. Yorke "scorns a lie, and deals in none of those conventional subterfuges that are shabbier than lies" (452).

The Yorke family are represented as assertively individual, but, says the narrator, Yorkshire has such families, "peculiar, racy, vigorous; of good blood and strong brain; turbulent somewhat in the pride of their strength, and intractable in the force of their native powers; wanting polish, wanting consideration, wanting docility, but sound, spirited. And true-bred as the eagle on the cliff or the steed in the steppe" (152). This sounds very much like a race of heroes. William Farren, who shares Caroline Helstone's interest in natural history, also attests to the stubborn independence of Yorkshire "blood." It is what "we call i Yorkshire 'clean pride,'" he says, in contradistinction to the curate Donne's offensive southern snobbery or "mucky pride" (324). A lack of docility and reverence and a determination to speak frankly and fearlessly typifies all the working-class characters in the story. Hortense Moore's assertive and rebellious servant engages her mistress in daily battles of opinion, while the cook at the Briarfield rectory grumbles, when county ladies come to visit, "I wish these fine folk would stay at home till they're asked" (86–87, 113). The contentiousness and rivalry among the

Yorke children is meant no doubt to suggest the dangers of a total absence of reverence in their personalities, but what Brontë's representation actually conveys is the engaging vigor of active, combatant minds. This vitality is especially attractive in the contrast it presents to Caroline Helstone's crushed and stifled energies in her attempted acceptance of women's conventional subordination. Rose Yorke expresses this contrast most graphically when she tells Caroline, "I am resolved that my life shall be a life: not . . . a long, slow death like yours at Briarfield Rectory" (399). While all these qualities of vitality, sincerity, and fearlessness are identified as inhering in Yorkshire "blood," they are also claimed to be essentially English, in a racial sense. Mr. Yorke's face is described as "thoroughly English, not a Norman line anywhere; it was an inelegant, unclassic, unaristocratic mould of visage" (46).

As a contemporary reviewer and more recent critics have recognized, the republican Yorke family exerts a powerful fascination upon Brontë's imagination.[21] What the novel represents, in the free discussions and vigorous debates among those characters of the Yorkshire "race," is a utopian glimpse of an inclusive community based upon a public code of sincerity as the discursive ideal, interpellating all speakers in relationships of mutual respect and regard. Yorkshire, in effect, becomes Carlyle's "whole World of Heroes," if hero means a sincere man — or woman, Brontë would add. Moreover, since Yorkshire is claimed to be the essential England, this inclusive local community, produced by a vigorous democratic discourse of sincerity, is, in petto, an image of the nation as it could ideally aspire to be. In imagining this ideal of heterogeneous social inclusion, Brontë, in the immediate aftermath of 1848, goes further than most other political commentators were willing to go. Like the dominant characters in the fictional world of *Shirley*, most commentators continued to imagine the social formation in terms of exclusions and divisions. Brontë also develops, much more fully than Carlyle, the democratic implications of community based upon an ethos of sincerity. Yet it must be noted that this ideal discursive community is never brought into any oppositional contact with the demand for reverence. The force of rule and the force of discussion remain quite distinct in the narrative of events.

If Yorkshire is a world of heroes in the Carlylean sense of fearless, vigorous speakers, it is also preeminently a place as territory and terrain. Yorkshire as geographical place is acclaimed as retaining its connection to the most ancient beginnings of the nation: the area named Nunnwood is "the sole remnant of antique British forest" (212). The central site of this originary landscape is described in suggestively feminine imagery as "a dell; a deep hollow cup, lined with turf as green and short as the sod of this Common; the very oldest of the trees, gnarled, mighty oaks, crowd about the brink of this dell: in the bottom lies the ruins of a nunnery" (213). It is in contemplation of this ancient spot that Shirley and Caroline recognize and seal their ties of race:

> "Our England is a bonnie island," said Shirley, "and Yorkshire is one of her bonniest nooks."
>
> "You are a Yorkshire girl too?"
>
> "I am — Yorkshire in blood and birth. Five generations of my race sleep under the aisles of Briarfield Church." . . .
>
> Hereupon Caroline presented her hand. . . . "We are compatriots," said she. (212–13)

These ties of blood and race are cemented in an imaginary England, a landscape of desire or dream of dawn. The language of a deep, enclosed dell, guarded by oak trees, is echoed in Shirley's mythic writing on the orphan Eva, wandering forsaken in a primal British geography. The representation of Yorkshire as an ancient, mythic place functions to exclude the industrial present of the region; even the mill, hardly ever working, is hidden in the Hollow. The imagined local community gains its identity through the members' mutual belief in the superior qualities inherent in their Yorkshire blood. Such heroic virtues are necessarily constituted in opposition to an unheroic other, imagined as affected, hypocritical, class-bound, and southern. In other words, despite the utopian vision of community, the notion of heroism remains tied to conflict. This subtext of longing for a place peopled by heroes should not be read in biographical terms, even though the novel was written while Brontë was almost overwhelmed by the loss of her brother and sisters. The myth of place inhabited by a race of heroes speaks powerfully to a general human desire to belong to greatness. During the course of the narrative, several characters indicate that if the repressive social exclusions and denial of a proper place in Britain cannot be overcome, they will emigrate to distant lands.[22] By the 1850s, British colonial expansion was well under way. It was justified in the name of English racial vigor, English pride in ancient Anglo-Saxon freedoms, and English bluff sincerity as opposed to the treacherous hypocrisy of all other races. As Helstone says in the narrative, Wellington is the fit representative of "an honest nation" (38).

There is a further danger in the ideological uses to which the code of sincerity lends itself. In *Shirley*, the narrator comments on Shirley's familiar, jocular abuse of the working people: "There is nothing the lower orders like better than a little downright, good-humoured rating" (355). It is easy to dismiss this as the kind of patrician condescension that was destroyed in World War I, but in fact the comment contains a shrewd and more lasting insight. The code of sincerity *is* flattering and seductive, especially to those who may suspect they are regarded as inferior. Sincerity interpellates on an intersubjective person-to-person basis, implying mutual esteem and trust. As such, the code of sincerity offers an appealingly inclusive mode of address to political leaders of mass societies. Britain in the 1840s was, like Coriolanus, needing to invent a new kind of leadership to that of a traditional nobility of the sword. It needed domestic leaders who could appeal to a heterogeneous society of diverse and conflicting interests, and interpellate it as a community. It needed to invent sincerity as charisma, as embodied in the character Shirley. This is a style of address and presence that subsequent nineteenth-century leaders (e.g., Gladstone) began to develop as a formidable ideology of inclusion.

The domestic world of an inclusive modern nation must find ways of avoiding the kinds of violent conflict that call forth the traditional hero of the sword. In turn, this means that the general desire to identify with power must be refigured and resituated. In the middle of the nineteenth century, this refiguring began to be effected by means of a bifurcation of imagined national identity. The actual domestic heterogeneous collectivity that was Britain was transposed into a mythic territorial community united by belief in heroic race and blood and by love of place as originary home. Colonial and imperial discourses constituted the national territory of Britain as an imaginary world of heroes, dissolving class, regional, and gender conflicts in an identifying sense of belonging (be*longing*) to national greatness. The yell of class hate that reverberates in *Shirley* gave way to the yell of tribal conquest. Dangerous ambitions and disruptive vitality could be displaced from the domestic world to far-away geographies where distance would lend glamour and heroic brightness to deeds of empire and leave unseen the bloody bodies in the dust and the human beings trampled like worms.

Shirley is a remarkable narrative: it gives powerful symbolic expression to a desire to belong, the yearning for a place or sense of home, at that moment in the nineteenth century when the traditional mechanisms of social exclusion were at maximum strain. It uniquely recognizes the force of the visual, "the desire of the eye," as constituting naturalized exclusions that are entangled with perceptions of class and gender. Brontë's imaginative insight into the powerful emotive resonance of place as an imaginary landscape intensely experienced and as a space of enclosure and security suggests a way we might begin to understand national identity as a passionate attachment to a particular geography. The persistent, ambivalent interweaving of realism and romance serves as a constant reminder of the inseparability of desire, both as regressive nostalgia and utopian dream, from political practices and pragmatics. Brontë's exploration of possible principles of social affinity and inclusion, in the form of an encompassing hero worship or as an egalitarian discursive code of sincerity, envisages, in the latter, the positive potential for democratic heterogeneous community founded on free discussion, but also skeptically foreshadows the more sinister and manipulative populist politics to which both hero worship and a code of sincerity would contribute.

Finally, we should recognize the implicit claims for inclusion, within an enlarged public sphere, put forward by the narrative voice. With its somewhat overemphasized refusal of conciliatory civility and rejection of readers' genteel expectations, it constitutes a performance of "sincerity." Readers are interpellated, at the beginning of the story, on terms of a rather brusque, take-it-or-leave-it equality. At the conclusion, the narrator proposes that "you and I must shake hands" (632). In the era of civility, handshaking was regarded as vulgar and overfamiliar; during the nineteenth century, it became part of the performative language of sincerity. What the gesture implies is continuing mutual respect despite possible divergence of opinion and hard bargaining. This is the kind of interpersonal regard that Brontë's narrative voice aims to communicate to readers. Brontë is seeking to speak within a newly-forming, more socially heterogeneous public sphere than that of civil society. Yet since she speaks as a woman, and from Yorkshire, her claims for inclusion also constitute part of the transformative pressures upon the public sphere to incorporate those voices and viewpoints formerly excluded. The uneasiness of narrative tone and the unsympathetic critical reception of the novel serve mainly to indicate that Brontë was ahead of her time in articulating a longing to feel at home, as a woman, within a fully national public forum.[23] In 1854, Elizabeth Gaskell was to use *North and South* to assert similar claims for women's right to a place in the public sphere. In *Romola* (1863), George Eliot set herself the task of demolishing John Stuart Mill's rational vision of the wholly dialogic national community that Brontë imagines, in petto, in *Shirley*.

CHAPTER FOUR

The History of Henry Esmond, Esq.

The Hero as Sincere Man

Henry Esmond (1852) is probably the most undeservedly underread nineteenth-century novel. Its narrative technique is ironic and sophisticated; its plot turns upon risky sexual ambivalence; and its handling of time is complex and masterly. Moreover, its political themes of citizenship, civic privileges, and sacrifices belong also to the modern world and remain largely unresolved. The historical perspective of *Henry Esmond* moves from the exclusive, aristocratic early family world of the eponymous narrator toward a much wider recognition of a national community, a community that newly encompasses Scotland as part of the post-Stuart political settlement. In this, the novel provides a contrast with *Shirley*, where, as we have seen, the known world of the main characters, while offering an image, in little, of heterogeneous society, always remains a local, regional community completely separated from the larger national and European world of public events. The widening perspective of *Henry Esmond* is structured as the political bildungsroman of the hero and narrator, whose ambitions, like those of Stendhal's hero in *Le Rouge et Le Noir*, drift between desire for clerical distinction and military glory. Henry Esmond ultimately rejects the scarlet and black for the public sphere of letters as a more modern terrain of leadership. This personal bildungsroman is framed within a larger political perspective. By analepsis, the text refers to Cromwell's execution of Charles I and the establishment of a republic; the time span of the main story coincides with the provision of a limited monarchy in Britain under the Hanoverians; and by prolepsis, narrative commentary looks forward to the American rejection of monarchical claims and the subsequent setting up of a republican order.

Castlewood House functions as a metaphor of this historical change. The most magnificent part of the ancient house was battered down by Cromwell's army and, although the family is restored to aristocratic status, the structural damage is left unrepaired, and the house, like aristocratic caste, is maintained on a less-grand scale (37). Henry Esmond retains a nostalgic affection for Castlewood House through an idealizing memory that forgets much of the unfulfillment and inequality of his life there. In a comparable way, conservatives in the 1840s were recasting the order of nobility in a haze of romantic nostalgia. It is Beatrix, the daughter of the Castlewood family, who points to the actual effects of subservience to birth when she recalls that "dismal old Castlewood that made us all gloomy, and dissatisfied, and lonely under its ruined old roof" (357). Henry Esmond builds a new Castlewood House in America, where he goes to escape the limitations of British political and social life. From this perspective, the narrator recognizes that in England "you take the house you live in with all its encumbrances, its retainers, its antique discomforts, and ruins even; you patch up but you never build up anew. Will we of the New World submit much longer, even nominally, to this ancient British superstition?" (373). Using very similar imagery, the *Westminster Review* noted that Britain was "not in the habit of pulling down" but of "patching" the political constitution of the country.[1]

The sense of temporal change, encompassed in the above quotation, is enhanced by the complex handling of time as narrative discourse shuttles constantly between narrative past and present and extradiegetic past and future. Despite this almost modern handling of temporality,[2] critical views of the novel's historicism have been varied. Many agree with Thackeray's biographer Gordon Ray, who praises *Henry Esmond* as a historical novel surpassing even the achievements of Walter Scott, but nevertheless concedes that it is the autobiographical elements within the domestic love story that empower the writing (178–80).[3] Georg Lukács offers the most sustained critical response to the historicism of *Henry Esmond*. He pays tribute to Thackeray's political disillusionment as expressed in the novel's exposure of the false heroism of great men within historical legend; nevertheless, this historical objectivity, Lukács argues, is dissipated by the failure of the main plot to engage with historical forces—namely, the "tempestuous development of capitalism" and "the new triumphant morality of the rising bourgeoisie" (243).

There is a sense in which Lukács and those critics (cited in chapter 1) who praise the novel's fidelity to eighteenth-century or nineteenth-century worlds are all partly correct. The limitation of the readings comes from a failure to recognize the complex connectedness of the novel to its own political times and the many continuities and parallels existing between the early eighteenth century and the 1830s and 1840s. The issues at stake in both centuries, and clearly recognized in the public debates of the 1840s, were political legitimacy and the struggles over inclusions to and exclusions from the recognized body politic of the nation. It is the long revolution of democratic social inclusion that is the focus of imagination in *Henry Esmond*—a revolution that is, of course, fundamentally aligned with the development of capitalism and the social and moral influence of the middle class. Thackeray, however, in *Henry Esmond*, is exploring the political dimensions of this long constitutional transition toward a principle of inclusivity.[4] Like Brontë, he is responding to Carlyle's lectures on heroes as well as to the general concerns, articulated in the public sphere, as to the kind of leadership required by a heterogeneous social formation.

Like Brontë, too, he looks to a discursive code of sincerity as a medium of community, as opposed to exclusion. The novel also stages a performative charismatic sincerity as a potential quality for popularly acclaimed leadership, but in doing so the narrative reveals the ironic contradiction between sincerity as public performance and sincerity as a quality of interiority. *Henry Esmond*, again like *Shirley*, recognizes a need, experienced perhaps with particular sharpness in the 1840s, that people have to feel they belong, that they have a place in the social world. In a wholly feudal order, the politics of "belonging" are not an issue since social identity and position are understood solely in terms of obligation and duty. *Henry Esmond* begins to ask those critical questions for a modern order. What is at stake in belonging to an inclusive collectivity? What are the duties and obligations and what are the rights and empowerments that constitute citizenship?

There has been a slow, often reluctant, but continuous evolution of political thinking in Britain—from the early eighteenth century, proceeding through the nineteenth century and remaining still ongoing at the beginning of the twentieth-first century—that sees a shift from birthright as an exclusive principle of legitimacy and privilege toward legitimacy vested in the inclusive national collectivity. One necessary initiating stage of this movement was what Linda Colley terms the "brutally reconstructed monarchy" of the Hanoverians (48). To offer the crown to George Lewis of Hanover, Parliament had to pass over more than fifty individuals who were closer blood relations to Queen Anne (49). Although this act in 1714 secured a limited monarchy in Britain up to the present time, it was revolutionary in import. It radically undercut the claims of birthright upon which not only monarchy but an aristocratic order depends for legitimacy. In *The Idea of a Patriot King* (1749), Henry St. John, Viscount Bolingbroke, revisioned a notion of monarchy dependent on national consent. The source of monarchical authority "is National, not Personal," he argued; "Kings are obliged to govern according to a Rule established by the Wisdom of a State that was a State before they were Kings, and by the Consent of a People that they did not most certainly *create*" (21).

The Reform Act of 1832 flowed logically from the implicit denial of birthright in 1714. F. M. L. Thompson, however, describes the loss of aristocratic authority as a gradual, long-drawn-out revolution (272). After 1832, Thompson argues, the force of national opinion began slowly to weigh in the balance against aristocratic influence, and by the end of the century aristocratic power was, in effect, a thin crust of assumed privilege resting on the substance of a mass electorate that had the power if not the will to set it aside (278). The partial abolition of the hereditary House of Lords at the beginning of the twenty-first century constitutes a further act in this reluctant revolution. Most historians agree that the aristocracy and the landed interest remained the dominant political force during much of the nineteenth century. Certainly, until the 1850s the most bitter political struggles were those of factionalism within the nobility. In that sense there was an obvious continuity between the eighteenth century world and the early nineteenth century. Internal feuding within the Tory nobility allowed the great aristocratic Whig families to preside over the Hanoverian succession, appropriating to themselves the virtues of disinterested patriotism, liberty, and progress. Similar Tory dissension and disarray, following Robert Peel's support for Catholic emancipation in 1829,[5] left the Whigs, in 1832, to usher in the Reform Act under the same claims of promoting national interest and liberty. Robert Blake, in his biography of Disraeli, suggests that Disraeli's understanding of eighteenth-century politics was actually based upon Disraeli's own mid-Victorian times (273).

Although the struggles over the retention of the Corn Laws to protect the revenues from land were frequently linked, in the contentions of the public sphere, with the Act of Settlement in 1701 and the Reform Bill of 1832, there was, in fact, a qualitative difference. The debates articulated a real challenge to the privileged status of land and territory as the fundamental defining principle of what constituted a disinterested stake in the country. Thompson pinpoints the conflict over the abolition of the Corn Laws in 1846 as the only moment in the nineteenth century when the challenge to aristocratic power was explicitly posed and vigorously defended (272). Robert Peel's support for abolition was perceived by the Tory nobility as the most bitter betrayal. Blake compares the political impact and fall out to that of Munich in the twentieth century (234).

The aristocratic class's fierce defense of the Corn Laws was motivated largely by economics: they sought to protect the value of land upon which their power ultimately depended. Yet it was also importantly ideological. With the rejection of birthright at the beginning of the eighteenth century, the justification of aristocratic prerogatives and privileges had to be refashioned. This was done in terms of a national epic in which landed property became the sanctioned principle justifying the right to power. The aristocracy began to figure themselves consciously as national heroes, defending territorial sovereignty with the disinterested patriotism available only to those having an immemorial stake in the land. Linda Colley provides a detailed description of the cult of heroism espoused by the nobility at the end of the eighteenth and the beginning of the nineteenth centuries that refigured class and factional interests as disinterested service to the nation. Aristocratic privilege and wealth became the means for a public projection of visually mythologized heroic patriotism and sacrifice.

The public exhibition of the painting of *The Death of General Wolfe* at the Royal Academy in 1771 began an artistic fashion among the aristocracy for massive portraits in classical and military style, and these were then crudely copied for mass production and consumption (Colley, 193). Gorgeous uniforms adorned with military swords, and rows of medals were specially created and worn for all public occasions. In effect, the aristocracy shrewdly recognized the importance of the public sphere, utilizing the charisma of conquest and landed territory to proclaim their disinterested patriotism and so gain popular assent for their exclusive position. This can be seen as a revival of "publicness," as Habermas terms it, although with a key difference. This is not the new, commercialized publicness of the second half of the century; rather, it is largely the same great people of the realm as in earlier times projecting the myth of their mystically endowed power and authority by means of visual presence within the wider public sphere as opposed to the court. Furthermore, this refeudalism also sought a material restoration of traditional codes of subordination, obligation, and duty. Despite, or because of, Chartism, conservative rhetoric of the 1840s projected a romantic myth of earlier relations of obligation between rich and poor. In *Bleak House*, Dickens satirizes these backward-looking illusions as a desire to "make the Vulgar very picturesque and faithful, by . . . cancelling a few hundred years of history" (173).

It seems almost the defining impulse of Thackeray's realism to debunk romantic idealizations. Nevertheless, throughout most of his writing there is an informed political attack upon privilege that postures as duty and upon hypocrisy associated with claims to noble disinterest. In his *Punch* series *The Snobs of England* (1846–47), he writes ironically of the nobility: "Your merits are so great . . . [that we, the people] shall enable you and the eldest born of your race for ever to live in fat and plenty. It is our wish that there should be a race set apart in this happy country, who shall hold the first rank, have the first prizes and chances in all government jobs and patronages" (14–15). John Sutherland comments on "the exceptional sense of emergency" conveyed by Thackeray's definitive writing on snobs and the anxiety he evoked in readers at the time (*Book of Snobs*, 4).

What made Thackeray's satire so dangerous was that he recognized and revealed that legitimacy had become a matter of representation, rather than substance. In his *Four Georges* lectures, he derides George IV as "nothing but a coat and a wig and a mask smiling below it — nothing but a great simulacrum" (7:686). *Henry Esmond* begins by emphasizing the uncharismatic actuality of the French king Lewis the Fourteenth. Without the glamour of distance, he is "but a little wrinkled old man, pock-marked," while, close-up, England's Queen Anne is "a hot, red-faced woman" (13, 14). Nevertheless, remarks the narrator, Lewis persisted "in enacting through life the part of Hero" (13). Royalty and nobility must delude themselves as well as others as to the inherent distinction of blood in order to so confidently assume their right to privilege and command. "A Prince that will wear a crown must wear a mask," Esmond tells the Pretender (414).

Throughout *Henry Esmond*, the myth of birthright as a mystical endowment of grace and plenitude is shown to be sustained and expressed by means of publicness: by a projection of charismatic style for the public sphere. The narrative is interspersed with ironic references to overflattering portraits of royalty and the aristocracy, frequently depicted as divinities or heroes. In *The Four Georges*, Thackeray writes of "that strange religion of king-worship" (7:642), and in *Henry Esmond* he writes of "worship of that monstrous pedigree" (322). The Dowager Viscountess Castlewood believes in miracles wrought at the tomb of the late King James II (189). The centrality of visual representation in sustaining this public mythologizing is suggested in the text by the vanity and concern over physical appearance in aristocratic culture. Viscount Castlewood is "not a little proud of his beauty," being "fond of the parade of dress" and spending "as many hours daily at his toilette as an elderly coquette" (73, 77). Frank Castlewood, Beatrix's brother, is early encouraged by his mother to "admire his beauty" (81). General Webb's pride in his lineage goes along with his vanity in believing himself "the handsomest man in the army" (242). While an imposing appearance can be taken as a gratifying indication of noble blood, it is, in an age of sharp inequalities of wealth and status, a less transcendent matter of good diet, confident bearing, sumptuous clothes, and splendid settings. Nevertheless, these qualities also provide all the advantages of distinctive presence required to convince in the public sphere of representation.

Worship of the nobility as charismatic figures endowed with almost divine grace is represented in the novel as part of a powerful and widespread imaginative impulse. It is not just an illusion imposed from above on the gullible. The text recognizes that there is a cultural willingness to endow physical beauty with special powers. In that sense, the text seems to support Carlyle's claim that ordinary human beings have a strong impulse of reverence, but the consequences of this are regarded far more critically than in Carlyle's writing. Throughout the story, a halo of luminosity suggests an imagined projection of divinity onto the merely human. The young Henry Esmond, dazzled by his first sight of Lady Castlewood's "golden hair shining in the gold of the sun," accepts her as a "*Dea certe,*" a goddess manifest (17). His spontaneous impulse of worship is mocked by the always irreverent Beatrix: "He is saying his prayers to mamma" (18), but later Beatrix seems to Henry to reveal herself like "a goddess in a flash of brightness" (414). When Beatrix and Frank are old enough to enter London society, their beauty wins them instant adulation and following. The narrator says of Beatrix: in her "dazzling completeness of beauty . . . there was a brightness so lustrous and melting, that I have seen a whole assembly follow her as if by an attraction irresistible" (217). Such are Frank's beauty and gaiety that "wherever he went, he charmed and domineered" (222).

The bringing together here of the capacity to charm and to domineer points to an exploration in the text of the contrasting relations to duty and disinterested-ness held by those of privileged and unprivileged social standing. Beneath the shining presence of nobility, a sense of special election, of near-divinity, gives to those who feel themselves so endowed a confident belief in their absolute right to regulate, and when necessary to dispose of, the lives of ordinary mortals. Young Frank Castlewood assumes "the calmness of patronage . . . as if to command was his undoubted right" (225). In the novel, the duke of Marlborough most fully epitomizes the chilling faith in a divine right to command human life. He has, says the narrator, "this of the godlike in him, that he could see a hero perish or a sparrow fall, with the same amount of sympathy for either" (237). Lord Castlewood is good-humored when he is flattered and indulged, but Lady Castlewood denounces the husband's absolute power over wife and children as "monarchical"; "in our society there's no law to control the King of the Fireside. He is master of property, happiness—life almost" (136–37). Frank Castlewood, like his father, is generous-hearted, but while still a child he sets up his court among the village boys, "already flogging them, and domineering over them with a fine imperious spirit, that made his father laugh when he beheld it" (96). As he grows older, Frank is impatient for the wider field of command and heroic figuring offered by military combat. The justification and self-identity of aristocratic caste as heroes and divinities is sustained, necessarily, by an ideology of conquest—of territory, women, and men. Lord Mohun is described as having the *bel air*, "a bright daring war-like aspect" (126). After Mohun has killed Lord Castlewood in a duel, Lady Castlewood, watching her son, Frank, in a mimic tournament with Lord Marlborough's son, despairs of the way such children are initiated into a nobility of the sword in which killing is idealized as heroism. She wishes she had never heard the word *gallantry* (178, 179).

In the novel, the fictionalized character Richard Steele tells the young Henry Esmond that there is no difficulty in persuading people to give their lives, disinterestedly, for a believed ideal: "everywhere multitudes die willingly enough" (65). Throughout his narrative of the war with France, Henry Esmond constantly uses the word *gallantry* to describe victorious English action, and he invariably follows this with an account of brutal carnage and plunder. On one occasion after battle, Frank Castlewood is represented, handsome and careless, singing and drinking at the center of an admiring group of fellow officers, the epitome of "disinterested" charismatic leadership unconcerned with personal safety or prudence. The narrator offers no explicit criticism of this thoughtless relish of battle as a sport, but says, "Great God! What a scene of murder is here within a mile of us; what hundreds and thousands have faced danger today" (264).

What the novel points to in such passages is the dangerous logic in the hero worship of kings and nobility. Reverence for the charisma of birth as almost divine inspires a faith and loyalty in the uncharismatic multitude that commands their genuinely disinterested obedience, even to death. This reverence is perceived by the nobility as conformation of their godlike right to demand sacrifice from others. "Tis for such as these," says the narrator, "that nations suffer, that parties struggle, that warriors fight and bleed" (418). If the aristocracy requires a cult of heroism and patriotic leadership to disguise their class interest, then inevitably they will have an investment in presenting national identity as territorial sovereignty. This not only demands an aggressive attitude to all other nations, it displaces sovereignty from the people, who thus become subjects for sacrifice and duty, rather than citizens.

An idealizing ethos of militarism and conquest under the guise of disinterested, heroic patriotism is represented in *Henry Esmond* as one of the necessary evils that result from aristocratic influence. Another, largely ensuing from this, is a pervasive culture of hypocrisy and deception. In *The Four Georges* Thackeray mocks the humbug of servility, which, at the opening of the Crystal Palace in 1851, had two noble lords "with embroidered coats, and stars on their breasts and wands in their hands, walking backwards for near the space of a mile while the Royal procession made its progress" (7:628). Such sights may seem merely ridiculous, but the show of humility by the noble lords was not disinterested. Public rituals of deference and reverence are the means of signifying power and authority held mystically as of right. In *The Four Georges*, Thackeray writes that royalty has flatterers but no sincere friends (7:691). In *Henry Esmond*, a social ethos based on the inherent hierarchy of birth produces either those like Tom Tusher, who superstitiously worships rank as a religion, or hypocrites who flatter from fear or self-interest. Tom's fawning behavior, says the narrator, is not hypocrisy but a natural inclination toward the great, to whom he is always obliging and servile (110). In contrast, the court in the final days of Queen Anne is represented as the location of self-interested hypocrisy by scheming nobility who pay lip service to monarchy to preserve or further their own fortunes and privileges.

Rachel Castlewood in her relations to her husband passes from self-deceiving servility to hypocrisy. In the early days of their marriage, "her lord was a god to her; his words her law. . . . She had been my Lord's chief slave and blind worshipper" (96). However, as he comes to hold her loyalty cheap, she learns to recognize him as far from godlike, although his legal and financial power over her remains unchanged. Where such disillusion with imposed authority exists, says the narrator, "the whole household becomes hypocritical, and each lies to his neighbour" (116). What the novel claims, by means of its constant analogy between family politics and relationships and national politics and social relations, is that any social order structured upon power held without consent or limit cannot be a community in any real sense since it is founded upon a simulacrum, an illusion, that necessitates a culture of deceit. Behind representation there is only emptiness. Beatrix, who is a voice of disillusion throughout the text, says bleakly, "We are all hypocrites. . . . We are all alone, alone, alone" (356). Collective hypocrisy and dissimulation make open and free discourse impossible. In that sense, the problem of community and belonging, as in *Shirley,* can be understood as a problem of language. The transformation of social exclusion as the structuring basis of society to social inclusiveness requires also a transformation of public communicative codes.

The political bildungsroman of the narrator as character, Henry Esmond, takes the form of a trajectory from slavish worship to self-responsibility, from an orphaned desire for a family identity based on blood relationship and landed property to freely chosen identification with a national community as its "people." The location of belonging is transferred from feudal vassalage to modern citizenship. While the narrative of Henry Esmond takes the form of a quest for heroism, it involves the rejection of the traditional fields of leadership: religion and war. Henry Esmond's growth of political independence is clearly to be read as an analogue of a national political bildungsroman. As a young child, Henry Esmond's first affectionate attachment is to Roman Catholicism as embodied in Mr. Holt, a Jesuit priest, who soon gains "an entire mastery over the boy's intellect," winning the child's "reverence" and "absolute fealty" (39–40). But Holt is soon replaced by Rachel Castlewood, Henry's *Dea certe.* She converts him willingly from Catholicism to the Anglican faith, since he "would have subscribed to anything she bade him" (74). To worship and adore her becomes the business of his life (72). However, alongside this impulse of reverence, there is another impulse of independence. This is represented as largely intellectual, pulling against the nostalgic desires of early affection and memory. From the outset, Henry observes for himself and begins to read and think beyond the range of the small family circle: "He read more books than they cared to study with him; was alone in the midst of them many a time" (74). At university, although ostensibly accepting his dutiful future role as family chaplain, his studies are eclectic and seek out religious and political controversy. Henry takes his family's Tory politics to college with him, but adds to this his own "dangerous admiration for Oliver Cromwell," enjoying student debates in which kings are crowned and deposed (112).

In addition to this intellectual development, Henry learns from his personal experience of the unhappy Castlewood marriage the way in which power corrupts social relationships. This teaches him to distrust fictions of reverence based upon a false belief in mortals as divinities. The final stage of demystification is marked by his recognition that Rachel is for him "goddess now no more, for he knew of her weaknesses" (210). Ironically, it is at this moment that their positions are reversed and Rachel begins to worship him, projecting upon him the luminosity of divinity: "I saw the golden sunshine round your head" (213). Subsequently, she appeals, "Let me kneel — let me kneel, and — and — worship you" (332). This abasement comes when she learns that he has foregone his legal right to the title of Castlewood. Henry's symbolic burning of his birthright can be read as the final stage in the process of separating himself from servility to a family name and blood that has deemed him an inferior because of illegitimate birth. He resolves, "If I cannot make a name for myself, I can die without one" (169–70). Subsequently, he comes to feel "a cheerful sense of freedom" to have escaped "the ignoble bondage at home" (199).

Linda Colley argues that British national identity was forged by war, particularly by conflict with Roman Catholic France: "From the Act of Union to the Battle of Waterloo in 1815, Great Britain was involved in successive, very dangerous wars with Catholic France" (19). Henry Esmond moves from independence of family for his sense of identity to chosen identification with an imagined national community by means of the experience of war. From book 2 onward, as Henry takes up a military career, the words *English* and *British* begin to appear quite frequently in narrative discourse. This experience initiates his disillusionment with military fame and heroes. Henry Esmond, as retrospective narrator, is far from glorifying war and British victories over the French. He is indeed bitterly ironic toward "You, gentlemen of England, who live at home . . . and huzzah for the British Grenadiers," while knowing nothing of the atrocities that are the other side of triumph (235). He is also critical of Addison's representation of war that leaves out all that is ugly and brutal. The fictionalized Addison's response to this criticism makes clear the ideological function of celebratory art in the construction of territorial might. It is the duty of the poet as a Briton, Addison says, to acclaim those heroic triumphs in which "every Briton has a share, and whose glory and genius contributes to every citizen's individual honour" (256).

Contrary to Addison's claim, it is not the experience of triumph and glory but that of suffering that produces Henry Esmond's identification with a national community, as opposed to the nation as territory. In this, Thackeray's understanding foreglimpses Benedict Anderson's emphasis on the symbolism of the unknown soldier's tomb in the imagining of nationhood and Ernest Renan's comment that "griefs are of more value than triumphs" in consolidating a sense

of national community (Anderson, 9; Renan, 19). The British armies under Marlborough win the battle of Malplaquet, but at a terrible cost in lives. It is this
episode in particular that drives home the casual account held of ordinary life by
those who regard themselves as endowed with a God-given right to dispose.
"Every village and family in England," the narrator says, "was deploring the
death of beloved sons and fathers" (319). For the first time in the text, the army as
a whole is perceived as a microcosm of the national community. Rank is largely
dissolved in the recurrent questioning: "Where were our friends? . . . Where's my
comrade? — where's my brother that fought by me" (319–20). It is immediately
after this traumatic event that Esmond tells Father Holt firmly that his church is
the church of his country, his faith that of "the countless millions of his fellow-
country men" (322). Religion here becomes an affirmation of a chosen national
identity, whereas previously Esmond's Catholicism and Anglicanism had been
merely a reflex of his hero worship, first of Holt and then of Rachel. It is at this
point, too, that Henry Esmond recognizes Stuart claims to divine right as "worship of that monstrous pedigree," and when Father Holt taxes him with republicanism, Henry does not disagree, but claims, "I am an Englishman" (322). In the
context of Henry Esmond's horror and repugnance at the carnage of Malplaquet,
this assertion symbolizes an unequivocal identification with the nation as its
people, not its territorial might.

   The final stage of Henry Esmond's political bildungsroman is completed
through his experience of the world of monarchical politics. Prince James Edward's ignorance of English language, morals, and liberties convinces the already
skeptical Henry that if Britain must have a monarchy, it must be such as "scouts
the old doctrine of right divine, that boldly declares that Parliament and people
consecrate the Sovereign" (416). Ultimately, he moves beyond even this tepid
acceptance of monarchical rule: "What cared he in his heart who was king? Were
not his very sympathies and secret convictions on the other side — on the side of
People, Parliament, Freedom?" (421). The next logical move from this is republicanism, and Henry, having always admired Oliver Cromwell, ends his days the
friend of George Washington (8).[6]

   In his *Four Georges* lectures, Thackeray declared, "We are with the mob in the
crowd, not with the great folks in the procession" (7:639).[7] The political and
social consciousness of Henry Esmond appears to be constituted upon similar
principles of inclusiveness, or what the *Westminster Review* had called the principles of affinity. This is represented, in part, as a recognition of the damage
inflicted upon people who are looked upon socially as unworthy and subordinate

and so excluded from equal regard and fellowship. As a child, Henry noticed how Viscount Castlewood's habitual "listless and supine" demeanor was suddenly energized by the self-respect he gains in defending his normally domineering wife against a no-popery mob (52). Henry himself looks back with "a bitter feeling of revolt at the slavery" imposed on him by deferential loyalty and gratitude to the family, and his energies waken and expand with a sense of freedom once he has taken control of his own fortunes (188). Beatrix speaks of her "sense of servitude" and "longing to escape" at the thought of her subordinate role in marriage (397).

More positively, the narrator's inclusiveness constitutes a sense of commonality with his fellow beings. Thackeray liked to quote the antislavery slogan "Am I not a man and a brother."[8] In contrast to Frank's imperious subordination and flogging of the village boys, the character Henry Esmond as a child associates with the servant lad John Lockwood as a "comrade" (46). The text draws attention to the shocking differences in justice meted out to rich and poor. Henry Esmond thinks back with shame to his insensibility at the misery of the common criminals whose conditions in Newgate were so very different from those of the gentlemen lodged comfortably there (181). He notes that the day on which Lord Mohun is set free after killing Lord Castlewood, "a woman was executed at Tyburn for stealing in a shop" (179). In *The English Humourists of the Eighteenth Century*, his lectures written just before *Henry Esmond*, Thackeray says that it is the task of the humorist writer to arouse "tenderness for the weak, the poor, the oppressed, the unhappy" (*Works*, 7:424).

The inclusive consciousness of Henry Esmond as character is constituted as a tolerant cosmopolitanism, an acceptance of what is other. He has encompassed Roman Catholicism as well as Anglicanism, but rejects the religious intolerance of both faiths. He comes to claim an English identity, but speaks French as his mother tongue (399). His father may have been a lord, but his mother came from a working-class family of Flemish silk weavers. Henry Esmond is constituted of many potential identities and assumes many names in the course of the narrative. The only strong antipathy he expresses is an antipathy toward the violent intolerance that is war. In the early part of his story, Henry is held by a nostalgic yearning toward an idealized, luminously remembered, aristocratic past. As he develops, he looks with greater hope to a future world: "Will we of the New World submit much longer, even nominally, to this ancient British superstition?" (373). The question within the story is ostensibly addressed to America, but the narrator speaks also to the novel's contemporary British readers in a political situation in which conservatives were yearning back to an idealized aristocratic past and progressive opinion was hoping for the beginning of a new, more inclusive political world, based upon principles of affinity, rather than exclusion.

Yet the narrative embeds, within the life story of its narrator, a utopian image of just such a community. At the end of his lectures on English Humourists, Thackeray proclaimed that the "great aggregate experience" of public opinion in the public sphere was the best safeguard against the self-interested hypocrisy that necessarily constitutes a world of exclusions based upon a mystique of birthright. The larger public world, he declared, always "detects a pretender" (*Works*, 7:617). He was probably familiar with the actual Richard Steele's view, as expressed in 1712 in the *Spectator*, that the only criterion for pleasing all the people, those below you as well as those above you, was "the Opinion they have of your Sincerity" (Bond, 2:592). In all of his writing on the English Humourists, and particularly on Addison and Steele, Thackeray emphasizes and praises the new code of directness that they brought to the public sphere. This was in sharp contrast to the insincerity imposed by a courtly discourse of subordination and flattery. Steele complained that "if any Man measures his Words by his heart . . . he can hardly escape the Censure of want of Breeding" (Bond, 1:430). The concept Thackeray reiterates again and again in praising the writing of Steele and Addison is that of "voice" to suggest the style of familiar, interpersonal inclusiveness that characterizes their direct address to the reader as a fellow being. Until Addison—"the most delightful talker in the world"—began to speak, says Thackeray, eighteenth-century language was "artificial" and "quite unlike life" (*Works*, 7:483). And "the great charm of Steele's writing," he declares, "is its naturalness . . . [he] make[s] the reader his confidant" (7:510). Steele may not be the greatest wit or most profound thinker, "but he is our friend" (7:514).

Confidant and *friend* are the implicit interpellations of a code of sincerity, posited upon a formal assumption of equality of regard as the basis of social relations. It is a performative act of communication demanding a response of mutual trust that is difficult to resist. The potential for manipulative force lies in just this performative logic of sincerity as interpersonal public code. As Adam Smith noted, "We trust the man who seems willing to trust us. . . . The man who . . . invites us into his heart . . . seems to exercise a species of hospitality more delightful than any other" (337).

In effect, Thackeray's writing demonstrates the contagious force of performative sincerity. Thackeray enters imaginatively into the world of eighteenth-century writers as into a known community based upon mutual esteem, friendship, generosity, and indifference to rank (*Works*, 7:541–42, 7:570, 7:585). In *The Four Georges*, Thackeray writes, "Delightful Spectator! Kind friend of leisure hours. . . . How much greater, better, you are than the King" (7:640). In *Henry Esmond*, the narrator's daughter informs the reader that "[her father] set the humblest people at once on their ease with him" (10). In the story, it is the tolerant quality of inclusive friendship offered by the fictionalized Steele and Addison, as opposed to their literary writing, that is foregrounded as an oppositional form of social relations to that of the divisions, self-interest, deceit, and hypocrisy of rank and court. Despite finding themselves on opposing sides during the bitter factional struggles that ended Marlborough's political career, their sincere regard for each other can transcend or respect difference of viewpoint. When Esmond bumps into Addison late at night, Addison greets him, "What cheer, brother? . . . Why should we quarrel, because I am a Whig and thou art a Tory? Turn thy steps and walk with me to Fulham, where there is a nightingale still singing in the garden, and a cool bottle in a cave I know of" (416).

Yet Henry Esmond as character aspires to more than brotherhood. He is ambitious for distinction and leadership, ostensibly to win the approval of Beatrix, who is as hungry for eminence as he is. What kind of hero or leader can achieve recognition by the great aggregate of public opinion that always detects a pretender? Not surprisingly, the narrative fashions the hero as sincere man. To this point I have been referring, somewhat indiscriminately, to Henry Esmond as character and narrator, ignoring Thackeray's typically complex narrative structure and technique. This structure produces a very ambivalent handling of the concept of a hero. George Levine argues that Thackeray's realism greatly extends the tradition of the unheroic hero (*Realistic Imagination*, 156). This is only partially true of *Henry Esmond*. The novel opens with an apparent debunking of heroic myths, pointing to the ironic split between aggrandized public identity and the familiar, undignified private self: Lewis the Fourteenth as he projects himself as hero and the little wrinkled old man; the noble Cato projected by history and Cato befuddled in a tavern. Yet we could recognize a similar formal split between Henry Esmond as character in the events of the story and Henry Esmond as the familiar voice of the narrator. Levine points out that Thackeray's novels "normally depend heavily on a narrator constructing a self by talking to his audience" (*Realistic Imagination*, 149). It was by means of this narrative technique that Thackeray contributed powerfully to the popularization of a code of sincerity in the public sphere. Henry Esmond as narrator is undoubtedly produced as a self through the performative act of talking to the implied reader, but the familiar self of the narrator is by no means identical with the character in the events of the story. This duality of identity, which actually fragments into a great many other named identities in the course of the narrative, produces a double perspective on the making of heroes analogous to Brontë's oscillating movement between distant glamourizing perspective on national leaders and a perception founded upon domestic skepticism.

The novel begins with a preface in which the daughter of Henry Esmond constructs her father unequivocally as a public hero: beloved by all, handsome, clever, a natural leader of men. Yet this is followed by a short introductory section that is the only part of the text to be written entirely in the first person. Addressing the reader in an informal, personal voice, the narrator, Henry Esmond, writing his memoirs near the end of his life, robustly dismisses heroic posturing of all kinds, just as later in the text he instructs his grandchildren to represent him "not an inch taller than nature has made him" (76). Early in the story, the reader is assured, "Henry Esmond has taken truth for his motto" (77). Appropriately then, the story of events constructs the character Henry Esmond as a Carlylean hero of sincerity in opposition to the self-deceiving projection of the aristocracy as divinities and "disinterested" national heroes.

Throughout the narrative of his early life, Henry is represented as quick to recognize sham and hypocrisy in others and to censure it in himself, as when he affects poetic sorrow at the death of Nancy Sievewright (90).[9] More usually, however, Henry is represented as courageously and disinterestedly speaking out the truth, however unwelcome to his hearers. So, scorning the Reverend Tusher's servility, he tells Lady Castlewood that her looks have been damaged by smallpox (88), and later he draws down her rage by attempting to speak out on behalf of her husband (130). Subsequently, he risks his life by confronting the dangerous Lord Mohun with the truth about his pretended attack of gout (144). At the end of the narrative, Henry, referred to at this point almost wholly as "the Colonel," authoritatively and fearlessly speaks his mind to the prince, who is so overwhelmed by Esmond's stern sincerity that he impetuously offers to go down on his knees and beg pardon (458). Sincerity thus figured as disinterested truth projects an irresistible Carlylean claim to leadership that even princes are forced to recognize. The man of truth speaks with disinterested charismatic authority, regardless of birth or rank. This implies that the hero as sincere man can heal the split, noted at the beginning of the narrative in the examples of Cato and Lewis the Fourteenth, between the familiar private "I" and the projected public persona. The publicness of charismatic sincerity claims a unity of identity of the public hero with the most intimate interior self.

What this plot structure, tracing the constitution of Esmond as hero of charismatic sincerity, simultaneously figures is a radical, even revolutionary transfer of power. Potency leaks away from those who have assumed authority and leadership on the basis of a false mystique of birth. It reappears in the style of the consensually acclaimed leadership required for an inclusive community. Power is relocated in the charismatic sincerity of the hero of the story. Acclamation of the hero is the function of all those commendations of Henry Esmond's intellect, wit, courage, and even fighting prowess that are made by university students and tutors, military officers, and even by bad Lord Mohun.

The underlying narrative logic has been indicated even before the story proper begins, when Esmond's daughter, in the preface, recalls Lord Bolingbroke's assessment: "Were your father . . . to go into the woods, the Indians would elect him Sachem" (10). There is a revealing fairy-story element here. It is as if a good spirit had hovered above Henry's lonely childhood bed and endowed him with the force to command his own terms of belonging in defiance of unacknowledged birth. He becomes "the dearest of benefactors" to those that kept him in subservience, and thus empowered with a kind of self-plenitude he becomes the object of desire and worship (367). Mother and daughter vie jealously for his love, and Lord Castlewood acknowledges that Henry with his superior qualities "ought to be head of our house" (155). Rachel kneels before him, as does James Edward Stuart. Frank Castlewood turns away from the undeserving Stuart pretender to the throne to Henry. "I fancy you are like a king," Frank says, and he subsequently declares, "I would die for you" (411, 421). Thus the narrative of hero making swings a full ironic circle. It begins by recognizing a dangerous willingness in people generally to worship charismatic aristocratic projections in which the familiar qualities of common humanity are mythicized as semidivine. This awed submission licenses the right of the great to dispose of the lives of the many. What the plot structure suggests is that all forms of charismatic leadership reproduce these inequalities of power and obligation that underlie a general readiness for reverence and sacrifice.

A hero of sincerity might seem to avoid this unequal power relationship by bridging the gulf between public persona and domestic person, thereby keeping such a leader in touch with a shared humanness. Yet the double narrative perspective of *Henry Esmond* also ironizes the claims of charismatic sincerity. Levine sees the narrator in Thackeray's fiction as "a gesture at community, a means of constructing a self by invoking . . . a community of private feeling" (*Realistic Imagination*, 149). This comes close to expressing my sense of the ideological functioning of a code of sincerity, with its interpellative promise of interpersonal regard based upon an assumption of common interiority. The narrative voice of *Henry Esmond* is certainly constructed as a gesture of community with the implied reader. By implication, the narrator signs himself "Yours sincerely." A relationship of familiarity with the reader is maintained throughout the narrative by intermittent first-person confessional forms of speech in which the narrator trusts the reader with revelations of his less-admirable motivations and aspirations: "I suppose a man's vanity is stronger than any other passion in him; for I blush even now as I recall . . ." (310). At other times, the reader's opinion is directly canvassed by questions: "Would you know how a prince, heroic in misfortunes, and descended from a line of kings . . . was employed . . . ?" (400). Moments like this are rendered the more effective by the sudden movement into first-person voice in the midst of the unusual formal third-person autobiographical form.

It is the masterly opening section of the novel, the only part of the story to be wholly in the first-person voice, that most fully establishes the special, intimate relationship between narrator and reader, so that, as Thackeray claims for Steele, the reader becomes friend and confidant. The tone and language of this opening section shift rapidly and continually between stately formality evoking the eighteenth century and informal colloquialism that seems to break spontaneously through the artificial decorum, drawing the reader into a shared community of sincere feeling as opposed to the pretensions of rank and pride. The first sentence sets the pattern of this style with the informal, personalizing phrase *as we read*, interrupting the cadence of "The actors in the old tragedies, as we read, piped their iambics to a tune, speaking from under a mask, and wearing stilts and a great head-dress" (13).

As the paragraph continues, the slight residual formality of the plural pronoun *we* gives way to the familiar *I*, and shortly the narrator is invoking the reader on terms of equality: "She [Queen Anne] was no better bred nor wiser than you and me" (14). This sense of voice is sustained by conversational phrases like *In a word* and by insertion of anecdote. By the end of the short opening section, reader and narrator are constituted as an imagined dialogic community, with the narrator confidently ventriloquizing both voices: " 'And I shall be deservedly hanged,' say you, wishing to put an end to this prosing. I don't say No. I can't but accept the world as I find it, including a rope's end, as long as it is in fashion" (16). What attracts irresistibly about this interpellative offer of community is the style of confessional sincerity, with its egalitarian inclusiveness: "I have seen too much of success in life to take off my hat and huzzah to it as it passes in its gilt coach; . . . I look into my heart and think that I am as good as my Lord Mayor, and know I am as bad as Tyburn Jack" (15–16). Who would not be disarmed and warmed by the "hospitality" of such openness?

Yet this is sincerity as style, rather than substance. Indeed, "man of truth" is a paradoxical self-figuring for the narrator, given that the self of the story is constituted within the text as multiple public identities: Henry Esmond, Mr. Esmond, the Colonel, Parson Harry, Don Dismallo, Aeneus, Don Quixote, My Lord Graveacres, bastard. What is more, the self-styled "sincere" narrator is perhaps the most duplicitous identity of all. Despite the confessional transparency of "I look into my heart," the narrator's interiority is not available to the reader in relation to the two most important aspects of his whole life. In the first place, two of the main characters, Rachel and Henry, are represented as persistently disavowing the knowledge they are, at another level, most conscious of: Rachel's passionate sexual love for Henry. The ironic subtlety and comedy with which Thackeray handles this repressed desire accounts for the shocked outrage of many of his nineteenth-century readers when Henry and Rachel marry, almost incestuously, at the end of the story.[10] Nevertheless, given the narrator's emphasis upon his motto of truth and that he is writing long after his marriage to Rachel, he is being more than a trifle hypocritical with his implied readers in those passages describing his and Rachel's relationship as only familial: "And as a brother folds a sister to his heart; and as a mother cleaves to her son's breast — so for a few moments Esmond's beloved mistress came to him and blessed him" (215).

The second area of silence on the part of the narrator concerns his ambitions for social distinction. In his retrospective account of his early life at Castlewood House, the narrator recalls only his feelings of slavish love and duty to the family. Yet Lady Castlewood remembers his "strong imagination and eager desires" (212), while Beatrix insists that he had always wanted to be worshipped: "of all the proudest wretches in the world Mr. Esmond is the proudest, let me tell him that" (363). His daughter, likewise, remembers that he was "familiar with no one," liking to be always "the first in his company." (10). This silence as to inner desire for acclaim on the part of the confidential narrator points to the contradictory paradox of charismatic sincerity as a style of popular leadership. It cannot allow transparent access to an interiority ambitious for power. Charisma in large part is the capacity to project a visual presence of self-completeness. To speak openly of ambition is to confess to self-interest — to acknowledge not a plenitude and fullness, but a lack. Charisma demands the disinterestedness of self-repleteness.[11] Charismatic sincerity therefore reinscribes hypocrisy at its heart; it, too, constructs a simulacrum.

While distance can project a romantic luminosity, familiarity often breeds contempt. Although the narrator declares at the beginning of *Henry Esmond*, "I would have history familiar" (14), he later admits that "as we turn the perspective glass, . . . a giant appears a pigmy" (244). The story is full of figures once perceived as divinities that are revealed on closer, more familiar knowledge to be only too commonplace. Discussing Rachel Castlewood's disillusionment with her husband, the narrator asks, "Who is to love what is base and unlovely?" (118). Beatrix, the voice of cynical truth, tells Henry that "a goddess in a mob-cap, that has to make her husband's gruel, ceases to be divine" (363).

The formal narrative structure of *Henry Esmond* embodies the contradiction and difficulty of inclusive leadership required to project a charismatic ordinariness. The plot constructs Henry Esmond as a character of inherent personal charismatic authority based upon a Carlylean sincerity to which all other characters willingly submit. The narrator retains a necessary silence as to his desires for such acclamation despite the early claim to a confessional interiority. Yet even so, as narrator he remains too close and familiar to assume a luminous identity for the reader. The code of sincerity has too successfully interpellated reader and narrator as a community based on equal regard. Henry Esmond as "I" remains preeminently a familiar voice, and none of the public identities enunciated by the narrator are invested with the imaginative presence or publicness required for charismatic power. "Charm and charisma," Pierre Bourdieu writes in *Distinction*, "in fact, designate the power, which certain people have, to impose their own self-image as the objective and collective image of their body and being" (208).

It is the character Beatrix in *Henry Esmond* who represents the visualized charm that imposes itself as presence upon the reader's imagination and who points, by comparison, to the absence of such specular publicness in the hero-narrator. The luminosity of physical beauty and grace, the text persistently suggests, exerts an irresistible attraction for most people. Beatrix is almost invariably represented in the text as a compelling spectacle. Most notably this is so when she is perceived for the first time by the narrator having changed from a child into a beautiful woman. Beatrix carefully stage-manages the publicness of her appearance, richly dressed, dazzlingly radiant, descending a great formal staircase, haloed in candlelight (217). The narrator pays tribute to the power exerted by her physical presence: "She was born to shine in great assemblies . . . and to command everywhere" (337). Yet he notes that part of her "dazzling completeness of beauty" comprises "perfect symmetry, health, decision, activity" (217). To a considerable extent, these qualities are the birthright, at all times, of wealth and privilege. Good food, good health, physical freedom, social confidence, stylish clothes, and costly jewels make up a large part of the impression of bodily attractiveness. Beatrix is born into such material plenitude; the ambiguity of her name suggests a blessed fullness of being, but also a yearning desire for what is beyond worldly reach. This contradiction between fullness and lack is embodied in the replete perfection of her physical being and her exclusion, as a woman, from social being, understood as participatory citizenship.

Throughout the story, there is a deliberate paralleling of the two characters Beatrix and Henry. Each is driven by a sense of unbelonging and, as a consequence, by intense ambitions and desires. Like Henry Esmond, Beatrix as a woman has no inherent legitimacy. Yet also like him she is aware of the superiority of her intellect and personal force compared with those in the family who assert authority over her. She demands, "Why am I not a man? I have ten times his [her brother Frank] brains, . . . had I worn a sword and periwig . . . I would have made our name talked about" (341). Beatrix has all the personal attributes for charismatic leadership, but there is no social space in which these can be projected as a compelling publicness for others. Taxed, as Henry is, with lack of reverence for family or religion, it is inconceivable that Beatrix could meet this challenge with the assertion of the prior claims of citizenship: "I am an Englishwoman." The only identity available for Beatrix is the domestic one of wife. The narrator recognizes that Beatrix's sincerity and her scorn of hypocrisy and servility stand in the way of her assuming this role.

While the narrative voice exploits the urbane code of social sincerity that easily encompasses concealment, Beatrix speaks out the passionate interiority of the outsider; the hunger for power, position, status, and identity of those beyond the pale of legitimacy: "Why should I not own that I am ambitious, Henry Esmond; and if it be no sin in a man to covet honour, why should not a woman too desire it? . . . I want my wings, and to use them, sir" (362–64). This constitutes a public confession of lacking the "disinterested" repleteness that defines charismatic force. More than that, Beatrix's naked assertion of self-interest repudiates what was regarded as the most sanctified aspect of woman's nature — the capacity for self-sacrifice and submission. This in turn highlights the contradiction at the core of an inclusive society that retains sharp inequalities of wealth and privilege. The self-interest of the more fortunate, whether of gender or class, depends upon a willingness for self-sacrifice and submission on the part of those less privileged. War is only the most extreme form of the sacrifice upon which social order is based. The ideology of "disinterestedness" is necessary to shield this system of differential rewards and duties from view. Not surprisingly, then, Beatrix is harshly punished for her rebellious presumption and honest declaration of self-interest. From being represented as a luminous divinity, she becomes, as Ninba Auerbach has shown (88–101), almost an archetypal figure of evil: her charm is "desecrated," "the roses had shuddered out of her cheeks" (459). Henry Esmond, as an "Englishman" and full citizen within a newly empowered but masculine public sphere, escapes the humiliating role of chaplain that was seen as befitting his illegitimate status. Beatrix's wings are brutally clipped by marriage to Tom Tusher, the servile family parson.

Perhaps Charlotte Brontë intuited such an outcome when she described the first part of the novel as "admirable and odious" (quoted in Ray, 173). Nevertheless, despite the ending to Beatrix's story and the intermittently misogynist narrative comments, the right of women to participatory citizenship and to legitimate aspirations for national leadership is never given more passionate voice, during the nineteenth century, than in Thackeray's representation of Beatrix Castlewood. In that sense, Eve Kosofsky Sedgwick is surely right in claiming that *Henry Esmond* "is perhaps most appropriately considered a proto-feminist text" (*Between Men*, 146). Moreover, *Henry Esmond* explores more fully than *Shirley* a new kind of domestic political leadership to displace the ideal of aristocratic territorial conquest: a leader able to project the public persona of sincere man, confident, and friend. In doing so, the novel foregrounds the inherent contradiction between a public code of sincerity based upon an ideology of open and equal interiorities and the charismatic performance of sincerity as the disinterestedness required for leadership of a democratic inclusive order. It points, too, to the ideological functioning of "disinterestedness" as the means of veiling and maintaining privilege and inequality in the distribution of social rewards and sacrifices. In *Romola* (1863), George Eliot focuses upon the civic ideal of willing sacrifice that underpins social order and subjects it to a radical critique.

Part III / The Constitution of the Public

CHAPTER FIVE

Bleak House

Interested Knowledge and Imaginary Power

Both *Shirley* and *Henry Esmond* participated in the debates in the public sphere of the 1840s that articulated a sense that a traditional aristocratic leadership of the sword, deriving from notions of territorial sovereignty, would have to transform itself to meet the needs of a more comprehensive domestic national constituency. The refashioning of leadership within the public sphere was indicative of a much larger transformative movement toward greater social inclusiveness. This involved the broadening of the public sphere under the influence of the mass platform of the Chartists and the public politics of the Corn Law struggles. The fact that leadership felt compelled to enter the sphere of representation marked the emergence of a new political force: the power of wider public opinion.

A generally recognized concept of "the public" as a nonexclusive national identity marks the formal shift from a conception of birthright and landed property as sole foundation of political legitimacy to a recognition of "the people" as legitimating aggregate of the nation. Not surprisingly, the public sphere of civil society came into being during the eighteenth century subsequent to the Act of Settlement that formalized rejection of divine right. The moment, in the nineteenth century, that marked its transformation into a heterogeneous public was probably symbolized for many people, at the time, by the Great Exhibition of 1851, which was attended by a spectrum of the entire nation — almost certainly the first occasion in history that such a collective event had occurred. It was the public demeanor of working-class families at the Crystal Palace that consolidated the post-Chartist view that the respectable laboring men could safely be accommodated, in some limited sense, as citizens of the nation.

However, this transformation of the public sphere was inseparably involved with a transformation in the nature and location of power. The relationship of osmosis between the public sphere and sources of power requires a model that is more dynamic and complex than Habermas's ideal sense of a public sphere of rational opinion that opposes the tyranny of the state's monopoly of force. In the first place, public opinion became, in the nineteenth century, a location of power that was certainly not always rational. To some extent, Habermas accommodates this development in his concept of manipulative publicness — a point to which I shall return in the next chapter. It also has to be recognized that the mass politics of Chartism always included, as a subtext, the message of the potential power of numbers. The respectable classes at the time certainly felt this as a force. Furthermore, although political leadership was relocated into the public sphere and separated, in representational terms, from identification with the power of a dominant class, nevertheless sources of wealth and political power remained largely vested in landed property for most of the century (see Price, 301–4).

Visible and experienced power meanwhile was increasingly situated within the impersonal machinery of public bureaucracy maintained by public officials who defined their responsibilities as public service in the public interest. Moreover, many of this new class of professionals within the public domain of the state came largely from the ranks of the lower nobility and the gentry, who were the section of traditional society that lost out most in the attack upon aristocratic privilege and nepotism.[1] Although separated by wealth from the great landowners, what was thought of more generally as the landed interest included the gentry within its fluid boundaries, and there were numerous interconnections with landed proprietors within the older legal professions, the church and the army, as well as shared perspectives and responsibilities sustained by intermixing on magistrates benches, in Parliament, county hunting, the London season, and public appointments, as well as by education and a sense of shared cultivation.[2] This class section had always represented the most articulate core of eighteenth-century civil society, and they continued in the nineteenth to exert considerable influence on public opinion, while at the same time becoming agents of a new form of bureaucratic state power. As well as necessitating a more complex under-standing of the nature of the nineteenth-century public sphere, this recognition of the interconnection of the ancien régime of aristocratic power with the new epistemologies and bureaucracy of the state suggests that Foucault's notion of a seamlessly imposed regime of governmentality requires some rethinking.

While the panoply of social reality encompassed as "public" can be divided, theoretically, into the public sphere pertaining to representation and the public domain of the state pertaining to power, notions of agency, public opinion, public interest, and public duty interact across the always porous division. *North and South* (1855) intervenes in this contested terrain to address the concern with the transformation of the public sphere from the privileged space of civility to the forum of a heterogeneous society. *Bleak House* (1851) is preoccupied with a trans-formation in the domain of power. Yet both novels explore the question of where power, influence, and agency reside in an order based on collective legitimacy, rather than a traditional, exclusive landed nobility.

Bleak House provides a fictional narrative of a transfer of the active power of the state from a dynastic, landed caste to an impersonal public state. In so doing, the text offers quite original insights into a transformation in the way power comes to be imagined in modern society. Power is disembodied, becoming imaginatively disassociated from national leaders, who function increasingly in the public sphere of representation. The demands, during the course of the nineteenth century, for increasing degrees of social inclusiveness required political leaders to project a quality of charismatic humanness: sincerity as recognition of a shared interiority. As a result of this transition from military might to domesticated charisma, power came to be imagined as impersonal and unlocalized. It assumed those qualities associated with it by Foucault and represented in the popular modern thriller genre as well as more serious literary forms: it became thought of as secret, amorphous, and omnipresent. This hiding away of located power at the moment when a popular political order was coming into being *may* represent the first phase in the establishment of the tentacular disciplinary techniques of mod-ern governance, but equally the disappearance of class identity and interests in the defining and locating of power has to be recognized as a convenient camou-flage for those social groups that retained their dominant position within the nation's unequal distributions of economic, social, and cultural capital.

Not that the landed nobility could be accused, during the late 1840s and into the 1850s, of seeking to disguise their central role in national affairs. The rhetoric of aristocratic influence was strategically shifted to assertions of disinterested patriotism. Calling upon the tradition of Edmund Burke, conservatives claimed that only those with an ancient, inherited stake in the land itself were to be trusted as disinterested guardians of the national welfare as a whole. The state was, Burke had maintained, "a sort of family settlement; grasped in a kind of mortmain forever. . . . We hold, we transmit our government and our privileges, in the manner in which we enjoy and transmit our property and our lives" (120). If power fell into the hands of other classes, patricians claimed, sectional or private interests would be pursued before those of the nation.[3] The great land-owners, on the other hand, were, in essence, the enduring nation. Opponents of continued aristocratic monopoly of government were quick to point out the narrow class investment behind this mythologizing of landowning as conferring a privileged and disinterested national identity. Within a political order based upon birthright as legitimating an exclusive prerogative to rule, there can be no clear-cut distinction between public and private interests. For an aristocratic caste, affairs of family seem equally and naturally to be affairs of the nation. A writer in the *Westminster Review* in 1851 summed up the critique: "By constant intermarriage and community of interest the entire landed aristocracy may be broadly regarded as one great family having privileges to defend which it is in the interests of the people they should no longer keep."[4] The opposition here be-tween landed interest and "interests of the people" marked out the discursive terrain of the struggle for active state power: conflicting claims were asserted in terms of a disinterested concern for the national or public interest.

At midcentury, threats to the national interest were imagined in two forms. One was the fear of social revolution of the kind that had overtaken France in 1848, leading to a brief democratic republic. Journalism of all political perspec-tives was preoccupied, from 1848 to the early 1850s, with accounts and explana-tions of current events in France, and invariably the opportunity was taken to stress the need for government in England to take timely heed of similar dangers at home.[5] *Bleak House* participates in these discursive warnings with multiple allusions to revolutionary struggles to gain state power: repeated references to the French Revolution of 1789, Boythorn's mentioning of the gunpowder plot, the ghostly Dedlock tradition dating back to the civil war, and Miss Flite's apoc-alyptic utterances. Miss Flite's allusions to the Book of Revelation echoes a re-viewer in the *Westminster Review* who wrote of the rapidity of revolutionary action in France: "We seem to have stood as witnesses to the opening of the seventh seal."[6] However, as perhaps the extraneousness of these allusions to the

narrative structure of the novel suggests, fear of social revolution was ebbing away in Britain by the 1850s. Chartism was a spent force, and in its aftermath the educated public was more willing to note the peaceable seriousness with which many non-physical-force Chartists had argued and organized.[7] The respectable demeanor of the large crowds of working-class people visiting the Great Exhibition provided the well-to-do with a graphic and welcome demonstration that the laboring masses might safely be included in national gatherings and events. As Harriet Martineau noted, the exhibition afforded "indisputable" evidence of a "change in the public mind . . . and inclinations of the multitude."[8]

As Brontë makes clear in *Shirley*, traditional models of leadership require conflict and conquest to constitute the charismatic hero of the sword. The duke of Wellington was called out of retirement to subdue the Chartists in 1848. Following this, there was no obvious adversary to sustain the conventional aristocratic form of leadership. After 1848, the most powerful threat to national well-being was perceived as amorphous, shifting, and hidden. It was the danger of cholera and disease generated in the appalling environs of urban slums. It was this shift of perception from the resolved danger of working-class demands to the present peril of poverty that helped consolidate that oscillating, dual perspective of the laboring population as both pauper mass and the respectable, individualized working-class man and his family. The cluster of anxieties associated with overpopulation, urban crowding, social massification, contagion, and criminality constituted a national danger that heroes of the sword were ill-equipped to subdue.[9]

It was around this perception of an unquantifiable and uncategorizable threat that a counterdiscourse of public interest to that of landed interest was articulated within the public sphere. This counterdiscourse was largely expressed in terms of a disinterested, professional knowledge that could offer an objective, dispassionate understanding of public problems, free from any sectional interest or bias. The impersonal public state founded upon scientific knowledge and principles became an ideal to affirm in opposition to the territorial family state of aristocratic rule. Civil servants and those, like doctors and lawyers, who gained public office in the expanding state domain of poor law provision, urban health, and penal and criminal reform, resorted continuously to the public sphere to enhance their status and importance with claims to professional expertise and professional dedication to an ideal of service to the public.[10] In opposition to aristocratic nepotism and patronage, they asserted the disinterestedness of their knowledge as scientific and of their professional conduct as vocational calling. Both doctors and lawyers were particularly active in the numerous statistical societies that flourished during the middle decades of the century. The factual "evidence" thus gained was used to underwrite claims to comprehensive and objective knowledge of national problems — especially the problem of population. As the boundaries of familiar, local, known communities were submerged in the amorphous flux of urban spread and social mobility, only the new social sciences seemed able to offer objective scientific analysis of what had become knowable only as aggregated mass society. It was this constant stream of statistical information into the public sphere that helped constitute the imaginative conception of an aggregated collective, of a general public, and of a mass society. Not surprisingly, for many this was a form of knowledge to be resisted, as threatening loss of individual identity in numbers and sameness.

Nevertheless, the expanded role and importance of professional experts within government was largely brought about by a general public perception, which the statisticians and similar officials had themselves created, of unseen dangers within the nation that urgently needed to be known and quantified. Inevitably, perhaps, the statistical and scientific reports produced by the new professional public servants — men like the omnipresent Edwin Chadwick — utilized highly selective, often lurid details of social evils that fed the fears of a lurking menace that only professional expertise could bring to light and regulate. One such public official wrote in typical mode: "Do we not find that each one of the social problems we have been . . . at pains to unravel strikes its roots into the substance of the nation, ramifying through a hundred secret crevices into classes apparently the most removed from its influence" (quoted in Corrigan and Sayer, 135).

Undoubtedly, professional service in the new public domain of the state offered expanded opportunities for improved social status and remuneration to that section of the middle class, largely the gentry, that was not attracted to industry and finance. Women also could claim a privileged form of expertise in many of the areas of social concern to the state.[11] Yet claims to disinterestedness were not merely cynical, self-interested promotion. The ideal of service to the national community, affirmed as part of the attempt to raise the esteem of professional careers, did much to popularize a concept of active, knowledgeable citizenship. Indeed, for the gentry, who largely shared the aristocracy's land-owning ideology, a sense of public duty was a long-assimilated and naturalized part of their sense of social legitimacy and value. Nevertheless, the transformation, by the professionalized gentry, of this class identification with the nation into a more universal sense of "public interest" was a progressive move toward an ideal of

egalitarian social inclusion. Without a concept of "public interest," no imagining of participatory citizenship or of the nation as a "community" would be possible. To gain a notion of "the public interest" is to move from an unthinking, passive acceptance of a naturalized feudal order of duty and obligation unchangeably inherited with birth to the necessary degree of distance at least to imagine civic responsibility and agency.

On the other hand, "the public interest" can function as the ideological cover for "interests of state." Foucault offers a starkly different interpretation of the instrumental reason of the rational state to that of Habermas's ideal of communicative reason as medium of the public sphere. Foucault associates the disaggregation of a public state domain from an earlier monarchical regime with the implementation of the bureaucracy, *savoirs*, and techniques of the multi-dispersed power of modern governmentality ("Governmentality," 87–104). The project of the savoirs and techniques of governmentality is the production of political subjects as dutiful and obedient citizens. By the 1850s, the industrious working-class, perceived as respectable and decent wage earners and their families, was no longer the prime focus for such moral normalization. It was the proliferating and engulfing body of pauperism, existing beyond the bounds of the moral rationalism of civil order, that was seen to constitute a social evil threatening the security of the state and requiring intervention.

Within Foucauldian discourse, the specialized use of *savoir* is distinguished from a science proper in that it is a functionalist practice of knowledge that transforms an abstract "scientific" epistemology—like, for example, political economy—into a "knowledgeable" interventionist program: the techniques and mechanisms of governance (see Procacci, 156). In that sense, a savoir functions across the terrain of the public sphere as the forum of informed public knowledge and the terrain of state power as interventionist force upon people's lives. Yet understanding the savoirs, constructed around the need to mitigate the social problems of pauperism, as acting at the interface between abstract knowledge, on the one hand, and regulatory interventions in social reality, on the other, should not be construed as implying that such savoirs necessarily produced any "factual knowledge" of the real substance of existence of that which they sought to control. What was produced as knowledge of pauperism was largely the myth of an otherness existing beyond the categories of order and civilized humanity.

Paradoxically, pauperism was conceived within this savoir as essentially unknowable: it was amorphous, unformed, indefinite, fluid, unsettled, multiple, massified, unboundaried, and uncontainable. It was associated also with disease, corruption, and leaking and miasmic contagion. Imagery of animal savagery, vermin numbers, depravity, delinquency, and bestial sexual breeding pervaded discourses on pauperism. In 1849, an essay in the *Christian Observer* typically resorts to imagery of fluidity and amorphousness when it warns that "vagrancy is now becoming the character of our common people . . . form[ing] a mass which rolls over the surface of the country."[12] In 1852, a writer in the *Edinburgh Review* called attention to the "plague" of delinquency that, acting like a contagious "disease," renders each criminal a sphere of "infection" that results in "a mass of at least 50,000 depraved and vicious lads, professionally living on the plunder and injury of society."[13] The paradoxical admixture here of lurid imagery of uncontainability with a gestural citation of figures to imply "scientific" knowledge is typical of discursive constructions of pauperism.

The quotations from the *Christian Observer* and the *Edinburgh Review* also provide a good demonstration of the force of nonrational discourse upon the public sphere. The imagined amorphous nature of the threat to civil order meant that the language could easily be displaced into other areas of social life. In this way, the focus of savoirs aimed at producing good citizens was extendible to any form of behavior or identity perceived as threatening to the settled boundaries of civil order. Sexual "irregularities" of all kinds, vagrancy and unemployment, irrationality and madness, any mode of nonconformity and insubordination could be represented as partaking of this amorphous otherness and thus in need of being brought within the order of categorization, regulation, and normalization. What in particular needs be noted here is the way the production of an imaginary threat to state security, as amorphous and unboundaried, produces, simultaneously, like a mirror image, an imaginary ideal of power and knowledge as also amorphous and unboundaried in response to the requirement to investigate all those unseen, leaking sources of contagion, those "hundred secret crevices" of deep-rooted social evils, which, the public servant claimed, he had been "at pains to unravel." It is this new, glamourous form of power as a sinister panopticon knowledge that *Bleak House* explores and questions.

Bleak House is clearly participating in the public criticism of aristocratic rule as incompetent to deal with the complexity of the social problems facing the nation. In a foregrounded contrast to the myopic vision imputed to an exclusive governing caste, the narrative perspective of *Bleak House* is panoramic and all-comprehending. The society comprehended within narrative perspective, however, is not imagined as an inclusive one: "great gulfs" exist between the classes (272). Nevertheless, it is represented as a social order in which boundaries cannot hold,

imagery of dissolution, floods, miasmic fog, tainting, staining, and disease everywhere imply the collapse of distinction and stability. The problem of social inclusiveness is articulated formally and thematically in the narrative as a problem
of perspective, and hence of knowledge. There is a slippage, closely related to the
dual perspective that constitutes the poor, between perception as aggregation
and perception as individualized and personal. This oppositional duality is not
stabilized in the formal division of the story between the omniscient narrative
and the first-person narrative of Esther Summerson. There is an oscillation
within the omniscient perspective itself between the personalized peroration at
the death of Jo the Crossing-Sweeper and the aggregated perception of the poor
as "maggot numbers" (272).

As the chapter entitled "National and Domestic" makes clear, the main thrust
of the critique of aristocratic government in *Bleak House* centers upon the inability of a landed, dynastic class to separate their private sectional interests from
the interests of the nation. Sir Leicester Dedlock's sense of patriotism is represented as most stirred to action by the shipwrecked state of the country in not
being able to provide generous pensions for the numerous noble cousins (211).
Sir Leicester continually fears the obliteration of class boundaries, but is blind to
the corruption of his class in its use of public office for personal and family
benefit. The Doodle, Coodle, and Dedlock ruling caste are represented in the
story as utterly lacking any sense of separation between public and private interests. The nation is understood by them only as a domestic territory on which
their lives are staged: "Boodle and Buffy, their followers and families, their heirs,
executors, administrators, and assigns are the first-born actors, managers and
leaders, and no others can appear upon the scene for ever and ever" (212). This
circumscription of the nation to the small circle of the nobility ensures that their
private and personal interests magnify to assume the proportions of affairs of
state, while the larger realities of national life remain unknown: "It is a world
wrapped up in too much jeweller's cotton and fine wool, and cannot hear the
rushing of the larger worlds and cannot see them as they circle round the sun"
(55).

Dickens's critique of a political order legitimated by birthright is the more
telling in that Sir Leicester Dedlock is represented as adhering to the highest
principles of his order. He is a Burkean figure acting up to his sense of honor,
chivalry, and dignified courtesy. His sense of family loyalty and the protection he
extends to the poorest distant relation are wholly admirable as personal qualities,
but these virtues become a source of corruption due to Sir Leicester's inability to

separate the private realm from the domain of the state. Like Edmund Burke, Sir Leicester is represented as imagining the nation as "a sort of family settlement." In 1848, a writer in the *Westminster Review* accused the aristocratic Whig government headed by Lord John Russell of obstructing progressive, forward-looking administration in attempting to perpetuate the hold of the nobility upon power by misrepresenting the prerogatives and privileges of caste as "the palladium of the state."[14] In *Bleak House*, Sir Leicester is represented as wholly convinced that the security of the country demands the unchanged existence into perpetuity of all those national orders and institutions made venerable by precedent and usage: "His family is as old as the hills, and infinitely more respectable. He has a general opinion that the world might get on without hills, but would be done up without Dedlocks" (57).

The Court of Chancery is one of the ancient obstacles to progressive administration that Sir Leicester particularly values. The satire upon its procrastination and entangled investments in hereditary suits should be understood not as a harbinger of the modern mystifying bureaucracy of governmentality,[15] but as part of the novel's attack upon the ancien régime as attempting to arrest time, of shutting out the rushing on of larger worlds. Echoing the *Westminster Review*, Chancery is referred to in the text as "the great Palladium" (314). Miss Flite is correct when she accuses Chancery of blighting the lives of youth. Young men like Allan Woodcourt, with a strong commitment to public service and proven ability, can make no headway on their own merits without aristocratic interest to further their aspirations. Richard Carstone, who rests his hopes of prosperity on the uncertainties of inheritance, only toys amateurishly with professional callings, developing "something of the careless spirit of a gamester, who felt that he was part of a great gaming system" (280). As was recognized at the time, a gaming system is indeed a good description of a political culture based upon the arbitrariness of patronage and influence.[16] Carstone's continual disappointment and subsequent growing sense of injustice and unfairness is represented as "smouldering combustion" (612). In May 1848, the *Times* warned of the political dangers embodied in a disaffected section of the youthful middle class, who were unable to secure the positions and careers they aspired to: "No country, not even England, is safe from the machinations of disappointed cleverness and disaffected education."[17]

A professional practice of knowledge is undoubtedly the ideal that the narrative affirms in opposition to aristocratic self-interest. Yet just what is involved in each of those terms — *professional, knowledge, practice* — is a matter of complex investigation in the novel. The figuring of a transference of power within the narrative structure is certainly not endorsing the ideology of an objective dispassionate knowledge as a rational foundation for mechanisms of an interventionist state. Within the world of the fiction, all forms of disinterested knowledge are shown to be mythic; knowledge is avidly sought by almost every character, but in all cases the pursuit is in the interests of profit or power. Claims or demeanors suggestive of disinterest are shown invariably to be duplicitous. The terms *interest* and *profession* are repeatedly brought together in the text in a foregrounded and questioning conjunction.

The representation of the professions is highly ambivalent. The newest profession, that of medicine, is most positively represented by means of the character Allan Woodcourt, who is praised for both his skill and his knowledge, but equally for his sense of service to his vocation. His treatment of the urban poor who cannot afford to pay fees indicates that his professional ambition is not driven by a desire for personal wealth. Neither does he seek knowledge in the abstract sense as purely an epistemology; Mrs. Bayam Badger tells Esther and Ada that Woodcourt's "strong interest" in medicine for all "that it can do" is what will provide "reward in it through a great deal of work for a very little money" (282). This insistence upon Woodcourt's understanding of medicine as combining both practice and knowledge implies a conception similar to that of a savoir, yet it is very differently judged. Woodcourt's dedication to his professional calling regardless of self-interest highlights, by comparison, Carstone's lack of constancy, his inability to be "settled" and "steady and systematic" (375). The text extends its representation of the varying professional capacities of characters to women as well as men. Women, in the 1850s, were just beginning to recognize the opportunities for active careers opening up within the expanding public domain of the state. Harold Skimpole provides Esther with a glowing testimonial: "Now, here is Miss Summerson with a fine administrative capacity and a knowledge of details perfectly surprising" (654).

The profession that is represented in wholly negative terms as the most blatantly self-interested is that of law. The sinister Mr. Vholes is a caricature of unscrupulous self-seeking masquerading as disinterested service. The character discourse of Vholes constitutes a sustained ridicule of the elevated moral rhetoric of selfless professional devotion to the client's interests. Vholes continually insists upon the unbiased, disinterested objectivity of his professional advice and knowledge. "I am not a self-seeker," he tells Richard Carstone as he fleeces him; "I never stoop to flattery. . . . I pretend to no claim upon you, Mr C, but for the zealous and active discharge . . . of my professional duty" (607, 610). The two other characters relentlessly satirized for broadcasting their disinterested and indefatigable devotion to public service are Mrs. Jellyby and Mrs. Pardiggle. This satiric treatment is Dickens's unsympathetic response to women's large-scale presence within the charitable sector of the public sphere. During the 1850s, women were attempting to enhance the status of their role in charitable work by utilizing the new discourse of professionalism. They were also genuinely seeking to base their activities upon sounder practice and knowledge. Dickens is shamefully ungenerous in his representation of these legitimate ambitions. In his defense, it can be argued that his primary thematic concern in the satirical treatment of Mrs. Jellyby and Mrs. Pardiggle is the way claims of disinterested service and knowledge are utilized to mask a desire for self-aggrandizement and the will for power over others. He is also highly critical of the distanced and uncomprehending form of knowledge that informs both their practices.

The characterization of Harold Skimpole positions him at the opposite extreme from an ethos of instrumental knowledge put to the service of public utility. Skimpole is a self-professed "perfectly idle man. A mere amateur" (659). Yet it is upon this basis that Skimpole constructs a counterclaim of possessing "disinterested benevolence" (884). This suggests the ideological development of rival projections of disinterestedness in the second half of the nineteenth century. The zeal with which some of the new class of professional men asserted the objective utility of their specialized scientific knowledge threatened the cultural capital of the traditionally educated. The identity of gentlemanly status and civility was destabilized from its secure foundations upon familiarity with classical culture. The collapse of once-secure cultural boundaries unsettled traditional social distinctions as well. Undoubtedly, the energy and passion with which reformers like Chadwick urged scientific and statistical knowledge as the means of dealing adequately with social problems, seemed to others (for instance, Matthew Arnold, Oxford professor of poetry) an overzealous and narrow form of understanding. It is evident that such earnestness could often be experienced as a bullying insistence upon all that was materially and physically offensive and frightening within national life. The relief with which John Jarndyce, in *Bleak House*, turns from the "east wind" effect of the assertive, self-publicizing demands of those working for public causes to the sweetness and light of Harold Skimpole indicates the attraction of an oppositional ideology of disinterested sincerity.

Vholes proudly confesses to "insensibility" in his zeal for duty, and Mrs. Pardiggle insists on her "business-like" love of hard work (607, 154). Skimpole, by contrast, disdains any form of utility with disarming candor. He projects an insinuating performance of sincerity based upon claims of freedom from the material concerns and encumbrances that characterize the more earnest and unimaginative characters. Skimpole's discourse elaborates a performative code that fuses a winning "sincerity" to a dematerialized, cultured "sensibility," as Mr. Jarndyce is pleased to call it (649). Skimpole's pose of disinterested "candour" is revealed as the story unfolds to work wholly in the interests of himself. Yet Dickens was to capitulate to the insinuating charm that Skimpole represents. In *Our Mutual Friend*, Skimpole is rehabilitated as Eugene Wrayburn, whose disinterested and transparent openness are constituted as the charismatic grace of a cultured being.

Despite the diametrically opposed public personas projected by characters like Skimpole, Mrs. Jellyby, and Mrs. Pardiggle, the criticism of them within the text is the same: their understanding of the destitute poor is based upon a mystifying or uncomprehending distance from the lived reality of total social deprivation. Mrs. Jellyby perceives only a "surplus population" to be shipped off to Africa, Mrs. Pardiggle's moral bullying is so insensitive as to what is actually happening to those she harangues that she fails to notice a baby dying while she speaks, and Mr. Skimpole sings pathetic romantic ballads about homeless orphans, but delivers Jo over to the police for a bribe. Yet, strangely, the representation of destitution within the omniscient narrative perspective is open to much the same criticism. What is conveyed in the passages dealing with poverty en masse is a sense of loathsome otherness. In the composite image of destitution presented in the text, *Bleak House* seems fully complicit with those savoirs that constituted pauperism a mythic and amorphous social evil. In the aggregate images of extreme urban deprivation, as represented by the slum inhabitants of Tom-all-Alone's and the contents of pauper graveyards, destitution is projected as an almost hallucinatory horror.

This unclassifiable otherness of poverty is most forcefully impressed as a tangible proximity by the repeated word *slime*, suggestive of a putrefying dissolution of matter, neither liquid nor solid. The slum and the graveyard alike are represented as sources of a leaking corruption that nauseously invades the most intimate senses of bodily security: "The poisoned air deposits its witch-ointment slimy to the touch" (203). The "tainting" pestilence of "Tom's corrupted blood" and "Tom's slime" is uncontainable, spreading across all the "great gulfs" of social divisions (683). The people of the slum are dehumanized as a fluxing, animal-like mass. The dislocated grammar of narrative language that transforms aggregated numbers into the singular of a shifting, vermin-reptilian image suggests the logic of condensation and displacement, rather than the objective documentation of reality that is the aim of empirical rationality and of realism: "These ruined shelters have bred a crowd of foul existence that crawls in and out of gaps in walls and boards; and coils itself to sleep, in maggot numbers" (272). Under pressure of such unclassifiable otherness, even the order of grammatical regularity gives way.

Jo the Crossing-Sweeper, as an individualized pauper, slides in and out of the oscillation of narrative perspective from aggregation to specification. As with the destitute mass generally, Jo's otherness is conveyed as approaching the nonbeing of putrefaction: he is "like a bundle of rank leaves of swampy growth, that rotted long ago" (686). Not surprisingly, Jo's identity cannot be brought within the order of categorizing knowledge: "He is of no order and no place; neither of the beasts, nor of humanity" (696). Lady Dedlock's response to the proximity of physically touching Jo figures the repulsion engendered by fears of otherness. She drops a piece of money in his hand, "without touching it, and shuddering as their hands approach" (279). Nevertheless, although he is "so loathsome" to her that she cannot bear to recognize any human likeness in him, the "deadly stains" of the graveyard "contaminate" her dress (278). Both narrative viewpoint and language foreground Jo as a problem of knowledge and perspective: "It must be a strange state to be like Jo!" (274). The paragraph that begins thus continues with an objective generalizing speculation on what is involved in a condition of total social illiteracy—all signs unintelligible. The narrative voice then shifts into a first-person mode as if to convey the interiority of Jo's "strange state," but the language remains that of educated discourse. What is implicitly confessed here is the inability to make this radical shift of perspective across a great gulf. The paragraph that purportedly begins as a knowledgeable discussion of the ignorance of the destitute classes becomes, in effect, an admission of the ignorance of rational, dispassionate knowledge.

Nevertheless, the text makes a clear categorical distinction between the industrious working-class poor, as represented by the highly individualized entrepreneurial Bagnet family and the self-improving Necket orphans, and a tainting otherness that spreads its threat of social dissolution beyond the confines of pauperism. The Bagnets, by contrast, are firm upholders of proper order. Although Mrs. Bagnet is the power behind the family's improving prospects, the traditional boundaries of family hierarchy are not obliterated: "Discipline must be maintained," Mr. Bagnet insists. The family's stability is put in danger by their association with the unsettled "vagabond ways" of Trooper George. Mrs. Bagnet praises her husband to George as a "hard-working, steady-going chap" and deplores George's inability to marry and so end his "flighty," "rolling-stone" habits (531, 533). Marriage and domesticity are upheld throughout the narrative as normalizing influences, anchoring individuals into the civilized order of the moral community. Pervasive imagery of taint and instability suggests the necessity of such mechanisms of regularization and discipline if order is to hold. This imagery of taint implies invisible currents of contagion that connect the sexual irregularity of Lady Dedlock, whose stained dress foreshadows her dissolution in the melting slush at the entrance to the graveyard, the irregular employment of "vagabond" George, Richard Carstone's "tainted" unsteadiness of purpose, Miss Flite's madness, and the criminality of Krook, who combusts into yellow slime. The narrative structure of *Bleak House* traces a shift in the location of active state power from a visible dynastic class to "impersonal," professional public officials, but what underpins the urgency with which the nature of power is examined within this narrative transition is an imaginary fear of the dissolution of proper order, articulated as an amorphous, spreading contagion.

An instrumental disciplinary savoir, that takes cognisance of and intervenes in all spheres of irregularity, is located in the figure of the lawyer, Tulkinghorn. He is the still, watchful point at the center of all flux. Tulkinhorn is represented as the epitome of newly professional authority: reticent, relentlessly persistent, dispassionate, and methodical in pursuit of knowledge, "going on in his business consideration . . . like a machine" (637). He responds to sympathetic or emotional appeals and accounts of actions and events in a "dry passionless manner" and a "perfect assumption of indifference" (540). His depersonalizing, instrumental approach to knowledge is suggested as he moves pieces of sealing-wax around on his desk in place of the human agents whose irregular connections he is determined to bring to light (182–83). People are thought of only as objects to be brought into a correct order: he discusses with Lady Dedlock his decisions on her fate "as if she were an insensible instrument used in business" (715). Although employed by the aristocracy, Tulkinghorn is always careful to indicate his independence, exhibiting no trace of toadyism.[18] "It is part of Mr Tulkinhorn's policy and mastery to have no political opinions," and he is ready to serve the ironmasters in the north as professionally as their Dedlock opponents in the southern shires (627). The representation of his character suggests a personality entirely given over to a dominating perception of unremitting professional duty. Tulkinghorn has no private life: his home, if such it can be called, is his place of work. If an aristocratic caste is wholly unable to separate the public domain of the state from the private realm of their personal interests, men like Tulkinghorn embody the entire absorption of the private and personal in the public office.

Ostensibly, Tulkinghorn is an employee of the nobility, but he is censorious and contemptuous of those he nominally serves (433). His assumption of the right to investigate suspected irregularities within the Dedlock title of legitimacy is an act symbolizing the shift, within the narrative, of substantive power from the titular nobility to a professional authority. In the story, Tulkinghorn's relentless investigations and interventions are activated not by a sense of service to the nobility, but by professional suspicion of deviancy of any kind, some obliteration of proper boundaries, or by the need for disciplinary authority. In particular, he is exercised by insubordination, disobedience, any resistance or independence of will. In every sphere in which he intervenes, the aim is always to impose conformity to required order. The Man from Shropshire is punished for presumption in demanding an explanation of the law, and Mr. George is bullied and then sold up when he does not immediately comply with Tulkinghorn's wish to see Captain Hawdon's letters. Mademoiselle Hortense is warned when she tries to defy him: "In this city there are houses of correction (where treadmills are for women) . . . the law is so despotic here that it interferes to prevent any of our good English citizens from being troubled, . . . it takes hold of the troublesome lady, and shuts her up in prison under hard discipline" (645).

The treatment of the poor, as embodied in Jo the Crossing-Sweeper, most fully exemplifies the mechanisms and the objectives of these disciplinary techniques: the aim is to produce what Tulkinghorn calls "good English citizens." Jo becomes an object of knowledge. As the focus of a passionless and implacable surveillance, he is watched, chivvied, and worried until he feels he has "no business here or there or anywhere" (274). Yet the aim of this watchfulness is not to know Jo in any real sense, as narrative perspective tries and fails to know him, rather, the constant presence of authority imposes a mystifying internalized guilt. "Deviancy" is produced by the machinery of order as the necessary ground for its normalizing intervention. The invented object of knowledge becomes the justification of practice. Like a mirror reflection, Jo is represented as also mythicizing the authoritative subject of knowledge: Jo is "possessed by an extraordinary terror of this person who ordered him to keep out of the way; . . . he believes this person to be everywhere and cognizant of everything" (694). Perceiving himself only as an object of omniscience and not as a subject that knows (he "don't know nothink"), Jo is constituted as an obedient "deviant" subject who is "wery truly hearty sorry that I done it" (702).

George Rouncewell, another vagrant who is evading proper order, has no difficulty in locating the ultimate source of these disciplinary techniques in Tulkinghorn, a man who has also "got a power over me" (699). What the text suggests, in the characterization of Tulkinhorn, is the danger of extreme specialization of administrative purpose and of total separation of the public and professional domain from the private sphere of personal relationships, affections, and emotional understanding. The pursuit of absolute professional dispassion and disinterestedness have their own risks; or, more properly understood, they may have hidden investments and partialities. In 1854, a writer for the *Westminster Review* alerted readers to exactly this danger of "a purely functionary state." The essay pointed out the increased risk of despotism from the "personal *interest*" hidden under the guise of an impartial government functionary. Such an official, the writer warns, "is likely to be all the more obstinate in his official resolves: — for that is his way of exercising power, attaining to consideration, and making his view prevail."[19]

The desires and interests of self do not wither in the absence of a private life: Tulkinghorn is represented as "always treasuring up slights and offences" to his dignity (457). The pursuit of duty, efficiency, and policy become ends in themselves, and he is represented as contemptuous of what seems to him the indiscipline of the lives and liaisons of his aristocratic clients. Above all, desire for power fills the vacuum left by the absence of other passions. Lady Dedlock describes Tulkinghorn as having no feelings of pity, compunction, or anger: "He is indifferent to everything but his calling. His calling is the acquisition of secrets, and the holding and possession of such power as they give him" (567).

In *Bleak House*, Tulkinghorn represents a panopticon savoir that misrecognizes itself as dispassionate professional knowledge, while at the same time it underwrites normative, regulatory interventions into people's intimate lives and subjectivities. The characterization of Tulkinghorn bears intriguing resemblance to Edwin Chadwick, also a lawyer by training and a leading proponent of professional knowledge put at the service of the state and embodied in mechanisms of investigation and regulation. Chadwick was frequently accused, during the late 1840s and early 1850s, of having sinister, secret plans to bring the whole country under his central control. On 8 July 1854, the *Times* wrote of his pervasive presence within the public domain in terms that strikingly evoke the Tulkinghorn character: "But universal as he is, he is still more mysterious. That accounts for his being everywhere, for what you find everywhere is always the most lurking and impalpable" (quoted in Finer, 1). We might also note that this demonizing description of Chadwick has marked similarities to a Foucauldian image of power. Dickens came to know Chadwick personally from about 1848 to 1852, the intermediary being Dickens's brother-in-law Henry Austen, who was appointed to the sanitary commission in 1847. Despite some cooperative endeavor and mutual interest in the campaign for improved urban sanitation, Chadwick did not become one of Dickens's large circle of friends among men in public life.[20] Lack of fellow feeling between the two men is not surprising since Chadwick is described by his biographer, S. E. Finer, as having no interest in literature or art and as "endowed with far less than the average degree of compassion, humour, or sympathy" (2).

In relation to *Bleak House*, it is perhaps also significant that Chadwick tried to exclude doctors from positions of influence in the domain of public health. His own fall from power was partly brought about by this conflict with powerful medical interest. Chadwick's uncompromising attitude to alternative views to his own is seen by Finer as a passionate determination to impose his own will underlying his projection of dispassionate, professional pursuit of knowledge and facts. He was a man, Finer says, wholly untroubled by self-doubt, "moving ruthlessly and fanatically to his own preconception of what he thought was good for other people while having dangerously little insight into human nature and no tolerance for its foibles and weaknesses" (3). Dickens seems to have sensed this investment in power in Chadwick and his frightening self-certainty. These qualities are transferred to the fictional lawyer Tulkinghorn, who is represented as "immovable in what he has made his duty, . . . absorbed in love of power, . . . determined to have nothing hidden from him in ground where he has burrowed among secrets all his life" (457). Tulkinghorn is represented as particularly hostile to women, holding them to be always potentially deviant. Their emotionalism and sexuality are seen by him as "created to give trouble the whole earth over" (642). His ruthless pursuit of Lady Dedlock most fully suggests the way a personal interest in power masks itself as professional zeal. Having asserted, in a coded fashion to the assembled Dedlocks, his knowledge of her shame and approaching public degradation, he is represented as repressing an almost physical exaltation: "There is a rather increased sense of power upon him, as he loosely grasps one of his veinous wrists with his other hand, and holding it behind his back walks noiselessly up and down" (31).

The insight underlying the representation of Tulkinghorn is the way a seemingly disinterested drive for knowledge — for hidden deviancies in the body politic — as a savoir to discipline and normalize subjects, slides imperceptibly into a ruthless investment in power for its own sake. Rationality is never wholly rational. The dispassionate, bureaucratic impatience with irregularities and the disorder of human affections and foibles too easily transforms itself into a fanatical puritanism that mistakes its own personal repugnance for interests of state. In this way, the public and the private boundaries again merge dangerously and invisibly into each other. The resulting regime of totalized authority in "the public interest" forecloses the space in which citizenship can be imagined as agency; all that is permitted are those "good English citizens" defended by the disciplinary apparatus of the prison, the treadmill, and the police. In its misrecognition of its own excess as "disinterested" professionalism, the regime of order can collapse into its own other of disorder and violence.

That Dickens came to fear this danger is suggested by the other figure, in addition to that of Chadwick, that lurks behind the characterization of Tulkinghorn: Maximillian Robespierre. Chadwick was popularly believed to be trying to replace British constitutional freedoms with French centralized "tyranny," and Raymond Williams describes him as "the most hated man in England" (*Culture and Society*, 53). For the majority of Britons in the immediate aftermath of 1848, the most readily summoned and fearful image of French despotism was still Robespierre, whose passion for order had plunged France into terror and an anarchy of death. Like Chadwick, Robespierre was a lawyer by training, and the two men shared other similarities of character. Both had reputations for purity and incorruptibility (Chadwick was ridiculed as Saint Chad), both had a fanatical hatred of disorder, each was driven by an unquestioned belief in their own rightness, and the enemies of both accused them of excessive centralization of power.

Contemporary accounts of Robespierre make much of his old-fashioned dress of knee breeches and silk stockings, and Dickens, in his representation of Tulkinghorn, draws attention to his "knee-breeches tied with ribbons, and gaiters or stockings" (58–59). Tulkinghorn is killed in his chambers by Hortense, who has visibly reminded Esther of "some woman from the streets of Paris in the reign of terror" (373). At the height of the terror, just before his arrest by his own revolutionary committee, an attempt was made on Robespierre's life by a young girl visiting his lodgings. Such details were general knowledge. However, in representing Tulkinghorn, Dickens is drawing closely upon Carlyle's influential and highly imaginative construction of Robespierre in his *History of the French Revolution* (1837). Carlyle also notes the punctilious, old-fashioned dress, but what he most emphasizes is the unyielding self-certainty. Robespierre is "acrid, implacable"; he is "not a man with the heart of a man, but . . . incorruptibility, . . . barren as the east wind" (2:246, 275). Dickens transfers the east wind to John Jarndyce, but writes of Tulkinghorn that he is a "hard-grained man, close, dry, and silent" (359). Carlyle also describes how an ancient serving maid, Catherine Théot, pores over the Book of Revelation until she becomes convinced that Robespierre will bring into being a new earth. It seems likely that this gave Dickens the first germ of the idea for Miss Flite. What is difficult to convey at all adequately by quotation is the way the tone of Carlyle's writing haunts the representation of Tulkinghorn. Carlyle depicts Robespierre as inscrutable, self-conversing, mysterious to others: "Robespierre for his part glides over at evening . . . or is seen stalking in solitary places . . . with an intensely meditative air" (3:277, 274). Dickens writes of Tulkinghorn: "In the late twilight, he melts into his own square . . . and high priest of noble mysteries [he] arrives at his own dull courtyard . . . gliding into the dusky hall" (639–40).

Tulkinghorn meets a violent death at the hands of a passionate and insubordinate woman whom he has threatened but failed to control. The narrator's comment on the death of Krook seems far more apposite as a comment on the murder of Tulkinghorn in the insistence that such death is the inevitable outcome of all misuse of power — "of all authorities in all places under all names soever, where false pretences are made, and where injustice is done" (511). This diagnosis and denunciation of despotic authority is couched in the discourse of a diseased and proliferating otherness: "It is the same death eternally-inborn, inbred, engendered in the corrupted humours of the vicious body itself" (512). A telling collapse of identity is enacted by the language here between the diseased body of pauperism and the embodiment of power that always first engenders the social pestilence that it claims to regulate. What *Bleak House* seems to suggest is that the new professional, rational, categorizing forms of knowledge, that underpinned the shift from visible, identifiable aristocratic class power to an impersonal public state, paradoxically produced new fears of amorphous, tentacular, unclassifiable threats to the interests of state. These fears then produce a form of pervasive interventionist power that was necessarily a mirror image of the perceived menace. The slippage of identities in the text from Chadwick to Tulkinghorn to Robespierre indicates the uncontainable excess that always lurks behind the rational face of disinterested public authority.

Yet perhaps this slippage needs to be read also in the reverse direction. What the language of *Bleak House* offers insight into is a new way in which power was coming to be imagined in the public sphere of the 1850s: it was being discursively constructed as impersonal and unlocated. In this apparent invisibility, the actual contingent, partial nature of knowledge and bureaucracy could assume imaginary demonic forms, as indeed Chadwick was demonized by the *Times* as sinisterly omnipresent and omniscient and as in the fictional world of *Bleak House* Jo comes to believe Tulkinghorn "to be everywhere and cognizant of everything" (694). What needs to be remembered is that Chadwick was always dependent on the patronage of aristocratic political leaders, whose grip on real power did not much relax. When Chadwick became overassertive, he was brutally ditched. Hazlitt's insight, shared also by Thackeray and Brontë, into a general desiring fascination with power as awful might, suggests the possibility that there is a wish for power to be powerful. When it becomes disassociated from the visible might of a privileged caste, it easily comes to be mythicized as hidden but everywhere, inescapable, and all-knowing.[21] In this way, we can become "good citizens" in obedience to an omnipotence we have conjured in our own imaginations. Through the character of Grindley, *Bleak House* reminds us that power is always located, identifiable, and accountable.

In the novel, Tulkinghorn's power, like that of Chadwick, is also shown to be partial. His professional savoir proves inadequate as an informed mechanism of control. He seriously misjudges Hortense and Lady Dedlock through an inability to enter into their perspectives and feelings. The narrative is at pains to link perspectives to epistemologies. So what form of knowledge is implicated in Esther Summerson's subjective first-person viewpoint? Esther has not proved a popular character with readers. The modest disclaimers of any special personal virtue or intelligence prove irritating in their frequency. Yet this is perhaps the point. Esther's narration begins with a somewhat self-contradictory assertion: "I know I am not clever . . . [but] I had always a rather noticing way . . . a silent way of noticing what passed before me, and thinking I should like to understand it better" (62–63). The artful juxtaposing of terms here should alert us to the fact that definitions of what constitutes "knowing" are being reconsidered. At very least, this comment suggests the need for a degree of epistemological humility: understanding is located as much in what is being contemplated as in the observer. This is a perception of knowing as a dynamic, dialogic process of exchange between object and subject. Esther's wariness of imposing knowledge contrasts with all those other confident pursuers of secret information as the means of holding power over others. Esther's desire for better understanding derives directly from her sense of herself as somehow illegitimate, even before she fully understands the term. This social illegitimacy provides the basis for articulating an alternative form of professional but interested knowledge: a way of understanding that bridges without collapsing public and private interests, subjective and objective perspectives, individual and aggregate realities.

The text is at pains to draw a clear distinction between Esther's practice of knowing and that of Mrs. Pardiggle, the regulatory, "inexorable moral Police-man" of the destitute poor (158). Dickens's representation of Mrs. Pardiggle provides fictional exemplification of the "close co-operation" that Richard Price notes had been forged by the mid-nineteenth century between evangelical moral reformers and the police (199). Esther tries to excuse herself from the visit to the impoverished brickmakers on the grounds that "I was inexperienced in the art of adapting my mind to minds very differently situated, and addressing them from suitable points of view. . . . I had not that delicate knowledge of the heart which must be essential to such work" (154). The kind of knowledge that Esther implies to be necessary is that produced by proximity of feelings, physical closeness, and shared perspectives, in contrast to the shuddering repulsion produced by imagi-nary proximity to otherness. Esther observes that "what the poor are to the poor is little known, excepting to themselves and GOD" (161). This suggests that the poor themselves are producers of knowledge, even though their awareness does not enter the public sphere but circulates only within their own marginalized com-munication. The knowledge that derives from a perspective of social exclusion is represented in the novel as always interested, in that it always identifies with a point of view. Guster, the mistreated orphan from the Tooting workhouse, recog-nizes Jo's similarity to herself, and her personal understanding of his "strange state" leads to intervention in the form of offering him food. Guster's personal knowledge and practice is juxtaposed to the Reverend Chadband's boast, in the same chapter, that Jo is "an instrument" to be used (412). Jo also arouses interested concern in Phil Quod, "who was found, when a baby, in the gutter. Consequently, it is to be expected that he takes a natural interest in this poor creature" (697). It is in elaborating a form and practice of knowing based upon proximity and interest as well as professional objectivity that the marginalized perspectives of Esther and Allan Woodcourt become crucial.

Esther's early life is represented as producing a sense of self that is outcast and separate. This acts as a spur to the acquisition of knowledge: she wants to under-stand her strange state better. The account of Esther's childhood represents her as grasping literally and physically for knowledge that will explain the mystery of her unwanted existence, of which she felt "guilty and yet innocent" (65). She desperately catches hold of her aunt's dress and hands in a effort to get a response from her, both as answer and as affection (64–65). When her aunt dies, Esther kisses her still face, entreating her "to give me the least sign that she knew or heard me" (67). From then onward, Esther's relationships with others are repre-sented by means of physical touching, often by kissing and sometimes by touching the person's face with her hands. So, for example, as Caddy Jellyby begins to confide in her at their first meeting, "I put my hand on her forehead, and said that it was hot now, but would be cool tomorrow" (93). Frequently, as here, touching implies a form of knowledge. When Esther meets Ada for the first time, Ada spontaneously kisses Esther, who thinks, "It was so delightful to know that she could confide in me" (77).

Esther and other characters are frequently represented as using the word *touch* figuratively to signify a sympathetic, interested form of understanding, as when Esther reflects on Ada's situation as a ward of Chancery: "It touched me, that the home of such a beautiful young creature should be represented by that dry official place" (78). Mr. Bagnet warns of his wife's strong response should George "touch her on the children," and Guster's pity for Jo "touches her nearly" (534, 412). The narrative consistently represents Esther's ability to enter imaginatively into the situation of others as a reaching-out impulse of physical contact. In a similar way, Guster's compassion for Jo leads her to pat him on the shoulder, "and it is the first time in his life that any decent hand has been so laid upon him" (417). Affectionate, tactile intimacy is represented especially as a feature of the supportive female community of Caddy, Miss Flite, Esther, and Ada. This is not a local, known community in the traditional sense; it is much more modern in the almost contingent coming together of different lives within the flux of urban space and social mobility. The community is formed and stays "in touch" by shared understanding and sympathetic interest.

Allan Woodcourt's mother boasts of his aristocratic lineage, but what is perhaps more important is that his ancient origins are Welsh and Highland Scots, both cultures at the periphery of national hegemonic identity — both, in a sense, "other." Moreover, Woodcourt lacks influential patronage and so has difficulty making headway in his profession. His practice of knowing is represented also as involving physical closeness to the object of his concern. Immediately following a denunciatory passage condemning empty speeches in Parliament on how the poor are to be put right in their absence "by force of figures, . . . or by high church, . . . [or] according to somebody's theory," Woodcourt is represented walking observantly through an actual slum area: "nor is he merely curious, for in his bright eye there is *compassionate interest;* and as he looks here and there, he seems to understand wretchedness, and to have studied it before" (emphasis added; 683–84). A similar distinction is made earlier in the novel, at the death of the law-writer Nemo, between the kinds of "interest" informing different practices of knowledge. A contrast is implicitly drawn between Woodcourt's "professional interest in death, noticeable as being quite apart from his remarks on the deceased as an individual," and that of Mr. Tulkinghorn, "in his unmoved professional way" (191).

Immediately before this contrast is made, Woodcourt is represented with his hand on the region of Nemo's heart. This is part of his professional examination, but the bringing together of hand and heart in the pursuit of knowledge is significant. What is foregrounded in every representation of an interaction between Esther and Allan Woodcourt with a character from the diseased world of destitution is physical, bodily contact—a knowledge and practice informed by compassionate interest, as opposed to telescopic, dispassionate professionalism, is embodied in intimate proximity. Woodcourt "knows that by touching her with his skilful and accustomed hand, he can soothe her [the brickmaker's wife] yet more readily." Although he believes Jo to be the cause of Esther's illness, Allan "making a strong effort to overcome his repugnance, go[es] very near to him. . . . He constrains himself to touch him" (684, 689). Esther similarly combines a practice that is administratively systematic with concerned personal interest. Smallpox marks her physically with the sign of her willing connection to the body of the poor. When her maid Charlie succumbs to the contagion, Esther is represented as "holding her head in my arms," and when she in turn is ill and feverish, it is Charlie who provides physical comfort: "I talked with Charlie, and felt her touch, and knew her very well" (495, 544). During her illness, Esther has nightmares of separation and isolation, and in describing these she stresses the need for systematic knowledge based on personal understanding that can inform practical intervention: "It may be that if we knew more of such strange afflictions, we might be better able to alleviate their intensity" (544).

A savoir is a practice of knowledge that interfaces between the abstract level of an epistemology and the intractable "real" of its invented object of study. It also moves across the terrain of the public sphere and that of interventionist power. As such. a savoir informs those techniques that aim to intervene and regularize what is publically imagined as disorderly and resistant to categorization. By means of its narrative structure, *Bleak House* warns of the coercion and the dangerous misrecognition of needs of state for public duty that may inhere in such interested professional practices. Importantly, though, the text also allows for a double reading that recognizes the way all distanced forms of knowledge tend to mythicize their object, even when that object is knowledge itself and power. An aggregated perception of "the destitute" or any other social group thought of as menacing to the "public interest" imaginatively produces the very antisocial "other" that is feared. In exactly the same way, power that is dispersed, impersonal, and largely invisible very easily comes to be imagined and constructed within the public sphere as "other" and menacing. The need for "professional experts" to match their claims to knowledge to the inflated social danger of the invented object of their savoir exacerbates this imaginative process of demonizing power.

To such distant, mythologizing epistemologies, *Bleak House* opposes a different kind of interfacing knowledge based upon the proximity of personal perspective and systematic professional practice. Such a praxis entails a double perspective: a cognisance of the community as an aggregated whole brought into dialogic relationship with the interested "in touch" compassion deriving from personal proximity. Moreover, it is an epistemology that recognizes that those at the margins, those like Guster and Phil Quod, are producers of knowledge, rather than objects to be known in the aggregate. As such it opens up a positive civic space in which active participant citizenship can be imagined as a form and practice of inclusive knowledge that constitutes the nation as the known community.

Bleak House endorses a democratic epistemology that encompasses the perspective of the marginalized as part of an inclusive practice of knowing. To mechanisms of mystification and mythic otherness, it opposes the understanding that derives from proximity of social relations. This is not to suggest that the novel is univocally progressive in its politics. Esther's radical capacity for knowing, deriving from an alienated sense of self and the experience of bodily contact, is recontained at the close of the story within the traditional domestic sphere. It is her husband who brings to the public domain of health the professional fusion of abstract knowledge and compassionate interest. John Stuart Mill was indignant at what he termed the "vulgar impudence" of Dickens's satiric treatment of Mrs. Jellyby to ridicule women's rights (quoted in Collins, 297–80). Mill's criticism was certainly justified, yet he missed the centrality of Esther's role within the novel's elaboration of a new practice of knowledge to inform the working of the public state.

As a sort of coda to the novel, we might notice a rather pleasing parallel between the marriage of Esther Summerson and Allan Woodcourt in *Bleak House* and the marriage of Harriet Taylor to John Stuart Mill in 1851. Mill paid great public tribute to the influence of Taylor upon his intellectual movement from the rational epistemology of political economy to a more comprehensive and inclusive imagining of society. Mill wrote of their collaborative practice of knowledge: "What was abstract and purely scientific was generally mine; the properly human element came from her: in all that concerned the application of philosophy to the exigencies of human society and progress, I was her pupil, alike in boldness of speculation and cautiousness of practical judgement" (*Autobiography*, 146–49). In *North and South*, Gaskell speculates upon women's future role within the public sphere and imagines the contribution they can make to the exigencies of human society and progress.

CHAPTER SIX

North and South

From Public Sphere to Manipulative Publicity

Feminist readings of *North and South* (1856) have challenged earlier criticism of Gaskell's representation of class conflict in the story by mapping it, in far more complex ways, onto the mediating role of the tale's heroine across the boundaries of class and those of the public and private spheres.[1] The novel, it is claimed, utilizes this mediation to suggest that industrial conflict and class antagonisms might be transformed by those qualities of personal and social relationship conventionally associated with the private and domestic realm. Following this line of argument, Catherine Gallagher shows how the narrative rejects the separation of public and private spheres inherent in both residual paternalist and dominant middle-class domestic ideologies of social ordering to affirm the moral force that women bring to the public world (168). Yet, Gallagher says, the text indicates that this is a force they acquire only by virtue of the private sphere.

Gallagher defends the romantic ending of the novel as strengthening the metonymic connections that the narrative has made between private and public life, arguing that Thornton and Margaret metonymically represent the best of their respective classes (178). Rosemarie Bodemheimer similarly upholds Gaskell's innovative representation of class relations. She argues that *North and South* is more radical than *Shirley* in the way it challenges the ideologies of both paternalism and laissez-faire. The novel, she says, achieves "a breakthrough in the patterns of conceptualization. . . . Revising paternalistic images of government, views of the working class, and the separate woman's sphere, Gaskell's narrative . . . takes us through a gradual breakdown of traditional ways of thinking about society" (55). This revisioning is largely brought about by means of the interrelationships between the triangle of strong-minded figures: Margaret Hale, the heroine, Thornton, the mill owner, and, Higgins, the trade unionist.

Building upon this rich line of critical investigation of the novel,[2] this chapter focuses in particular upon the narrative's mapping of the transformation of the public sphere of civil society into a fully inclusive heterogeneous forum. Within the actual social world of the mid-1850s, such a transformation of the public sphere did indeed involve a reconfiguration of gender and class subordination and a restructuring of the dynamics connecting the private, public, and state domains. Early in the story of *North and South*, Margaret Hale refers complacently to her own "very comprehensive taste: I like all people whose occupations have to do with land; I like soldiers and sailors, and the three learned professions as they call them" (50). She is equally categorical that her comprehensiveness does not include those in trade. They do not share the same "standard of cultivation" (50), and neither, it seems, should they presume to: "What in the world do manufacturers want with classics, or literature, or the accomplishments of a gentleman?" (72). These disingenuous comments are typical of the unobtrusive irony that pervades Gaskell's representation of the heroine, an irony frequently unnoticed in complaints about overidealization. Nevertheless, Margaret's individual perception of who is to be known and the actual fictional world of the novel's first chapters is a fairly precise representation of the boundaries of civil society as it had existed since the eighteenth century. It was a world that encompassed the county gentry, the two universities, the professions of law, the clergy, the navy and the army, and polite London society. It was not a world based on similarities of wealth but on private property of some degree and, most importantly, a shared sense of cultivated rational sensibilities. This cultivated rationality, founded upon strong underlying class interests, was the ethos and discursive code that regulated the public sphere of civil society.

The narrative structure of *North and South* traces the bypassing of this order of civility in its fictional world and its transformation into an inclusive formation. As in *Shirley* and *Henry Esmond*, this is shown to entail a crisis of language; what Gallagher refers to in her discussion of the novel as "a kind of anarchy of signification" in which the text dwells on the difficulties characters have in understanding one another (181). Gaskell, like Brontë and Thackeray, sees the resolution of this problem of discourse in the replacement of a code of civility with a code of sincerity, but she, too, explores the contradictions inherent in an ideology of sincerity within a popular public sphere. Gaskell also asks what kinds of leaders and what kind of influence is possible and appropriate within a new inclusive society. She picks up on a term just beginning to appear in a new way within the discourse of the public sphere of the 1850s: *a representative man.* The oscillation in the meaning of this term from denotation of aggregation as a typical specimen of others of the same kind to denotation of individualism as standing in for others in an exemplary way highlights the anxieties aroused by imagined massification of the social order.

The novel is equally alert to the main forces for change as they were experienced at the time and as they informed the contentions within the mid-1850s public sphere that was itself the focus of debate and conflict. These forces can be summarized as, first, an expansion of access to cultural spaces and tastes, second, new oppositional forms of knowledge and expertise, and, third, the greater inclusion of the working class in national political and social life.

The democratization of cultural tastes and pursuits was most fully symbolized in the open access of the Great Exhibition to all classes. Harriet Martineau in the *Westminster Review* greeted this radical expansion of cultural experience with enthusiasm: "At the concert on the terrace there are no reserved seats. Everyone can carry a chair to the place he likes best. The conception is entertained for the first time, that such pleasures as these — luxuries requiring money, knowledge, and taste for their formation — are within the reach of the poorest, for free use as well as awe-struck contemplation."[3] In a similar spirit, the establishment of a National Gallery of Art in London, in the early 1850s, substantiated the recognition that, ideally at least, taste and culture should be the inclusive inheritance of all the nation. As well as art galleries in London and the major provincial cities, orchestras and concert halls were established in the capital, and the provinces offering concerts to a wide social range of audiences.[4] As Fanny Thornton proudly tells Margaret in the novel, the latest London music and literary fashions could be ordered from local suppliers (140). As Fanny implies, claims to discrimination and judgment could no longer be preserved as the unquestioned, exclusive endowment of the traditional possessors of cultural capital.

This more comprehensive perception of holders of taste put into question the identity of those who had previously felt themselves to constitute civil society and to form public opinion. The conservative voice of *Blackwood's Magazine* some-what irascibly expressed the growing anxiety about the changing nature of "the public" and its power: "The public — the public, and none but the public — shall have a National Gallery, [with] committees of taste, to tell this public what it wants, which it ought to know very well itself, if the said public had any individual bodily existence."[5] The same magazine took a similar dim view of the confusion of class boundaries brought about by the expansion of consumer taste: "The home of the trader is now more luxurious than was the dwelling of a nobleman fifty years ago."[6] The ostentatious display of Mrs. Thornton's household in *North and South* would doubtless have seemed to the reviewer a fictional example of the obliteration of the once-secure division separating the civil from the vulgar. In 1851, Gaskell wrote with obvious glee to a correspondent that "the Dickens have bought a dinner-service of *gold* plate," adding that her informant belonged to the "capital circle in London too" (Chapple, 175).

The expansion of those deemed acceptable within the "capital" cultural circles of London and the provincial cities also contributed to the displacement of the regulated rational urbanity that had formed the medium of social intercourse within a more homogeneous public sphere. The discursive shift toward a code of sincerity is clearly expressed in an article by Herbert Spencer in the *Westminster Review* in 1854 in which he complains of precisely the kind of cultured rational-ism that had informed the eighteenth-century public sphere: "Who is there that has not, from time to time, felt how cold and flat is all this talk about politics and science, and new books and new men, and how a genuine outflow of fellow-feeling outweighs the whole of it."[7] Spencer particularly associates this lifeless civility with the intercourse at dinner parties held to further the careers of rising men. Furthering social ambitions is also represented as the aim of the elegant hospitality organized by Edith and her husband, Captain Lennox, in *North and South*. The character Mr. Bell is represented as having similar thoughts to those expressed in the *Westminster Review:* "I can't stand the restraints of such a proper-behaved and civil-spoken set of people as these are" (465). The same journal printed another article on language use in which it argued for a return to the "native vigour" of the word *man* as opposed to the feudal modification of it into *gentleman*. The terms of the article are strikingly close to those used by Thornton in his argument with Margaret about the relative merits of the two words (218).[8]

Habermas has been criticized for not noting more fully the exclusion of women from the public sphere. Yet the *Westminster's* reference to dinner parties held to further careers of rising men suggests that there was considerable traffic across the public and private worlds. In *North and South*, Margaret Hale's own identification with civil society suggests that women did not feel themselves wholly excluded. In a recent detailed study of women of the gentry class in Lancashire around the end of the eighteenth and the beginning of the nineteenth centuries, Amanda Vickery demonstrates women's multiple involvement in the proliferating public sphere of literary societies, lending libraries, musical events, theatrical occasions, daytime lectures, and fashionable benevolence. "By the early nineteenth century," Vickery argues, "although their family duties remained, the public profile of privileged provincial women had reached unprecedented heights" (288). This involvement of women in the public sphere increased as the century progressed. Nevertheless, it was only restricted acceptance; women's access to the public institutions of learning and the professions remained firmly blocked. In *North and South*, the heroine's struggle to read Dante with the help of a dictionary indicates both her intellectual aspirations and the barriers impeding their fulfilment (55).

The universities of Oxford and Cambridge, as seats of learning still based preeminently upon a classical curriculum, underpinned the cultural values that gave cohesion and assurance to civil society. In the 1850s, these institutions were coming under strong criticism for the narrowness of their learning and for the social exclusiveness of their student bodies, their fellows, and scholars. In criticizing the trend toward tyrannizing centralized authority as perceived in the parliamentary commission set up in 1854 to investigate Oxford and Cambridge, *Blackwood's Magazine* invoked the public sphere in its ideal role of opposition to state power: "The public . . . have an interest in these great public institutions . . . and have a right to a voice in the question."[9] Yet the journal was appealing to a notion of the public of civil society that was already becoming outdated. New scientific forms of knowledge and new sources of expertise were informing public debate and undermining the authority of cultivated opinion in the more exclusive, traditional sense. The parliamentary commission into the universities was meeting the demands articulated in the widening public sphere for greater comprehensiveness in the body of knowledge taught and in the social composition of the colleges. In particular, Oxford fellowships of the kind that Mr. Bell, in *North and South*, is represented as holding were regarded as no longer tenable.

At the same time, the civil service was subjected to even more rigorous reform of its aristocratic culture. Government posts were no longer to be distributed on the basis of high connections within civil society but were to be awarded competitively on the basis of merit alone. The *Westminster Review* argued strongly against selection of candidates on the basis of classical scholarship. Such outmoded perspectives could provide no "independent search for new truth"; what was needed were "men of original power, with but little learning; [who] pay but little respect to the bounds of former knowledge . . . they carry their generation far beyond them."[10] Such a description might well apply to Thornton, Gaskell's character, who opens Mr. Hale's mind to a whole new world of possibilities. Margaret's conventionally cultivated suitor, Mr. Lennox, is also placed within the value system that the novel is investigating by the comment in the *Westminster* that lawyers are preeminently examples of learned men so conservative as to be unable to offer any new progressive ways of thinking.

It was particularly the new forms of empirical and statistical knowledge propounded by those who supported the social sciences that were perceived as threatening to cultivated civility. The unease felt at this new "scientific" and "progressive" methodology was threefold. First, aggregated, comprehensive information asserted a claim to disinterested knowledge that began to undermine the traditional force of "public opinion" as the corporate expression of each individual's discrimination, taste, and sensibility. Second, statistical investigations were seen as leading to an expansion of the public domain of the state in the social spheres of education, health, sanitation, and industrial legislation, thereby infringing upon the rights of individual responsibility and private property. The *Edinburgh Review*, for example, argued that widespread parental neglect in what it termed "the perishing classes" necessitated the "grave question" of whether "some legal authority must be given, not to persuade, but to command" the care and education of the children of the poor.[11] The third area of fear associated with the expanding emphasis upon numbers and quantification in the discourse of the public sphere was a sense that quality and distinction were being obliterated in sheer quantification. Those private individuals of like cultivation and property who made up civil society seemed threatened with collapse into a sense of the public as mere aggregate of the population.

Again *Blackwood's Magazine* expressed conservative anxieties. Two long articles in response to the collection of statistical information in the 1851 census attacked the encroaching role of the state and the new authority of science on the grounds that both undermined older forms of learning and the traditional sense of social distinctions. The title of the articles, "Civilization—The Census," neatly summarized the perception of opposed interests between the cultivated values of civil society, on the one hand, and, on the other, those of the new statistical sciences. The writer described the amassing of details about the entire population and their subsequent categorization and aggregation as the "doings of a public Busybody." It was further argued that the "accumulation of mere facts and figures" overvalued a form of knowledge that was hostile to those individual virtues that sustain civilized society.[12] In the second article, the writer concluded that "it has been shown how, since 1801, our statisticians have encroached upon the Englishman's home, his 'castle' " (524). The *Westminster Review* rarely found itself in agreement with *Blackwood's*, but in 1854 one of its reviewers expressed similar concern over the shift of meaning in the notion of "the public" so as to sink individual judgment and opinion into an aggregate of the population: "The terms 'the public' and 'nationality' are often so used as to express an untruth. The 'public,' the 'nation' are but aggregates of individuals, and no quality, power, or right resides in the aggregate which does not previously exist in the component individuals. We have no national conscience; but one by one we are accountable." The reviewer concludes that while man exists, "the nation is a mere convenient abstraction."[13]

In *North and South*, this anxiety over the tension between individual security and liberty of opinion and the requirement of the mass of the people as aggregate is expressed as a concern for those fragile human lives, perhaps the perishing classes referred to in the *Edinburgh Review*, that are "passed by in the swift merciless improvement or alteration" (204). When Margaret Hale returns to Helstone to discover it is no longer the place represented in her most cherished personal memories, the experience of "all-pervading instability" produces a sense of "individual nothingness" (488). Yet the following day she recognizes that change, although painful to some individuals, is right and necessary for general progress. As the narrator comments elsewhere: "In all measures affecting masses of people [there] must be acute sufferers for the good of many. The question always is, has everything been done to make the suffering of these exceptions as small as possible" (108).

Public opinion, understood as the corporate expression of civil society, acquired its imaginary ideal as a forum of rational critique through opposition to arbitrary and unaccountable central power. This ideal, evoked by Habermas, came into being in the eighteenth century, but the power opposed was the threat of absolute monarchy. During the nineteenth century, both conservative and liberal opinion continued to evoke the force of the public against centralized authority, but the distinction between public, private, and state realms of influence and agency became increasing blurred. Although the encroaching role of state intervention was vocally contested within the public sphere during the 1850s, response to the enlarged domain of the state was genuinely ambivalent.

This is because the expanding managerial responsibilities of government in the social spheres of education, health, sanitation, and criminal reform offered to three social groups — the gentry, middle-class women, and working-class men — crucial opportunities that they were all eager to grasp.

The public role of the state provided the gentry, the core of civil society, with a social space in which to reinvent itself as a professional class of state officials and public managers. Salaried careers opened up an alternate means of income and status to that of dwindling private resources. In *North and South*, Mr. Hepworth, the energetic vicar who replaces Mr. Hale in the village of Helstone, is a fictional representative of the new professionalism of those who saw themselves in some way as public servants. Mrs. Hepworth's enthusiasm for the new curriculum she is introducing into the village school indicates the opportunities that an expanded public domain offered women for more professionalized activity and recognized participant citizenship. A good example of the interactions that were increasingly linking together the expanding state, the new social sciences, and the public sphere was the passing in 1854 of the Juvenile Offenders Act, largely as the result of widely publicized statistics. The act allowed for state funding to voluntary groups, involving many women, for the further expansion of this public-sector work. Finally, for the leaders of the working class, the state and the public sphere constituted potential powers that they might influence to produce legislation to mitigate the inequalities of labor in relation to capital.

The aim of influencing public opinion gave working-class leaders an investment in consolidating that dual perspective of the laboring population that separated industrious individual working people from the irresponsible "perishing classes." Their aspirations were met in so far as there was a growing perception among the governing classes, by the mid-1850s, that the body politic would have to become more socially comprehensive. As yet, this was not a recognition that mass democracy was inevitable or necessary. It was, though, an acknowledgment, after the fact, that respectable working people had earned the right for their voices and viewpoints to be admitted to the public sphere of opinion. In 1854, the *Westminster Review* conceded, "In every country . . . those who merely labour have been more or less feared, in the mass, by those who merely possess. . . . We cannot hope to dislodge this feeling amongst ourselves by simple force of argument: we must trust rather to time and experience. The extension of suffrage must be won by degrees and as a consequence of growing confidence on all sides."[14] In effect, the working class would have to persuade public opinion of its fitness for inclusion in the body politic. An article in the *Edinburgh Review* asserted that while universal suffrage might prove the "surest instrument of despotism," nevertheless it would be beneficial to include the "elite of the working-classes" within the suffrage so that "the really worthy, competent, and educated of all ranks should be blended in one comprehensive and respectable constituency." Given the pride those chosen from the ranks of labor would feel to be thus recognized, the reviewer declared, "we are by no means sure that they would not become the *elite* of the constituency also." However, universal suffrage and the franchise of women were dismissed "as changes which, since no legislature will listen to them, it would be idle for us to discuss and silly to pronounce on."[15]

This perception of an alignment between the most able of the working class and property-owning society was further developed in the *Westminster Review.* In an article on " 'Strikes' and 'Lock-Outs,' " the reported attitude of the employers is the one that Gaskell represents as Thornton's: "The men shall choose between obeying the union committee or obeying us." Yet, the reviewer says, if seen from the point of view of the workers, such struggles would demonstrate "virtue under almost all its forms; of constancy under suffering, self-denial against temptations, loyalty to their leaders, sacrifices for their fellows, devotion to their cause."[16] In very similar terms in *North and South,* Nicholas Higgins compares the idealism upholding the worker's industrial action to the heroism of the soldier. Moreover, the writer in the *Westminster* goes on to say that while factory workers are quick to resent being addressed as servants since it degrades their independence, "there are no labourers who talk more than do factory operatives about the feasibility and propriety of making the relation with manager and capitalist one not only, as at present, of veiled, but also of professional partnership. They long to be called partners — to free themselves from the fetters of service" (143). Those who were left out of this projected new managerial disposition of power within the political and industrial realms were the perishing classes and women of all classes. Yet as the perceived need to manage the perishing classes for the good of the nation as a whole grew more pressing, the public domain of the state began to merge with and incorporate into itself the public sphere of benevolent activities. Women, particularly those of the gentry class, were quick to develop this new managerial space opening out from their earlier charitable role within the public sphere.

The structural transformation of the public sphere was brought about by the pressure of these cultural, epistemological, and social forces converging toward greater comprehensiveness. The code of civility facilitating communicative relations within the confines of civil society collapsed under the strains of greater social inclusiveness. By the 1840s and 1850s, the passionate demands of Chartism, the bitterness of the struggles over the Corn Laws, and the growth of trade unionism had all served to demonstrate that conflicts of interest could not be meliorated by rational debate to produce a consensus that was genuinely in the same public interests of all. Underlying economic structures entailed indissoluble opposition of interest between different social groups.

In this new, contested, heterogeneous public sphere, Habermas argues, critical publicity as the basis of rational debate began to give way to manipulative publicity by interest groups attempting to persuade by selective presentation. Instead of functioning to inform and engender disinterested debate to arrive at reasoned consensus, the aim of publicity shifted to that of gaining the passive acclamation of a targeted audience. Publicness as aura was reinstituted within manipulative publicity to win consent by means of the glamour of charismatic presentation. Meanwhile, the critical opposition between state as central authority and the public sphere based on private property was transformed by the increasing functionalism of each sector. While the state became increasingly managerial, offering a new sphere of professional activity to the displaced gentry class, and more gradually to women, private ownership of large industries declined and salaried managers and directors assumed charge of operational strategy. State and industrial managers and trade union leaders came more and more to share similar education, interests, and even goals, while the perspectives of the different sectors they served were entrusted to the publicity industry to be stylized as a show for public acclamation and identification. Thus the public sphere was "refeudalized" to become only a commercialized court of public opinion staging displays of authority, personality, and glamour for consumption. I would add to Habermas's account here that a central element of this new form of publicness would become the staging of manipulative sincerity.

Gaskell wrote *North and South* at the moment in the mid-1850s when the public sphere was vocal in its opposition to the encroaching power of centralization and in defense of individual liberty and private property. Yet, as I have argued, it was equally the pivotal moment when the identity of the public sphere became exposed to the forces of its transformation. *North and South* figures in multiple forms the coercive power of any imposed authority over the individual conscience. Mr. Hale is forced to dissent from the authority of the established church, being unable "to make a fresh declaration of conformity" (68). To Margaret, his honest doubts make him "an outcast," while her brother is literally "an outlaw" due to his defiance of the despotism of a naval commander invested with the full authority of the state (76, 66). When Margaret is discussing Frederick's case, she asserts the force of public opinion in opposition to the arbitrary power of the state: authority "brutally used," she argues, is rightfully withstood, and if "people [could] know what you did" and the motive for action, it would be "elevate[d] . . . out of a crime into an heroic protection of the weak" (326). The authority of the state is also defied by Thornton in regard to its perceived "meddling" and "interference" with the rights of private property owners to manage their own businesses — "even though that meddler be called the High Court of Parliament" (125). Yet Thornton contradicts himself, as Margaret Hale notes, when he espouses the dictatorial government of an Oliver Cromwell; the collusion of the state with private property is further indicated when soldiers are drafted in to protect his mill from strikers and make the men "feel the power of authority and order" (236).

By refusing to offer his employees the reasoning behind his management of the mill, Thornton sets himself in opposition to the critical rationality of the public sphere and aligns himself with arbitrary and secret practices of power. It is subtly suggested that Thornton also initially imagines the role of husband as a form of benign power: at one point he anticipates how Margaret "might droop, and flush, and flutter to his arms, as to her natural home and resting-place" (251). It is worth remembering that even the timid Hale decides his family's future in secret without consulting them in any way. The trade union, represented as an authority that cannot be challenged or gainsaid, is also accused, by Margaret, of tyranny (296). The union is seen as typical of most of the forms of authority questioned in the text, in that to pursue the good of the aggregate it must seem indifferent to the needs and rights of the individual who differs. Margaret is persistently represented as upholding an opposing inclination: while acknowledging a public duty to society generally to teach in the village school, she is "continually tempted off to go and see some individual friend — man, woman or child" (48). At the end of the novel, she reaches the conscious understanding that "love for my species could never fill my heart to the utter exclusion of love for individuals" (488). Significantly, in view of the ending of the story, Thornton, too, is said to have "no general benevolence, — no universal philanthropy" (275).

This individualism as opposed to aggregation of interests is stressed in the conversation in which Mr. Hale assures Mr. Bell and Mr. Thornton: "You are neither of you representative men; you are each of you too individual for that." Margaret responds by saying that "there is a difference between being the representative of a city and the representative man of its inhabitants" (412–13). The latter formulation sinks the individual into the aggregate or type whereas the former sees the individual as an exemplary embodiment of a distinctive set of cultural values. A representative in this sense could be understood as enjoying a form of publicness. It is in terms of the tensions within this new notion of representativeness that the novel interrogates modes of leadership in an inclusive social order.

The assertion of the independence of the private individual cuts across what is often read as the public/private divide in the novel and across gender demarcations. Thornton declares that northern manufacturers as private property owners "stand up for self-government, and oppose centralisation"; for his mother, the house and the mill are inseparable: "all belongs to him and . . . his is the head that directs it" (414, 214). His right, as owner of his own property, to impose employment conditions is frequently identified with the right of private householders to employ those domestic servants that suit them. On the other side of the class divide, Nicholas Higgins compares the private relations between employers and employees to that between husband and wife—not to be meddled in by those outside (384). For Nicholas, the domestic sphere of home is the location of his autonomy as an independent individual; people enter only on invitation, and, he says, "it would take a deal to daunt me in my own house" (419).

Margaret's mediating role in the story needs to be understood in terms of her representative social identity, rather than that of her gender. Margaret and her father are the representatives within the text of the gentry's traditional role within the public sphere of civil society. In the same way that Bell could be understood to represent the ideals of Oxford, Margaret and her father exemplify those values of civility, culture, and informed and rational opinion ideally associated with the public sphere. Margaret identities herself with this sphere early in the novel when she categorizes those cultivated people falling within her "comprehensive taste." Despite this class narrowness, Margaret and Hale are represented as exemplifying the civility of manner that treats everyone with a formal, outward assumption of equal regard. Hale punctiliously addresses Nicholas Higgins as Mr. Higgins and places a chair for him to sit upon. Margaret exerts herself to put Thornton at ease in her father's absence, despite her perception of him as a tradesman: "She felt no awkwardness; she had too much the habits of society for that. Here was a person come on business to her father; and, as he was one who had shown himself obliging, she was disposed to treat him with a full measure of civility" (99). The force of Margaret's civil dignity overthrows Thornton's own normal assumption of authority, and throughout the story insistent references are made to the impact of Margaret Hale's presence in any company. Mrs. Thornton's impatient question about Margaret and her mother, "What do they do?" entirely misses the point (117): Margaret's status resides in the aura of assuredness that is her inheritance as a cultivated woman. She insists, "I am myself a born and bred lady through it all, even though it comes to scouring a floor, or washing dishes" (116). A similar point is made in the contrast between the two households: the tasteful charm of the Hales's drawing room that so attracts Thornton serves no purpose. It simply expresses the presence of cultivated values, "the graceful cares [that] were habitual to the family," whereas Mrs. Thornton's uncomfortable rooms, dazzling with expensive but showy taste, are kept under wraps until there are visitors to impress (120). Bessy Higgins is represented as fearful that Margaret may be overpowered by the splendor of a dinner party at the Thornton's, but Margaret is able to reassure Bessy that she feels unperturbed by the honor of meeting members of Parliament and the mayor of Milton: publicness is her inherited mode of being.

It is this self-confident self-sufficiency, the aura endowed by cultural capital, that creates the semblance of disinterest and constitutes Margaret and Hale as a kind of dispassionate, nonpartisan public forum to which the opposing manufacturing interests of workers and owners bring their arguments. Thornton continually seeks to convince Hale and Margaret of the logic and economic rationality of his values and strategy as a substantial mill owner and private entrepreneur: "It was a duty he owed to himself to explain, as truly as he could, what he did mean" (125). The mill workers, likewise, are anxious to put their case before the representative tribunal of Hale and Margaret; the workingmen come to Hale "with their earnestly-told tales of suffering and long-endurance. . . . Here was this man, from a distant county, who was perplexed by the workings of the system into the midst of which he was thrown, and each was eager to make him a judge, and to bring witness of his own causes of irritation" (204). As Margaret and her father confront each side with the arguments of the other, they constitute the critical rationality of the public sphere in opposition to the threat of arbitrary authority and despotic power, whether of state or money or numbers. They provide the justice court of publicity in which conflicting viewpoints can be put to the test of critical reason. Insofar as the narrative is formally structured upon this dialogic interchange, Gaskell is deliberately positioning her story within the contestations of the 1850s. The novel is participating in the traditional role of literature within the public sphere; it is providing the basis for rational-critical debate.

In the world of the novel, the expanding role and importance of cultural values and tastes in supporting claims to recognition within the public sphere of local communities is indicated by Fanny Thornton's concertgoing and piano playing. Thornton is represented as pursuing a more serious concern to become cultured, taking lessons in the classics with Mr. Hale. Importantly, though, while Thornton comes to Hale for the culture of antiquity, the text makes clear that he gives far more than he receives. Bell and Hale belong to an educational and cultural tradition that is losing authority and relevance; the processes of change everywhere apparent in the text are pushing it into the past, as their deaths imply. Well-meaning though Hale is, his attempts to offer education to the workingmen are represented with almost Hardyesque irony as a course on ecclesiastical architecture (191). When he complacently asks Thornton whether the "recollection of the heroic simplicity of the Homeric life" did not nerve him up during the early years of struggle, Thornton simply laughs, exclaiming, "Not one bit!" (127). Mrs. Thornton dismisses Hale as "a worthy kind of man [but] . . . too simple for trade" (192).

By contrast, it is Thornton who nerves up Hale's intellect and imagination with new knowledge of the power of steam and the advances of technology and machinery, which "shall compel all material power to yield to science" (122). This entirely new realm of intellectual endeavor whose horizons are being advanced by men without traditional scholarship seems to Hale like a tale from the Arabian Nights, with reality stretched at one moment "from earth to sky and filling all the width of the horizon" and at the next obediently encompassed by a child's hand (122). When this rejuvenating intercourse with Thornton ceases, Hale appropriately goes to Oxford to die in his sleep. Mrs. Thornton bluntly suggests that the constitution of a new, enlarged public sphere is bypassing the traditional one of civil society: she tells Margaret and her father that although the name of John Thornton is unknown in "fashionable circles," it is known and respected among men of business throughout England and Europe. At this moment, father and daughter have enforced upon them the uneasy consciousness that the world Mrs. Thornton refers to "was not their world of Harley Street gentilities on the one hand, or country clergymen and Hampshire squires on the other" (160). The sphere of publicity is shifting, and with it the nature of reputation and public renown.

It is not just new forms of knowledge that Thornton represents; he also introduces a new code of social intercourse. At the conclusion of their first meeting, Thornton advances to shake hands, while Margaret follows the practice of civility and distantly bows. She does not recognize, says the narrator, that to shake hands "was the frank familiar custom of the place" (127). The words *civil* and *civility* are much used in the text and subtly juxtaposed to the words *friends* and *friendship*. At the beginning of the story, Margaret regulates her own standards of social behavior in terms of "civility," as when she accords Thornton, on their first meeting, "a full measure of civility" (99). However, Mrs. Thornton expresses a different estimate of civility when she instructs Fanny: "We will be civil to these Hales: but don't form one of your hasty friendships with the daughter" (142). Immediately after this conversation, Margaret is represented as responding to Bessy Higgins's request to describe Helstone: although Margaret has avoided speaking of the place since she left it, "her heart was opened to this girl" (144).

What the text opposes to the code of civility, with its formal assumption of cultivated equality, is the code of sincerity that functions as an interpellative mode of intersubjective mutual regard based upon the recognition of shared but different interiorities. As with Thornton's handshake, itself part of the code of sincerity, what is implicitly promised by such an interpellation is the frankness of trust. Jenny Uglo argues that by 1854 Gaskell had come to feel that "the cornerstone of a new ethic must be respect based on sympathy" (370). The code of sincerity implies a somewhat more vigorous form of respect based on an acceptance that other viewpoints and interests may differ radically. While Hale's civility shrinks from giving his wife pain and so leaves her uninformed of his worries and intentions, the relationship between Thornton and his mother is typified by their "daring" to speak out unpalatable truths to each other, so showing "reliance on the firm centre of each other's souls" (137). By contrast, the Hales, although man and wife, seem to lack any language in which to speak sincerely to each other, even of Mrs. Hale's imminent death. *Daring* is the key word in the description of the Thorntons' discourse. Implicit within textual notations of sincerity or frankness as an ideal regulating discourse is the acceptance that views may differ, that conflicting interests may be at stake. Although Margaret's "cultivated taste" is oppressed by the excess of delicacies served up at the Thornton dinner party, she quickly appreciates the superiority of the manufacturers' intercourse: "They talked in desperate earnest, — not in the used-up style that wearied her so in the old London parties" (216).

In London, the neighbors of Mrs. Shaw are "called friends because she happened to dine with them more frequently than with any other people" (36). Margaret comes to desire a return to her "former position of antagonistic friendship" with John Thornton as relief from the intolerable sameness of polite urbanity of her cousin's London life (303). As also in *Shirley*, the code of sincerity is represented in *North and South* as an invigorating, active clash of opinion in a communicative, interpersonal pursuit of truth as opposed to the code of civility that aims at urbane consent. Gaskell herself wrote to a friend in 1850: "I suppose we all *do* strengthen each other by clashing together, and earnestly talking our thoughts and ideas. The very disturbance we thus are to each other rouses us up, and makes us more healthy" (Chapple, 116). Precisely the opposite feeling guides Lennox when he entertains Bell with one conciliatory view of the cause of Hale's dissent as lack of intercourse with men of "equal cultivation." Seeing that this explanation angers Bell, he smoothly expresses the opposite opinion that there "is something fine" in Hale's integrity (466). He is quite unaroused by the subject or the beliefs in question, aiming only at civility. And it is Lennox who insists that Edith must be "civil" to Thornton when he is invited to her dinner party. Edith is proud that her dinner parties are so much more modern than her mother's; they function across the public/private spheres, serving to further the intercourse and careers of rising professional men of the day. The invitation to Thornton, which causes Edith uneasiness less he is unable "to sound his h's," indicates the widening of the public sphere (521). In keeping with the code of civility, Lennox is courteously anxious to avoid giving Thornton the mortification of having to admit his business failure, but Thornton adheres to the code of sincerity and publicly acknowledges, "I have been unsuccessful in business, . . . I am on the lookout for a situation" (524).

Another character, too, is represented in the story as frequently using the word *civil*: Nicholas Higgins. He meets Thornton's brusque dismissal of his appeal for work by retorting ironically: "Yo' made a remark, sir, on my impudence: but I were taught that it was manners to say either 'yes' or 'no' when I were axed a civil question," and he concludes the futile interview by thanking Thornton for "yo'r civil way o' saying good-bye" (397–98). Higgins also teaches Margaret that there are discourteous insensibilities in her code of civility when she patronizingly assumes the right to visit his family without being invited, although he shrewdly recognizes that she is inclined to think "I might ha' spoken more civilly" (112–13). Nevertheless, Nicholas is represented as having little real concern with civility. Although he frequently describes Thornton as not "o'er civil," he insists that he gives Thornton as good as he gets; what Nicholas wants is not civility, as understood by a Lennox, but "I should like to get speech o' them . . . tell 'em my mind" (203). As with Thornton, Higgins's ideal of social intercourse is sincerity: he commends Mr. Hale for not being a hypocrite, and the greatest concession he feels able to offer Thornton is a promise to "speak to him in private

first" if he saw him going wrong as an employer (397). Significantly, their agreement to try to work together is ratified by a handshake. As with Thornton's
relationship with his mother, so Nicholas's with his daughter is represented as
based upon an openness that rejects any genteel veiling of disagreeable realities.
Margaret is shocked by the apparently brutal sincerity with which Nicholas
accepts Bessy's claim to be dying, and Nicholas also refuses to soften his view of
industrial conflict to give her a false tranquillity: "Poor wench — poor old wench
— I'm loth to vex thee, I am; but a man mun speak out for the truth" (112, 133).
Bessy's and Nicholas's close relationship is based upon the mutual trust and
respect necessarily inherent in "antagonistic friendship."

Nicholas Higgins not only offers Margaret a form of social intercourse based
upon a code of sincerity rather than civility, he also offers new forms of knowledge. He instructs her on the realities of industrial conflict from the perspective
of the factory workers. He insists upon the economic logic of low wages, on the
one hand, and, on the other, upon the idealism underlying the workers' struggle.
In doing so, he addresses her with the same challenging familiarity that he uses to
his daughter: " 'My lass,' said he, 'yo'r but a young wench, but don't yo' think I
can keep three people . . . on sixteen shilling a week? Dun yo' think it's for mysel'
I'm striking work at this time? It's just as much in the cause of others as yon
soldier' " (183). Bessie Higgins also contributes knowledge of working lives when
she explains that the need for drink as relief from monotony is not to be equated
with drunkenness (185).

In *North and South*, both sides to industrial dispute recognize the need to put
the "facts" of their case and experiences before the public. Thornton assures
Margaret, "I shall be only too glad to explain to you all that may seem anomalous
or mysterious . . . especially at a time like this, when our doings are sure to be
canvassed by every scribbler who can hold a pen" (165). Just like their employers
the mill owners, the leaders of the union that Higgins represents are eager to
publicize their cause and to take their arguments against the owners to the court
of public opinion. Bessy explains to Margaret how the committee of the union
had carefully planned on "carrying th' public with them" by demonstrating they
were "steady thoughtful men . . . good citizens, who were friendly to law and
judgement, and would uphold order . . . who would ne'er injure property or life"
(259–60). Nicholas claims, "We had public opinion on our side, till [Boucher] . . .
and his sort began rioting and breaking laws. It were all o'er wi' the strike then"
(366). Hale expresses the ideal of a fully inclusive public sphere based upon an
ethos of rational frankness, maintained by means of a code of sincerity, rather

than civility, when he says, "But let us know each other, and speak freely to each other about these things, and truth will prevail" (290).

Yet with understated irony, the chapter in which Hale represents this utopian possibility goes on to indicate the limits of interpersonal sincerity within a wholly inclusive public sphere. When Hale attempts to persuade Higgins of the rational truth of political economy, Nicholas questions the assumption that consensual agreement is always the result of a public examination of different viewpoints. He says with sincerity, rather than civility, "There's two opinions go to settling that point . . . in time I may get to see the truth of it; or I may not. I'll not be bound to say I shall end in thinking the same as any man. . . . Same bones won't go down wi' every one. It'll stick here i' this man's throat, and there i' t'others" (293). At the end of the chapter, when Margaret describes the union as a tyranny in its attempt to impose a uniform will and discipline upon labor in the mass, Higgins does not really deny this, but he responds by pointing out the historical necessity of solidarity. Unified opposition to the power of property may well "be like a war" in which, inevitably, some will perish. Yet for unpropertied laboring men to withstand injustice, past, present, or to come, "our only chance is binding of men together in one common interest . . . whose only strength is in numbers" (296). Higgins remains unanswered; there is no gainsaying his assertion, which points to underlying structural inequalities within the social order that no amount of respect for the other's sincerity can weld into a consensual interest of the whole nation.

Higgins is represented as never relinquishing his active role of leadership within the union. In the matter of the works canteen that Thornton wants to initiate, Higgins acts as spokesperson for the men. As a Union leader Higgins is concerned that strikes are well "managed" and, as even Thornton admits, "respectable" (182, 414). From this managerial perspective, Higgins feels protective pity for the likes of Boucher, but very little in common with him. Yet while Higgins, in this sense, retains the dual perspective for representing his class, Gaskell challenges previous social-problem novels, including her own earlier *Mary Barton*, by representing the "unrespectable" poor, the Boucher family, in individualized terms, rather than en masse. When Boucher ruins the strike by undisciplined behavior, Higgins is represented as even more angry with him than are the mill owners. Boucher has destroyed the union's carefully planned strategies of publicity upon which the union depends to win its case within public opinion. Boucher is representative of what the *Edinburgh Review* called the perishing classes; Higgins refers to him as a weed and implies that either a union or central government has to take responsibility — often coercive — for those like Boucher who cannot take care of themselves (367, 366).

It is with Thornton that Higgins comes to share an antagonistic friendship. This is often read as the moral transformation of industrial conflict into personal understanding brought about by the intermediary of womanly concern.[17] Yet the text equally suggests that mutual respect between Higgins and Thornton grows out of common, if frequently conflicting, concerns over the functioning of the workplace. When Thornton initially agrees to employ Higgins after the strike, Higgins tells him that he will "need a deal o' brains to settle where my business ends and yo'rs begins" (405). As Thornton is transformed from a private owner concerned wholly with profits to a manager interested in the effective functioning of the system, he comes to share this perspective with Higgins. Thornton's evolved vision of industrial cooperation reads like a utopian blueprint of management and union interaction to produce an effectively functioning system: "But I would take an idea, the working out of which would necessitate personal intercourse; it might not go well at first, but at every hitch interest would be felt by an increasing number of men, and at last its success in working come to be desired by all as all had borne a part in the formation of the plan" (525).

Thornton is given the opportunity to develop these experiments in new forms of management when Margaret Hale becomes owner of his mill and insists upon funding him. Prior to this, Margaret has staked out an independent life for herself in caring for the perishing classes. The text has been at pains to emphasize that Margaret, too, like Thornton and Higgins, has a "genius for management" (98). Thus the narrative concludes with a glimpse of a newly forming inclusive consensual public sphere comprising the functionalism of industrial, union, and state managers — both men and women. Those that remain excluded from this inclusive community are the poor, the unemployed, all those who cannot manage for themselves and who yet refuse to perish.

Gaskell has been criticized for returning her heroine to the enclosure of marriage and domesticity at the end of the story.[18] Yet, as Gallagher and Bodenheimer suggest, nothing in the final interchange between Margaret Hale and Thornton suggests that their antagonistic friendship is to be dissolved into deference to male authority. Gaskell met Florence Nightingale in 1854 while she was writing *North and South*, and her correspondence indicates her mixed feelings toward this charismatic figure. On the one hand, she was full of genuine admiration for Nightingale's abilities and ambitions. "I have not half told you about Miss Florence Nightingale . . . she is thinking of becoming the Matron of one of the great London Hospitals," she wrote to Catherine Winkworth (Chapple, 309).[19] On the other hand, she was rather repelled by Nightingale's lack of personal warmth: "That exactly tells of what seems to me *the* want — but then this want of love for individuals becomes a gift and a rare one, if one takes it in conjunction with her intense love for the *race*" (320). Gaskell recognized that Nightingale's combination of physical beauty, powerful intellect, and "unbendableness" allowed her to overcome resistance to her entry into an active public life. Josephine Butler was a similarly charismatic figure — beautiful, flamboyant, and passionately determined: her husband, royal commissions, and MPs all willingly succumbed to her power. In Gaskell's letters, comments on her fictional heroine Margaret Hale are immediately followed by remarks on Nightingale. Clearly, the two heroines are connected in her imagination. While Gaskell is careful to reverse love of race into a love for individuals in her heroine, she endows Margaret Hale to the full with a force of charismatic presence that sweeps away resistance. The representation of Margaret in *North and South* foregrounds her qualities of forceful leadership — her aura of authority. Mrs. Thornton recognizes what she thinks of as Margaret's "glamour," which imposes itself as a power "over many people" (391).

This force of personality and the capacity for leadership are emphasized throughout the story at every moment of crisis and call for action. Margaret plans and executes the move from Helstone standing "calm and collected, ready to counsel and advise," during the trying process of removal (89). She subdues unruly family servants, commands the doctor to inform her fully of the nature of her mother's illness, takes charge of the sickroom, defies a police constable, and, of course, challenges a mob of rioting men. No other nineteenth-century heroine is so deliberately represented as eminently capable of sustaining a leading role in public life. After the riot, Margaret is represented as experiencing a "deep sense of shame that she should thus be the object of universal regard" (249). Such a shrinking from publicity was a common fear expressed by nineteenth-century women when they first became involved in public activities and campaigns. Although Margaret suffers from this sense of exposure, she resolves that should justice demand it, she "would do it again": "I did a woman's work" (247). This resolve undoubtedly suggests the moral force that women bring to the public sphere, but the linking of the words *woman* and *work* is significant more specifically in relation to women's position in the public sphere in their own right.

The 1851 census had caused alarm by revealing a "surplus" of women over men in the population. This statistic and the public awareness it prompted of "the woman question" were largely welcomed as useful publicity by the determined body of women campaigning during the 1850s for greater opportunities in women's lives.[20] Many of these women were Unitarians or came from Unitarian backgrounds, and as such were known to Gaskell.[21] They quickly recognized that the expanding public domain of the state offered a space in which women could find fulfilling employment and look to gain professional training and status. By 1851, Mary Carpenter, for example, was organizing a conference of professionals and specialists, men and women, working within the field of criminal delinquency. A great many of the women reformers in the 1850s belonged to the Social Science Association (SSA), which offered them opportunities to speak and read papers at its conferences, to network, and to organize campaigns for sanitation, ragged schools, and other causes. The SSA was at the forefront of the midcentury movement for professionalization, and its officials typified this rising social group: the general secretary was G. W. Hastings, the barrister, son of Dr. Sir Charles Hastings, founder of the British Medical Association, and the assistant secretary was Isa Craig, an independent, single woman (see Yeo, 128). During this period, women began to use the term *social workers* to describe themselves, and Emily Davis argued that even married women might legitimately spend part of their time "in definite professional work . . . or in unpaid public services, which, when seriously undertaken, constitute something of a profession" (quoted in Yeo, 126).

The characterization of Margaret Hale in *North and South* looks immediately forward to the significant entry of women into the public sphere of professional and social activity by the end of the 1850s. Of course, this expansion of women's aspirations did not occur without vocal criticism. In *North and South*, Edith begs Margaret above all else not to be "strong-minded" (509); *strong-minded* was a favored term of abuse directed at "emancipated" women (see Yeo, 129, 138). Campaigners for women sought to mitigate prejudice by arguing that, while motherhood remained women's most natural and elevated role, those women who were unmarried could properly become "social mothers."[22] Their "maternal" qualities of nurture, foresight, and moral influence could be offered to the "perishing classes," where lack of a decently managed home was perceived as a primary cause of delinquency, disease, and destitution. Gaskell seems to be suggesting a similar role of social motherhood for her heroine. Margaret is represented as most enjoying those moments with her little nephew when they "battle" over his "stormy passions"; she has "a firm power which subdued him into peace, while every sudden charm and wile she possessed was exerted on the side of right" (495).

At the end of the novel, when Margaret "[takes] her life into her own hands," she is able to do so, the narrator says, because she has thought through "that most difficult problem for women" of how much of their time may be "set apart for freedom in working" (508). Again the concept of work is introduced, but the shift in language from *a woman* to *women* suggests a widening of the context to encompass the need of purposeful and fulfilling public responsibilities for all women. Furthermore, in this passage *work* is aligned to *freedom* and placed in opposition to *obedience to authority*. In this revisioned binary, women's work and agency in the public sphere take the traditional place of cultivated opinion in opposing tyranny. In this sense, the character of Margaret is representative, not of women in the aggregate but as a charismatic embodiment of the ideal values and qualities that women will bring to the public sphere and the state domain.

The novel represents workers and manufacturers using persuasive, even perhaps manipulative, publicity to gain acceptance for their competing claims. The novel itself can be understood as part of the publicity aimed at gaining consent for women's greater involvement in the public sphere and state domain. The tall, finely made figure of Margaret Hale is described, in the opening chapter, as offering the perfect means of displaying Edith's rich Indian shawls to best advantage (39). So, too, the charismatic figure of the heroine is the means by which Gaskell publicizes, in most persuasive form, the claims of women for active citizenship.

The representation of Margaret Hale has been criticized by P. N. Furbank as overidealized. However, the "curious and special 'heroine' style" that Gaskell uses should be understood as part of a pervasive formal and thematic concern with representation as the staging or performance of identity to win consent in the enlarged public sphere.[23] Higgins's desire to project the union and the strike in the most favorable light to the public can be seen as a *mise en abyme* for the general recognition, throughout the novel, that identities and values are produced within the transformed public sphere for public consumption. Throughout the novel, Gaskell figures taste in terms of food and meals as a trope indicating the constitution of identity as a form of visual consumption. By so doing, she recognizes the initiating moment of a shift within the public sphere from the dominance of the cultured world of letters to the visual world of commodity consumption. The most obvious example of this is Mrs. Thornton's dinner party, at which the abundance of expensive delicacies functions visually to publicize her son's wealth and material success, although to Margaret's London cultivation, the excess announces vulgarity of taste (213). Nevertheless, Mrs. Hale also takes pains to impress the London lawyer, Lennox, with the civility of domestic management at the country parsonage by arranging dessert on the sideboard in formal order (59). When this is declined in favor of pears from the garden, Margaret presents the fruit to best advantage by displaying the pears on a beet leaf, "which threw up their brown colour admirably" (59). The informal spontaneity of the conclusion of the meal in the garden provides a narrative opportunity for Gaskell to "publicise" the tasteful sensibility of her heroine. Likewise, within the story characters are concerned to find opportunities for tasteful displays of self for the benefit of others. When Edith wants to represent herself as an ideal soldier's wife, she acts out a little performance of making tea, scalding herself heroically on the great kitchen kettle (45). Later, her husband expects her to enhance their visible public identity as a fashionable young couple: "He was anxiously attentive to Edith's dress and appearance with a view to her beauty making a sufficient impression on the world" (459). Social identity and social acceptability are largely constituted visually in the public sphere by means of self performances and displays of consumer taste.

Margaret is represented as coming to recognize that taste is not an inherent attribute of a cultivated sensibility but an acquired inclination that may therefore be made more comprehensive by new experiences and perceptions. When her father accuses her of being prejudiced against Thornton, she says, "He is my first olive: let me make a face while I swallow it" (221). She goes on to admit that with study she will come to appreciate the type. By the end of the narrative, the public sphere of London dinner parties has also acquired a taste for olives in the form of industrialists. The changed perception of manufacturers as a socially acceptable type is shown as largely produced by personal familiarity with their individual representative man, John Thornton. As is made clear in the earlier conversation between Margaret's father and Bell, Thornton is the personable exemplar of the best values of industrialists, not a representative of the type as aggregate.

The way in which identity is produced as visualized public representation is most clearly illustrated by the general misreading of Margaret's intervention in the riot. Even Thornton interprets her actions as indicative of regard for him: that was the socially agreed meaning attached to such a performance by a woman. Margaret's sense of her own identity is damaged and shamed when she perceives herself as others, especially Thornton, are perceiving her. Her own assured sense of self, based upon a cultured position, is threatened by the image of herself held up before her imagination by a different public opinion. Her response is an "impetuous wish to shake off the recollection . . . in the company of others" (257). To erase a projection of her identity that she finds degrading, she needs to represent her self publicly and visually in a role she finds more acceptable. She cannot wholly reinstate her self-image privately; identity has to be constituted in the regard of others. The company Margaret seeks out is the Higgins family, but there she discovers that Nicholas's hopes of representing the striking workers to the public sphere as "good citizens" have been ruined by the riot (259). Both women and workers have to combat stereotyped identities that exclude them from legitimate presence and activity as citizens and project into the public sphere a performance of identity that begins to reeducate social taste toward a more comprehensive range of acceptability. Publicity in this sense is aimed less at provoking rational debate than at producing and even manipulating acquiescence.

Thornton's own self-perception is also represented as severely damaged, not so much because Margaret does not return his love, but by the image of him she conveys through her response to his declaration. The "icy tone" of affronted civility in which she tells him that his "whole manner offends" her suggests to him that she feels "tainted" in being loved by one of his uncultured insensibility (253–54). His response is a defiant rejection of gentlemanly civility and an assertion of the larger claims invoked by the code of sincerity: "And the gentleman thus rescued is forbidden the relief of thanks!" he broke in contemptuously. "I am a man. I claim the right of expressing my feelings" (253). Thornton is represented as visually staging this reassertion of his identity in terms of an ethics of sincerity over those of civility. He buys a rich selection of choice fruit and carries it publicly through the streets to Mrs. Hale in person, offering it to her before the assembled family.

The fruit, selected to prove irresistible to the most delicate of appetites, is presented for consumption, but what is proffered with it is the idealized self-image of the giver reconstituted in the regard of others. Thornton represents this action to himself in terms of sincerity in opposition to Margaret Hale's disdainful civility: "I will not be daunted from doing as I choose by the thought of her. . . . A pretty joke, indeed, if, for fear of a haughty girl, I failed in doing a kindness to a man I liked!" (275). Taking the fruit personally rather than having it sent constitutes a publicly recognizable gesture of sincerity. And this is how Thornton stages it before the family: as a personal impulse overriding the code of civility: "If you will forgive this liberty, — my rough ways, — too abrupt I fear" (276). As an exercise in public relations, Thornton's fruit-giving is highly successful; even Mrs. Hale accuses Margaret of stubborn prejudice for her lukewarm acknowledgment of Thornton's goodness. The sincerity of Thornton's sympathy for

Mrs. Hale is not put in doubt by this publicizing episode, but its narrative force serves to demonstrate how persuasive the performative staging of sincerity can be.

Higgins is represented as a character who also values sincerity above civility, priding himself on his refusal to evade uncomfortable truths. Yet the identity of the laboring people that he seeks to project upon the public sphere is carefully manipulated to display their best qualities, rather than to represent the aggregate of the class that would then have to include those like Boucher who would mar the carefully fashioned image of respectable citizenship. The novel, in this sense, makes public the tension between a new code of sincerity in public discourse and the need to produce social identities acceptable and persuasive within the public sphere. This tension arises from the structural transformation of the public sphere at the midcentury. The expansion of "the public" from cultivated men of independent means to include manufacturers, gentlewomen, and the organized working class fractured the consensual court of public opinion. Under pressure, rational-critical debate began to give way to staged publicity in which sectional interests aimed to win general consent for their perspective or claims. While, on the one hand, within the public sphere there was a movement toward the massification of the public through aggregated statistical forms of knowledge and ideology, by contrast, on the other hand, conflicting values and interests were increasingly personalized in charismatic figures able to represent causes in the most glamourous way. What this entails is a shift from the authority of the traditional cultural capital of letters to a mass culture of evaluating visuality. As part of the new personalized appeal of publicness, a performed code of sincerity has dual utility: it insinuatingly addresses each person within the targeted audience as a unique interiority, but by that same token interpellates them into the proffered viewpoint as like-feeling fellow beings.

From the eighteenth century onward, novels played a key role in originating and sustaining the critical discourse of the public sphere. *North and South* offers itself formally in this mode: the text provides a court in which conflicting opinions are publicized and subjected to rational challenge. Yet in its use of highly personable, individualized representative men to exemplify the manufacturers and the working class, and most especially in its charismatic representation of the heroine, the novel reveals that its real aim is persuasion. The agenda of *North and South* is the transformation of the public sphere through the inclusion of those groups offering new forms of knowledge to those of traditional cultivation and a new code of social intercourse to that of civility. However, Gaskell's linkage of

Margaret's charismatic presence to the aura of class authority that she inherited as cultivated gentlewoman is intriguingly suggestive. The independent means of the gentry diminished throughout the century. The public sphere of the state offered a space for reinvention as a professional class. It may be that the gentry were also particularly suited to the new ethos of publicness dependent upon visualized charismatic presence that came into being along with mass forms of the media and culture industry in the second half of the nineteenth century.

Part IV / Embodying Mass Culture

CHAPTER SEVEN

Romola

The Politics of Disinterestedness

The problem that engaged the collective imagination, especially that of the "cultivated" classes, from late in the 1850s into the mid-1860s was how to maintain social distinctions within a mass society and how to reconcile the individual duties and responsibilities, required for civic order, with amorphous massification and aggregation. For most of the nineteenth century, as Gillian Beer has shown, writing on scientific subjects was still fully interactive within the general discourse of the public sphere (*Darwin's Plots*, 6–7). The works of Chambers, Lyell, Spencer, and Darwin were read at least as widely as literary writing, and the language of their texts drew upon novelistic metaphor and imagery and narrative plotting.[1] The first edition of *The Origin of the Species* (1859) sold out immediately, and a second edition had to be rushed out by January 1860.

In this way, widespread dissemination and acceptance of generalized evolutionary ideas, from the middle decades of the century, had convinced a majority of informed opinion in Britain that society itself was an evolving form and that the movement was irresistibly toward ever greater aggregation and complexity. Herbert Spencer, in particular, had propounded this idea tirelessly throughout the 1850s, a social-Darwinian before Darwin. His fullest statement is contained in the essay "Progress: Its Law and Cause," published in the *Westminster Review* in 1857, in which he claims: "This law of organic progress is the law of all progress. Whether it be in the development of the Earth, in the development of Life upon its surface, in the development of Society, of Government, of Manufacturers, of Commerce, of Language, Literature, Science, Art, this same evolution of the simple into the complex, through successive differentiations holds throughout" (2:10). In 1860, in another essay in the *Westminster Review*, he again outlined his views on "The Social Organism," emphasizing that intrinsic to the evolution of societies into ever more differentiated and complex wholes was the increasing mutual interdependence of each part of the whole upon all the others (1:272). In an earlier essay, "The Genesis of Science," he uses the term *consensus* to designate this process of active intercommunication and interdependence of the complex parts of the yet more complex wholes (2:40–41).

Blackwood's Magazine took a less sanguine view of the movement toward a more heterogeneous society, but the periodical nevertheless conceded, in 1860, that "a great many people in the country are fatalists on the subject of democracy, and imagine that it is as impossible to resist its encroachment as to stop the waves on the shore. . . . Mob-rule is coming certain as the grave."[2] Less apocalyptically, Matthew Arnold, in "Democracy," written as the introduction to *The Popular Education of France* (1861), accepted that the general process toward democracy "has been brought about by natural and inevitable causes" and that the evolution of society toward popular government was "identical with the ceaseless vital effort of human nature itself" (*Complete Prose Works*, 2:7–8). For John Stuart Mill, the age was characterized by a process of assimilation in which "formerly, different ranks, different neighbourhoods, different trades and professions, lived in what might be called different worlds; at present to a great degree in the same. . . . And the assimilation is still proceeding" (*On Liberty*, 274).

As early as 1851, in an article on the census of that year, a writer in *Blackwood's Magazine* had warned, somewhat ironically, "Perhaps . . . you never considered that you have only right and title to a certain limited area to live and breathe in, . . . People are approximating fearfully. You may come to touch very disagreeable people; at present you are only a few yards apart. There are two things according to this Census, threatening you — 'density' and 'proximity.'"[3] Certainly, ten years later, fears of being engulfed in the anonymous density of numbers and a visceral repugnance at the proximity of what seemed brutish forms of life were exerting powerful pressures upon the ways in which an evolving inclusive society was imagined. As Beer notes, many Victorians registered evolutionary ideas with "a physical shudder" (*Darwin's Plots*, 9). In *Romola* (1863), this dread of the tactile proximity of fleshliness turns George Eliot away from a radical perception of community based upon a quality of sympathetic tenderness. Ultimately, her evolutionary understanding of human nature as a slow, organic progression from animality to sensibility denies the possibility that the mass of the public can attain to the ideal of the common good upon which genuine community depends.

It was not surprising that most people by the 1860s accepted the view that society was fast evolving toward an aggregated mass culture. The public sphere had been transformed into a multivoiced forum, in which public opinion was a new and as yet unpredictable force. The cultural authority of letters and literature that had traditionally sustained the polite public sphere was increasingly usurped by mass forms of publication and, more particularly, by pictorial media and spectacle. The Great Exhibition of 1851 marked a reorientation of popular sources of knowledge from the written to the visual. Whereas previously information about distant lands came entirely from written accounts, visitors to the exhibition gained knowledge, so it seemed, at firsthand from the spectacles on show. The Great Exhibition set the trend for similar events in the provincial cities and was repeated ten years later in London in the vast International Exhibition, staged in 1861. The similarity between the visual displays of artefacts in the galleries of the exhibition and the commodities on display in the new department stores was underlined when, after its closing day, the International Exhibition reopened as a bazaar so that the "bargain-loving public" could compete to buy goods from around the world.[4]

Traditional forms of cultural capital that had given authority to the "cultivated" classes as arbiters of taste and distinction seemed threatened by the mass production of imitation fashions in clothing, jewelry, furniture, and architecture. Mill wrote that increasingly all people "now read the same things, listen to the same things, see the same things . . . have their hopes and fears directed to the same objects" (*On Liberty*, 274) Articles on "taste" abound in the journalism of the time. Taste even formed the subject of a leading article in the *Times* (1863) — a piece that began, "There is probably no subject upon which party spirit runs so high in the present day as on that of Art."[5] The *Quarterly Review* voiced typical concerns when it pointed to the prevalence, among the British articles on display in the International Exhibition, of mass-produced veneered furniture. It blamed the "semi-detached" stratum of society, that "last strong-hold of bad taste," for wanting to "combine the maximum of show with the minimum of cost."[6] Habermas argues that when heterogeneous public opinion and commodified culture become the most dominant forces of the transformed public sphere, rational critique is degraded into manipulative publicity. In *North and South*, Gaskell's manner of depicting her three leading characters as exemplary representatives looks forward to this form of persuasive publicness. In *Romola*, the representation of Tito suggests that the character shapes himself and stages his political identity in terms of manipulative publicity.

Gaskell, in *North and South*, is concerned with what kinds of men and women and what kinds of influence come to the fore in an inclusive society. As in *Shirley* and *Henry Esmond*, so, too, in *North and South* a performative code of sincerity is advocated as a medium of community that can interpellate a heterogeneous public sphere as both one and many. By the 1860s, sincerity as a public discursive mode, seemingly proffering mutual regard and confidential trust, had become preeminent political capital. Once political leaders had to operate in the public sphere almost as much as in the closed world of Westminster, *insincerity* became a favored term of political abuse to denote a betrayal of the public's confidence. *Blackwood's Magazine*, for example, wrote of a "revulsion in public feeling" at the "duplicity and insincerity" of the Whig Ministry.[7] In April 1863, the *Times* praised Lord Palmerston in terms that indicate the efficacy of sincerity as a performative code. He talks to the operatives and workers "as confidentially and unreservedly as to the House of Commons, and, taking them into his councils as colleagues in the internal government and foreign policy of this empire, he recounts the various successes . . . which we have all achieved together and which have made England on the whole so prosperous, so happy, and so respected."[8] Invited into this manipulative fiction of partnership in world government, the operative class might be excused for forgetting they did not even have a vote. For the *Westminster Review*, though, Palmerston was a representative man in the derogatory sense, deriving his political power by appealing to the most illiberal aspects of public opinion.

> Lord Palmerston represents, under all circumstances, the feelings, the judgements, the prejudices and the passions of the average British character. He represents the average head and heart of an age singularly devoid of high aspirations . . . an age peculiarly intolerant of eccentricity, . . . delighting only in easy and ephemeral pleasures, . . . hostile to anything which draws heavily on the intellect, whether in art, in literature, or in statesmanship. That is the England which Lord Palmerston admirably represents.[9]

Dickens's views are frequently closely aligned to those of the *Westminster*, and Palmerston is a far more convincing and telling model for Podsnap than John Forster. Certainly the national culture that the journal associates with Palmerston is almost identical to that which Dickens calls by the name of Podsnappery.

One response of the "cultivated" classes to the anxiety aroused by what seemed an encroaching aggregation of sameness, vulgarity, and mediocrity was to reconstitute cultural distinction as the inherent attribute of an evolved sensibility. A tradition of thinking that identifies moral discrimination with a cultured sensibility can be traced back to Shaftesbury in the eighteenth century. In the middle of the nineteenth century, it was Herbert Spencer who was particularly influential in propagating this perception of human nature in the guise of evolutionary scientific knowledge. In his essay "The Social Organism," he had declared: "The classes engaged in agriculture and laborious occupations in general are far less susceptible intellectually and emotionally than the rest, and especially less so than the classes of highest mental culture" (1:276).

Paradoxically, while seeking to identify the fullest development of humanness with distance from physical animality, this ideology continually located classification in the visual appearance of bodies. Spencer argued that beauty of appearance was an index of superior mental and moral evolution (2:387–99). Matthew Arnold described the "raw" urban working class of British cities as "the least enviable-looking" in Europe (*Complete Prose Works*, 5:18). Eliot expresses the same idea of differentially evolved sensibility, indicated by physical appearance, in her essay "The Natural History of German Life." She says, "This explains why the old German painters gave the heads of their subjects a greater uniformity of type than the painters of our day: the race had not attained to a high degree of individualization in features and expression. It indicates too that the cultured man acts more as an individual; the peasant, more as one of a group. . . . Many thousands of men are as like each other in thoughts and habits as so many sheep or oysters" (*Essays*, 274). This perception of human nature, in which interiority was no longer a shared attribute of human kind that could serve as a basis of mutual confidence but rather the location of an evolved distinction from the mass, was the ideology underlying the further transformation of the public sphere in the later decades of the nineteenth century, dividing it into the realm of elite culture and the popular realm. The narrative structures of both *Romola* and *Our Mutual Friend* are deeply implicated in the physical shudder that impelled the cultural division of the public sphere and the shift to social categorization based upon bodies.

John Plotz has argued that in response to fears of the unwashed masses, literary writing functions to reconstitute a spacious inwardness to which the jostling, restless, animal energy of the multitude has no entry (190). The development of Eliot's psychological realism can be seen to follow this trajectory toward a sanctioned inner space. The critical elevation of George Eliot, during the 1950s and 1960s, into first place among nineteenth-century novelists was based largely upon claims for the moral seriousness of her representation of a character's evolving interiority, as a medium of truth leading to a widening of human sympathies.[10] What has been less noticed is the way this psychological realism functions ideologically to reposition sincerity from being primarily an aspect of interpersonal, often public, communication to a value inhering only in the inner sensibility of special individuals. For Carlyle, the hero is preeminently the sincere man who speaks out an unwelcome truth to combat cant and falsity. In Eliot's fiction, heroism is identified with an active struggle for truth to self, against the prejudices and stupidities of common opinion, certainly, but even more by transcending the clinging webs of self-deception. In her novels, very few characters indeed attain the self-sincerity of unclouded inner truth and wisdom that can alone constitute moral sympathy or more frequently moral sacrifice of self for the good of others. In her essay "The Natural History of German Life," she castigates Dickens for his false sentimentality "in encouraging the miserable fallacy that high morality and refined sentiment can grow out of harsh social relations, ignorance and want" (*Essays*, 272). The bracketing together here of morality with refinement indicates Eliot's indebtedness to the Shaftesbury tradition.

Evolutionary theories helped to redefine and naturalize social distinction as the highest form of evolved human nature: it was sensibility as refined mental and moral interiority far removed from animality, although signified by bodily grace. The corollary of this was that the mass of humankind had to be perceived as largely driven by dull stupidity and physical appetites. As a *Westminster* reviewer had earlier explained, human nature in its present evolutionary state ranged from "loathsome animality to high and divine morality."[11] The problem such a view posed for inclusive forms of democracy was how the unleavened mass, lacking moral and intellectual interiority, could yet be imbued with sufficient idealism and disinterestedness to feel a concern for the common good. How were they to be dissuaded from pursuing a redistributive notion of class justice of the kind that *Blackwell's Magazine* had termed "mob plunder."[12] As a character in *Romola* puts it, how can the "vulgar . . . conscious of nothing beyond their own petty wants of back and stomach" be expected to "rise to the sense of community" (91). When the mass of the people, lacking moral refinement, gained the power of the vote, how were they to be instilled with the corresponding duties and obligations of citizenship?

Matthew Arnold's response to this question was to turn to classical culture as a way of "fostering in the mass of the peoples . . . a greatness of spirit" (*Complete Prose Works*, 2:6). His essay "Democracy" (1861) provides the most generous expression of this goal. Following the Hyde Park riots, the conclusion of *Culture and Anarchy* (1869) makes clear that if the laboring people refuse this offer to remake themselves in concordance with these patrician values, their anarchic animal impulses for retaliatory justice are to be crushed by heavy authority. Two other solutions to the problem of imparting the ideals of community to the masses were expressed in the early 1860s: one was rationally argued in Mill's writings, and the other was seen as much more dramatically expressed in the heroic struggle of Garibaldi to unite the divided and disparate parties of Italy into one nation. Catherine Gallagher (*Reformation of English Fiction*, 219–67) has pointed to the intertextual influences existing between *Felix Holt*, Mill's *Considerations on Representative Government*, and Arnold's *Culture and Anarchy*. In *Romola*, Eliot challenges the ideal of popular leadership symbolized by Garibaldi, and she rigorously interrogates the main body of Mill's political writing and the cultural "solution" that Arnold first set out in "Democracy."

The national movement to unite Italy riveted the attention of all Europe during the late 1850s and early 1860s. It was widely reported in the British daily and periodical press, and when Garibaldi visited England in April 1864 he was given a spontaneous and rapturous reception in London. A writer in the *Westminster Review* saw Italian unification as one of the most important struggles ever for the civilization and progress of the world; it was "the war of the future against the past."[13] The skillful political leadership of the Italian patrician Count Cavour ensured that unification posed no threat to the interests of property or traditional elites, but, admitted the *Westminster*'s reviewer, it was the popular leadership and inspiration of Garibaldi, son of a fisherman and ardent republican, that lent the movement its "life, poetry and moral grandeur." Garibaldi, with his disinterested passion for freedom, provided democratic ideals with a hero that even Hazlitt could have admired.

The qualities attributed to him in the *Westminster* — his love of truth, his "soul" that burns with the fire that "makes martyrs and heroes," his passion for the regeneration of Italy, his political unworldliness — evoke many aspects of Eliot's representation of Savonarola.[14] The parallel between the two heroes is further strengthened by the thunderous excommunications with which the pope attempted to outlaw the unification struggle. Also like Savonarola, Garibaldi aspired beyond narrowly particular national interest, envisioning Italy as part of an evolving universal order of freedom and peace. The *Westminster* reviewer wrote that "he instinctively feels the brotherhood of people with people, and the bonds that unite their future destinies in one . . . he belongs . . . to a new and possible order of things" (194). Perhaps what impressed opinion in Britain most favorably was what was seen as Garibaldi's ennobling influence on the common people: his inspiration had regenerated the formerly "untutored masses and a lifeless, passionless multitude" endowing them with disinterested patriotism and principled beliefs in universal ideals (192). In *Romola*, Eliot represents two popular leaders sprung from the people: Savonarola, modeled, at least in part, on Garibaldi, and Tito, a cynical self-publicizer. The narrative structure traces the downfall of a traditional charismatic visionary leader of the people and the rise to popular power of Tito through adept manipulation of public opinion.

The fullest response to the issue of democratic inclusiveness in the early 1860s was articulated in Mill's three great essays *On Liberty* (1859), *Utilitarianism* (1861), and *Considerations on Representative Government* (1861), in which he sought to provide an ethical, civic, and political framework for inclusive society. In *Romola*, Eliot challenges Mill's thinking almost point by point. In that sense, the questioning dialogue that the novel constructs with the three essays can be seen as exemplary of rational critique in the public sphere of letters. The double irony is that the public sphere was already losing even the potential for rational critique, at just that moment when Eliot was intent on showing that the ideal of disinterested debate was always unrealizable. By the 1860s, Mill's early radicalism was somewhat tempered by his fear of "collective mediocrity." He saw that in many ways the threat of coercive authority had passed from the state to the force of moral conformity as expressed in the most vocal public opinion. Conventionality and aggregation of taste and opinion were coming to dominate national culture, he believed. When people live in crowds, he argued, "peculiarity of taste, eccentricity of conduct, are equally shunned with crimes: until by dint of not following their own nature they have no nature to follow: their human capacities are withered and starved" (*On Liberty*, 265). As the references here to human nature and capacities suggest, Mill does not take a pessimistic evolutionary view of the predominance of animality in the mass of people; instead of physical stupidity and inertia, Mill blames the Christian tradition, with its overemphasis on obedience and sacrifice for the collective servility that constitutes public opinion (*On Liberty*, 255). Christian renunciation and fleshly repression, Mill argues, need to be balanced by the Greek ideal of self-perfection that encompasses bodily energies as well as the spiritual, and it needs also to be supplemented with the classical civic tradition as a counterweight to narrow concern with purely individual salvation (*On Liberty*, 266, 255–56).

Mill is often seen as the champion of individual liberty. He is so only insofar as he opposed what was the new conservative force of public conformity. In every other respect, his ideals and politics are essentially collective. His advocacy of the public sphere is as passionate as that of Habermas, but, unlike Habermas and his eighteenth-century ideal, Mill believed in a fully heterogeneous public forum where every divergent interest could speak out freely. This democratic public sphere is the single force that Mill pits against intolerant religious authority, public conformity, state tyranny, and commodified mass culture. Free debate is the essence of a healthy democracy for Mill. He rejects any idealized individualist notions of truth as strengthened and purified by oppression and sacrifice, citing the example of the silencing of Savonarola (*On Liberty*, 238). He also rejects notions of revealed truth as contemplative private interiority.

Enlightenment for Mill is by definition collective: the result of a democratic, dialogic contest of living voices. Without the struggle of dialogue, the vigorous debate of opposing principles, truth degenerates into commonplace and dogma: "The human faculties of perception, judgement, discriminative feeling, mental activity, and even moral preference, are exercised only in making a choice," he insists (*On Liberty*, 262). As his words suggest, the faculties he lists here as constituting humanness are not restricted to the evolved sensibilities of the few; on the contrary, it is by entering into the national dialogues and debates that "even" the manual laborer "becomes consciously a member of a community" (*Representative Government*, 469). The Italian people were prepared for civic responsibilities, he claims, by the Italian patriots encouraging them to demand it (*Representative Government*, 379–80). The British working class should not be enjoined to dumb obedience and duty to religious and state authority. Only participation in democratic dialogue and processes will ensure that they acquire the disinterested concern with the common good of the nation as a whole and rise above the narrow interests of class and belly (*Representative Government*, 410). In flat contradiction to pessimistic evolutionists, Mill insists that there is no reason why the necessary "amount of mental culture sufficient to give an intelligent interest" in the general well-being of humanity "should not be the inheritance of everyone born in a civilised country" (*Utilitarianism*, 261).

Belief in the collective capacity for benevolent intelligence grounds Mill's thinking on civic justice and order. He rejects notions of any religious or transcendental authority as the foundation of justice and notions of punishment and duty. These abstract ideals, he says, are the spontaneous outgrowths of two inherent impulses that are "in the highest degree natural" to all human beings: the instinct for self-defense common to all animal life and the impulse for sympathy, the wish to be in unity with our fellow beings (*Utilitarianism*, 248). It is this second impulse that transforms the narrowly personal concern to retaliate a hurt or to secure the self from harm into the disinterested generalized obligations that constitute justice. Civic duty and disinterest are the rational, consensual extensions of particular individual requirements for security and well-being. The sense of justice operates so powerfully upon the generality of people precisely because of its foundations in the instinctual imperatives of all physical existence. Hence, the most commonly shared sense of justice is that a person should obtain what he or she deserves. For this reason, Mill argues, breaches of promise and friendship, betrayal of trust in the hour of need, and accepting a benefit and then denying a return rank as the highest social wrongs, exciting intense resentment in the person suffering and in sympathizing spectators (*Utilitarianism*, 256). This is exactly the situation from which the plot of *Romola* springs and the means by which Mill's optimistic and secular view of justice is tested.

Before turning wholly to *Romola*, it will be helpful to further clarify Eliot's thinking generally upon human sympathies, an important concern in all of her fiction and represented as the only means by which a perception of community can be achieved as the active principle impelling a character's actions. The ideal of human sympathy is closely related to her understanding of sincerity as the means to true knowledge. In contrast to Mill's collective notion of truth, Eliot's is essentially individualistic, although very far from any version of materialist, self-interested individualism. Eliot's individualism consists, paradoxically, of heroic self-transcendence. She was pervasively influenced in her thinking by the philosophy of Shaftesbury as mediated by Kant and his followers and, more specifically, by her association with Carlyle, Spencer, and Lewes, as well as by Comte and Feuerbach.[15] Most of these latter contemporary thinkers shared a view of history and of human nature and ethics as propelled by an integral organic progress that evolved from primitive simplicity to multiply complex structures of interdependent parts. Given this view of reality in all its forms, they also shared a belief that scientific knowledge and truths were not to be obtained merely by statistical accounts or by observation of empirical particularity.

Gallagher recognizes that, by the 1860s, Eliot's novels "manifest a deep skepticism about the principle of mere aggregation in literature as well as politics" (*Reformation of English Fiction*, 224). Carlyle's practice of history writing provided an important model for Eliot in transforming empiricism into idealism. Carlyle began with painstaking research into all the particularities of French life and politics at the time of the French Revolution, but it was an act of imaginative energy, he claimed, that brought all these complex parts together in their related-ness and allowed him to conceive the whole. Comte, in similar fashion, argued that "art rises above science, as better adapted to promote the development of true unity" (*Appeal to Conservatives*, quoted in Myers, 94). As George Levine has shown, Lewes made a similar argument for scientific truth properly understood. Reality in its fullness can only be grasped by a dual approach: there must be meticulous study of empirical particulars but this has to be accompanied by an intense inward contemplation that comprehends the separate physical units as part of a larger, systematic wholeness. Lewes writes, "But opposed to this discontinuous Cosmos perceived there is the continuous cosmos, which is conceived" (*Problems of Life and Mind*, quoted in Levine, "Eliot's Hypothesis," 10). Thus comprehended by means of both sensory observation and intellectual intensity, knowledge of reality becomes "an intuition embracing the Universe" (quoted in Levine, 9). This is an intuition, however, "given only to the highest minds" (quoted in Levine, 24). As did Shaftesbury, Lewes links this refined capacity for comprehensive understanding with moral sensibility; hence, he says, "so much immorality is sheer stupidity" (quoted in Levine, 16).

Eliot's thinking interacted closely with that of Lewes, and in an unpublished essay on "Form in Art" she set out the role of the artist in very similar terms to Spencer's and Lewes's ideal of scientific knowledge. The earliest sense of form that human beings acquire, Eliot says, derives from proximity; from our sense of touch as the first most tactile relationship the child has with its physical world (*Essays*, 432). Later, as knowledge grows beyond immediate sensory experience, "it arrives at the conception of wholes composed of parts more and more multiplied and highly differed, and yet more and more absolutely bound together by various conditions of common likeness or mutual dependence" (433). The word Eliot uses to convey this active interdependence of parts is *consensus*, the term Herbert Spencer uses with exactly that meaning in his essay "The Genesis of Science." The highest example of artistic form, Eliot concludes in her essay, is that of "multiplex interdependent parts to a whole which is itself in the most varied and therefore fullest relation to other wholes" (433). Such art, in its transcendence of empirical particularities through an act of intense contemplative energy, facilitates a widening of human sympathy by comprehending the smallest human life or incident in a life within the "ideally illumined space" of human history as a whole.[16] Mill believed, certainly rather optimistically, that active engagement in national debates could instil in all classes a sense of community and concern for the general good. Eliot's fiction suggests that very few, even of the most idealistic, can so overcome those "spots of commonness," shared with the generality of humankind, as to achieve the capacity for "sympathy" as she understands it. "Community," therefore, and benevolent compassion for the general good are concepts not easily available to the average person.

Eliot's construction in her fiction of an expansive narrative perspective has been seen by Elizabeth Ermarth as conforming to the humanist grammar of realism that asserts "this world is one" (98). Within the all-encompassing consciousness shared by narrator and reader in Eliot's novels, Ermarth claims, a unified community of awareness is constituted in which all differences of understanding are ultimately resolvable within the all-seeing comprehensiveness of narrative temporality. The narrative perspective in *Romola* certainly moves persistently from detailed empirical knowledge of the particulars of daily life in late-fifteenth-century Florence to the universal grammar of overarching laws of human nature: "under *every* guilty secret"; "circumstances *never* fail"; "*all* who remember"; "marriage *must* be" (emphases added). While the inclusive narrative *we* appears to construct a community of awareness with readers, this altruistic consciousness, able to comprehend the smallest particularity within the vast complexity of a universal order, is unavailable to a single character within the story.[17] Indeed, as we shall see, the novel denies the possibility of any communal pursuit of truth as enlightened public opinion. The rarefied transcendental wisdom of Eliot's narrative consciousness does not produce an inclusive social world founded upon mutual sympathies; rather, it constitutes a panopticonism of pity in which the stupid and insensible are distanced as objects of a "disinterested," but always inherently evaluating compassion and assimilated into a cosmic order so vast and abstract that they are virtually dematerialized.

Yet, paradoxically, Eliot continues to insist that the imaginative drive toward idealizing contemplation must begin from and retain contact with the most primary tactile responsiveness to physical bodily existence. In *Romola*, the motif of trial by fire serves to focus attention upon fleshly testimony. Without that exigent proximity, human sympathies are narrowed into abstraction, false idealism, and even fanaticism. It was the belief—held by Mill, Comte, and Lewes—that literature is especially able to fuse particularity with generality that persuaded Eliot to turn to novel writing. In *On Liberty*, Mill urged those who would teach political principles to find discursive forms that would convey the conflict of living ideas enunciated from the partisan positions of those who are committed to them. In *Romola*, Eliot puts Mill's views to just such a dramatic testing.

The city of Florence is Eliot's most fully imagined inclusive political community, and, as she represents, it would seem to be the ideal location for a collective, dialogically informed public opinion. At first impression, it might well be an image of Mill's envisaged democratic ideal in which disparate classes, different neighborhoods, and various professions and trades are united into genuine community through inclusive civic dialogue in the public sphere. Clearly, Eliot is foregrounding debate as a possible forum of public enlightenment. Even in the Proem, the returning ghost of fifteenth-century Florence warmly remembers the "humming piazze" and the "eager life" of the city whose members "were conscious of having not simply the vote, but the chance of being voted for" (4). The quotations that were to have headed the first chapter proclaim, "Florence, city eager to talk" and "The Florentine mind is sharp and in every respect energetic" (597 n. 1). Truth as an active edge to cut through falsity is a frequent image in the text, perhaps most fully embodied in the voluble barber, Nello, whose tongue seems as quick and incisive as his razor. Nello associates his calling with an ideal of disinterested truth, preferring the "liberal art of the razor" to the "narrowing business of authorship." He claims, "Now a barber can be dispassionate; the only thing he necessarily stands by is the razor" (35). The opening chapter gives us the battle of wits between Bratti Ferravechi and Tito, followed by the stir and buzz of many voices in the marketplace as the death of Lorenzo Medici and its likely consequences to the politics of the city are enthusiastically debated. Throughout the narrative, the many different parts that constitute the whole of Florentine society — the popular life of the streets, scholarly circles, and religious orders — are represented as sharing a common, contested, discursive space. There is nothing spaciously contemplative about this dialogic interaction; it is eager, energetic, and restless. Such terms, *eager, energetic, restless,* are of course frequently associated with the more animal energies of the masses. In her author's introduction to *Felix Holt,* Eliot represents the "multitudinous men and women" of manufacturing towns as characterized by "eager unrest" (79), while for Matthew Arnold a popular order is "pushing, excited and presumptuous."

Thus, when we ask how effectively the dialogic clash of opinion against opinion in the public sphere of Florence progresses toward the establishment of enlightened civic views, it becomes clear that Eliot is questioning Mill's optimistic belief in the triumph of a disinterested rationality through free debate. An ironic warning that "the human soul is hospitable and will entertain conflicting sentiments and contradictory opinions with much impartiality" is first sounded in the Proem (5). The opening chapter, with its references to streets ringing with "the shout and clash of fierce battle between rival families" or simply noisy with "unhistorical quarrels and broad jests of wool-carders" (11), similarly implies that rational enlightenment is not always the motive for or the result of exchanges of opinion and beliefs. Party interest and calculation dominate all aspects of Florentine politics. As one character puts it, "a popular government in which every man is to strive only for the general good, and know no party names, is a theory that may do for some isle of Cristoforo Colombo's finding, but will never do for our fine old quarrelsome Florence" (344).[18] By implication, Eliot's main criticism of Mill's view of rational critique as the driving force of social and political consensus is that he fails to recognize the strength of other interests and passions that are entangled in human reasoning. Despite his insistence that physically derived energies and desires are equally needed for the full development of the pagan ideal of human perfection, he rarely, if ever, considers their force.

Eliot suggests in *Romola*, as in her other fiction, that egoistic self-interest, in the fullest narcissistic sense of the term, is the passion that most often blinds individuals to wider perceptions of truth. Even an individual's most altruistic aspirations may provide a screen for projections of self-aggrandizement; indeed, narcissism even disguises itself as a disinterested pursuit of culture, scholarship, and wisdom. The utility of "culture" as a means of elevating social status is most comically represented in the chapter entitled "A Learned Squabble," in which Tito is able to use his knowledge of ancient Greek to defend the beleaguered classical reputation of Bartolommeo Scala, secretary of the Florentine Republic, and so favorably launch himself into the highest social circle of the city.[19] Nevertheless, a similar narcissistic self-regard underlies Bardo's scholarly ambitions. Bardo loftily denounces the commodification of culture by "mechanical printers who threaten to make learning a base and vulgar thing," repudiating "the multiplication of these babbling lawless productions" (50, 62). Yet his own concern for knowledge of the classical world is entangled with narrowly personal desires. This is clearly indicated when his attempt at Stoic disinterestedness deserts him as simply "lip-born maxims . . . powerless over the passions" at the prospect of his unregarded cultural capital: "it is not fair that the work of my brain and my hands should not be a monument to me" (57).

Nevertheless, in commenting on the estranged relationship of Romola and Tito, the narrator remarks: "They were too hopelessly alienated in their inner life ever to have that contest which is an effort towards agreement" (399). Here, it does seem to be suggested that a sincere exchange of views might bridge the gap of understanding between them and establish a truer, more sympathetic knowledge of each other. Romola herself comes to hope for this, "dwelling on the possibility that this confession of hers might lead to other frank words breaking the two years' silence of their hearts" (411). There is, of course, no fulfillment of these hopes for clarification and reestablishment of trust. Gaskell's concept of "antagonistic friendship" based upon mutual openness is alien to Eliot's focus upon individual interiority. In *Romola*, the narrator explains, "genuineness implied confession of the past . . . and Tito had as little bent that way as a leopard has to lap milk when its teeth are grown" (416). Read carefully, what these comments imply is that mutual sincerity would not produce a new, shared, consensual truth through an extension of sympathy for the differing viewpoint, or truth, of the other. Truth is unified and essential; it always already exists to be revealed in a "genuine" confession. Truth is not collective or a process, but resides within each individual, to be discovered and confessed.

Sincerity as confessional truth is a central concern of the text. Savonarola tells Romola, during the meeting that changes the direction of her life, that "the chief gate of wisdom is the sacrament of confession" (363), but he also tells her that self-renunciation is "the portal of wisdom" (361). Sincerity is here linked to self-transcendence as a means of achieving the highest form of knowledge. Much earlier in the story, the narrative represents Tito's hesitation over selling his father's ring for his own personal gain rather than setting off to ransom him. His thoughts are presented in the form of an inner dialogue; this, says the narrator, "was his first real colloquy with himself" (98). However, Tito lacks inner capacity for self-renunciation, and his self-questioning evades the rigor that might have produced greater self-knowledge or a wider, more compassionate perspective than that of narrow self-interest. Tito's failed colloquy, indicating lack of a complex sensibility, does point to the potentially positive function of confession: inner confession as sincerity to self involves a dispassionate scrutiny of interior motivation to detect egoistic interests. An antagonistic self-colloquy provides a safeguard against what is termed "the stupid inflexibility of self-confidence" (573)—words that recall G. H. Lewes's assertion that much "immorality is sheer stupidity" due to a coarseness of intellect unable to apprehend the manifold wholeness of ideal reality and the complex interrelation of parts. In *Romola* the narrator comments, "To the common run of mankind it has always seemed a proof of mental vigour to find moral questions easy" (523). Such words echo Mill's fear of the intolerance of mass conformity, but the response of each writer is quite different. In *Romola*, only an active inner sincerity, which continually scrutinizes self-perceptions, can avoid the stupidity of egoistic self-confidence. In that special sense enlightenment is dialogic, an agonistic process of expanding

personal awareness to encompass an increasingly complex, disinterested understanding of the "many-twisted conditions" of particular human lives (561).

Savonarola's many self-colloquies provide the most complex examination of
the obstacles that impede the wisdom that should result from confession as a
sincere interior dialogue. His tragedy, says the narrator is "the struggle of a mind
possessed by a never-silent hunger after purity and simplicity, yet caught in a
tangle of egoistic demands, false ideas, and difficult outward conditions, that
made simplicity impossible" (490). Savonarola, like Lydgate in *Middlemarch*, is
"spotted" (235). As with Bardo's scholarship, even Savonarola's altruistic ideal of
a universal regeneration of human kind is not entirely disinterested or sincere in
Eliot's sense. It is represented as partly a projection of his own desire for power
and glory and this self-interest obscures the wholly disinterested clarity of vision
needed for transcendence to unimpeded human sympathies. In addition, there is
the danger that idealism becomes fanaticism, so that, as in the case of Dino, a
passionate yearning for transcendence results in a damaging narrowing of sympathies due to the loss of proximity to material existence. Transcendent knowledge, for Eliot, must always derive from empirical particularity. In commenting
on Dino, the narrator insists that there is no "wisdom apart from human sympathies which are the very life and substance of our wisdom" (160).

Paradoxically, though, too much proximity to the particularity of the social and
political world is represented as also obstructing the "inward light" of intellectual
energy in its track toward an "ideally illuminated space." As Savonarola becomes
more hard pressed by "difficult outward conditions," his self-colloquies become as
restless and busy with "crowding thoughts and passions" as the noisy, tumultuous
public squares and streets beyond his cell (522). Indeed, the outer and inner unrest
become identical. Savonarola's goals are slowly transformed from expansive universal ideals to much narrower limits by the pressure of coarser public demands
that are able to envision only the particular and the immediately beneficial.
Savonarola's prayers are increasingly "drowned by argumentative voices within
him that shaped their reasons more and more for an outward audience" (524).
Urban populousness is represented here as a state of mind; the restless, swarming
multitude of the populace outside has surged inside, engulfing and drowning
Savonarola's finer self. In contrast, the disinterested wisdom to be gained by
sincere confession as interior dialogue requires a sanctioned inner spaciousness
that is far removed from all din and hubbub.

The ideal image of contemplative but strenuous self-communing, safely distanced from the conflicting interests of contested public opinion, is represented

at the very beginning of the narrative by the "night-student," who questions "his own soul, for that hidden knowledge which would break through the barrier of man's brief life and show its dark path, that seemed to bend no wither, to be an arc in an immeasurable circle of light and glory" (1). Such contemplative distance from the particularity and striving restlessness of social life is consistently shown in the text to be necessary for the expansion of those inner energies that lead to enlightened comprehension of the greater whole. What remains unclear is how such a dispassionate perspective can simultaneously remain in touch with empirically felt human sympathies that are "the very life and substance of our wisdom" (160). Nevertheless, such an expansive awareness of the complex relationships of the particular individual life within the compass of a universal order is associated by the narrator with justice: the recurrent light of day "shines on, patiently and impartially, justifying or condemning by simply showing all things in the slow history of their ripening" (536). Truth and justice in this sense depend upon a charismatic individual struggle for wisdom as a heroic redirection of egoistic energy into a transcendent sincerity that, in the words of Lewes, constitutes "an intuition embracing the universe."

Such disinterested wisdom is at the opposite pole from Mill's dialogic sense of collective truth and justice as the basis of a democratic community. The knowledge gained from interior dialogue can lead only to individual self-government and self-renunciation, not to active, participatory citizenship.[20] Indeed, as the case of Savonarola indicates, participation precludes the conditions required for disinterested thought. Furthermore, the text makes clear that for most people the necessary intellectual refinement for self-transcendence is beyond their reach; they remain confined within the particularity of purely sensory knowledge. Their "dullness of sensibility" requires an external form of authority to exact obedience to the law (561).

Eliot was not only skeptical of Mill's faith in dialogic sincerity as an open debate of contesting interests and principles. The character of Tito provides the basis for a critique of Mill's grounding of justice and civic duty in physical instincts and his advocacy of pagan self-delight as a counterbalance to the Christian ideal of sacrifice and renunciation. Tito is one of Eliot's most ambivalently imagined characters—the location at once of intense currents in the text of desire and loathing.[21] In the early chapters of the novel, as representative of pagan self-delight, he seems to embody the irresistible joy of physical life untouched by trouble, age, or lack of any kind. He is associated with arcadian images of sunshine, grapes, honey, and milk.[22] As he recalls Romola from the clinging sorrow of her brother's death, "now in the warm sunlight she saw that rich dark beauty which seemed to gather round it all images of joy—purple vines festooned between the elms, the strong corn perfecting itself under the vibrating heat, . . . round limbs beating the earth in gladness with cymbals held aloft, . . . all objects and all sounds that tell of Nature revelling in her force" (177). The imaginative charm of Tito's being seems to draw even from Eliot herself what must be the most sensuous language of her fiction.

The plenitude associated with Tito recalls Freud's description in "On Narcissism" of the "charm" of the child's primary narcissism (Freud, 83). In the child's imaginary, blissful self-repleteness, Freud says, we find an irresistibly attractive image of our own repressed childhood narcissism, a glimpse back to an imaginary lost world without sorrow, absence, or renunciation of pleasures (85). It is a world before the development of interiority. In the novel, it is appropriately Tito who links the image of the child to Epicurean philosophy and to a remembered Golden Age (*Romola*, 34). Tito's sudden appearances to Tessa in moments of unhappiness are represented as having just that magical charm of imaginary delight experienced in infancy: "He was . . . something come from paradise into a world where most things seemed hard and angry; and she prattled with as little restraint as if he had been an imaginary companion born of her own lovingness and the sunshine" (107). In this sense, Tito is the Great Tempter of Dino's nightmare; Tito represents the seductive, nostalgic yearning to regress to the imaginary perfection of primary narcissism, a blissful state in which sacrifice, renunciation of the pleasure principle, is inconceivable. Such sensuous plenitude, an arcadian self-delight, "would be paradise to us all," the narrator says, "if eager thought, the strong angel with the implacable brow, had not long since closed the gates" (110). The pleasure principle must give way to rationality and realism, but the gates of repression should not be closed so tightly that, as with Dino, all sensual joy and fleshly delight is lost. Human sympathies are born of and nourished by recognition of common, fleshly needs and vulnerabilities. Moreover, as Freud suggests, primary narcissism is never eradicated; what the adult "projects before him as his ideal is the substitute for the lost narcissism of his childhood in which he was his own ideal" (88). In just this way, we might understand Tessa's view of Tito as "born of her own loving kindness," Romola's projection of Tito as all that is good, Savonarola's ideal of a just society, and Bardo's yearning for scholarly immortality.

Despite his association with the joy of unfettered physical life, Tito is represented as Epicurean[23] or Utilitarian in Mill's positive sense of an instinctive

human desire for community with fellow beings. In representing Tito as Epicurean, Eliot does not participate in the cruder condemnations of Utilitarianism
as offering license to the lowest desires. Tito is not remotely swinish in his
pleasures and is not attracted by merely animal contentment: "His fibre was too
fine, his intellect too bright, for him to be tempted into the habits of a gross
pleasure-seeker" (*Romola*, 299). In *Utilitarianism*, Mill argues that the basis of all
moral feeling is the rational extension of our natural "desire to be in unity with
our fellow creatures" (*Utilitarianism*, 231). Tito is represented as having a childlike enjoyment in popularity—"he basked in approving glances" (*Romola*, 216).
Nevertheless, Tito's desire to be in unity with his fellow beings is utilitarian in the
more general sense of the word and in a particularly self-interested way; it enhances his sense of ease with the world: "He cared so much for the pleasures that
could only come to him through the good opinion of his fellow-men, that he
wished now he had never risked ignominy by shrinking from what his fellow-
men called obligations" (*Romola*, 161).

The obligation from which Tito shrinks is the need to rescue his adoptive
father from slavery. This represents an example of the duty that Mill places at the
center of the notions of civic justice: the acceptance of a benefit and denying a
return in the benefactor's hour of need. Mill writes, "Few hurts which human
beings can sustain are greater, and none wound more" (*Utilitarianism*, 256). Eliot
embodies this sense of hurt to the full in her representation of Baldassare, but in
her characterization of Tito she attempts to demonstrate how even Mill's most
positive form of Utilitarianism cannot offer a firm basis for the sense of moral
obligation, as a willingness to sacrifice self for duty, that underpins any social
order. In a passage that directly engages with Mill's criticism of religious fear and
ethos of punishment, Eliot insists that for the majority of people only some
internalized dread of an unseen power or authority can restrain selfish desire and
compel the fulfillment of obligations. Few sensibilities, the text suggests, can rise
heroically to the refined wisdom of disinterested altruism. Tito's education has
been "as active as a virulent acid" in eliminating any dread of unseen authority,
either in the form of pagan "awe of the Divine Nemesis" or the "more positive
form" of Christianity "still felt by the mass of mankind as a vague fear" (*Romola*,
116). Tito "felt himself too cultured and sceptical for that"; the erudite familiarity
with opposing principles and belief systems that Mill saw as collective enlightenment has commodified forms of belief for Tito, making commitment to any
particular creed seem merely "a matter of taste" (*Romola*, 117).

In expressing and acting upon such skepticism, Tito also represents a critique of Arnold's faith in culture as a means of inculcating in the masses a sense of disinterested and Stoic civic duty. Tito's absence of ideological baggage, his "unimpassioned feeling of the alien toward names and details that move the deepest passions of the native," is what allows him to act toward all people and parties with sweetness and light (216). His bodily grace, his ready smile, his prevailing charm epitomizes exactly that flexible ease of manner, that apparently "natural simplicity," that Arnold associates with the aristocratic "grand style" of high culture. Baldassarre thinks of Tito in terms of a physical plenitude that seems to speak of a disinterested repleteness: "It was as if that beautiful form represented a vitality so exquisitely poised and balanced that it could know no uneasy desires, no unrest" (99). Tito would seem to epitomize Mill's notion of pagan self-delight and Arnold's ideal of cultured "sweetness." Yet Tito has no disinterested concern for classical culture for its own sake; it is not for him an inherited tradition in which he can identify himself as part of a much larger whole. Culture for Tito has always a utilitarian function. It has always been the means to an end: a means of livelihood, approval, and an elevation in social status. For Tito, culture has always represented "cultural capital," and his first reference in the novel to his learning expresses his sense of its value as a commodity, quoting the worldly monk who advised him: "Florence is the best market in Italy for such commodities as yours" (30). Tito facilely appropriates the rhetoric of enlightenment to disguise his economic interest, justifying the sale of Bardo's library for profit as a disinterested, humanistic dispersal of knowledge (283).

There is a political dimension to Tito's commodified perception of value systems: they allow him to please all interests. Tito is represented as smiling at all comers. His education has given him access to the rhetoric of many forms of belief. Yet far from furthering Mill's ideal of rational critique, Tito finds he can adapt his language to accommodate all sections of Florentine society (102). His duplicitous sincerity is most clearly figured by the act of translation. Throughout Eliot's story, he wins favor by an ability to translate various languages in ways that meet the receivers' desires or expectations. His listeners perceive translation as a transparent act of communication, yet Tito always omits or modifies the account of meaning he offers. The narrative suggests that Tito's "facile ability" to be all things to all men is exactly what is expedient for the charismatic form of leadership demanded by a democratic political order (472). In a political culture epitomized by the passions of vested party interests, Tito's dispassionate manner takes on the semblance of a disinterested sincerity. Tito is represented as unhampered by a developed interiority. He fashions himself upon a manipulative form of publicness. As he duplicitously performs a public code of sincerity in the form of an unassuming and conciliatory urbanity, he has "a keen pleasure in the consciousness of his ability to tickle the ears of men with any phrases that pleased them" (312).

Savonarola represents the Carlylean charismatic prophet of the people: his power rests in popular recognition of the sincerity of his impassioned belief that he reveals God's truth.[24] Savonarola, however, uses his authority to demand sacrifice and self-renunciation for the greater good or for abstract principles, as when he commands Romola to return to her place and the lot appointed her (356–57). The populace, lacking the disinterested wisdom of an expansive intellect, cannot for long comprehend the common good of the city. Savonarola's charismatic power fails because he demands too many sacrifices of the masses.

Tito, by contrast, represents the domesticated charisma of the popular political leader, able to embody in glamourous form the people's own narcissistic desires for well-being: "that bright face, that easy smile, that liquid voice, seemed to give life a holiday aspect" (96). Despite being so favored by the gift of physical charm and the opportunities of Florentine party politics, Tito wears his good fortune "so easily and unpretentiously that no-one has yet been offended by it" (96). Tito can perfect the style of persuasive sincerity because, lacking a complex interiority, he is without passionate investment in any principle, belief, or party beyond himself. Tito begins by seeing his charismatic charm as a means to win general popularity as a source of pleasure, but "now it flashed upon him in the shape of power — of such power as is possible to talent without traditional ties and without beliefs" (347). In contrast to genuinely disinterested leaders like Savonarola or Garibaldi, Tito is attracted into politics not by principle of any kind but by desire for wealth, status, and above all his own narcissistic gratification. "What motive could any man really have, except his own interests," Tito thinks (476). He is represented as enjoying the urbane familiarity of his welcome among the Florentine elite, but he is equally ready to win the cheers of the crowd with spirited republican sentiments: "It was very easy, very pleasant, this exercise of speaking to the general satisfaction" (263). We might properly understand Tito as the first representation in fiction of a modern politics of manipulative sincerity as pure style.

Tito has the domesticated charisma of the common touch; he projects an undemanding promise of ease and sufficiency. His education and culture ensure that the crowd tends to look to him for leadership, to speak for it, but Tito is a representative man who never sets himself apart from the aggregate. Tito is always ready to enter into the spirit of the streets. Indeed, as Eliot represents it, the crowd shares an essential aspect of Tito's character; the crowd is driven by utilitarian desires for immediate pleasure, "ready to sacrifice a stray individual to the greater happiness of the greater number" (103). Tito is represented by Eliot as, by origin, one of the people. His education was the gift of his adopted father, who raised him out of a life of "beggary, filth and cruel wrong," remaking him in his own cultured image (97). The narrative suggests that had Tito remained in his "appointed" place he might well have proved good and contented. In the little family circle he establishes with the contadina, Tessa, and their two children, Tito is loving and responsible. Significantly, the narrator points out that "obedience made up the largest part of Tessa's ideas of duty" (293). Tessa has not lost her dread of unseen authority through a process of enlightened education. It is Tito's self-interested rejection of his adoptive father's claims to recognition that degrades Baldassarre's scholarship and culture into a brutality that in its visual appearance of coarseness is indistinguishable from the poorest of the mass. Thus the two most powerful father figures in the novel, Savonarola and Baldassarre, are both, in different ways, pulled down into the multitude, losing the distinction of an elevated cultural identity. This is imagined as a shockingly physical degradation when, to the brutal, ribald delight of the mob, Savonarola is literally stripped of authority prior to his execution. This nightmare image of a submergence of a refined identity by which the cultured sensibility knows its self perhaps accounts for the intensity of hatred directed in the text at Tito.

Eliot uses the representation of Baldassarre to radically challenge what she sees as the dangerous inadequacy of Mill's utilitarian definition of justice as the animal instinct to retaliate a hurt, rationalized into a disinterested principle by natural human sympathies. The narrative suggests that the underlying psychology of retaliatory justice is politically destabilizing, rather than serving as the foundation of social order. Mill uses the term *thirst* to express what he sees as the strong, natural instinct for revenge; Baldassarre's need for vengeance is repeatedly called an "unquenchable thirst," but the violence of his passion is too fierce to be checked by any rational extension of human sympathies. On the contrary, extension of Baldassarre's sympathy is represented as serving only to swell the current of his hate. He speaks pityingly to Tessa, who has befriended him, but her kindness is powerless to "reconcile him to the world"; instead, it seems that she is "with him against the world, that she was a creature who would need to be avenged" (298).

Although Baldassarre's thirst for vengeance is frequently represented as an animal ferocity, it is shown to be inextricably entangled in human desires. Vengeance is provoked most passionately by wounds to the ego, not the physical body, as the narcissistic mirror logic of Baldassarre's speech to Tito indicates: "I saved you — I nurtured you — I loved you. You forsook me — you robbed me — you denied me" (308). Baldassare adopted Tito so that Tito would, in turn, love and nurture him. In the aftermath of Tito's rejection, Baldassarre looks into a pool of water at his own face and his passionate desire for vengeance splits off from the suffering identity that he sees reflected there and assumes the form of a power apart from the self (269). Ironically, Tito's educated cynicism eliminated any superstitious dread of divine punishment for wrongdoing, but the wound he inflicts on Baldassarre's narcissism is projected out into the transcendent form of outraged justice as an irrevocable nemesis.

It is in the preaching of Savonarola that Baldassarre first hears the words of vengeance that come to him "like the promise of an unquenchable fountain to unquenchable thirst" (230). A similar psychology of narcissistic projection, it is suggested, underlies Savonarola's faith that "the sword of God's justice" is held in readiness over a corrupt world. He has "seen his belief reflected in visions," but, says the narrator, the real force of demonstration lay in "his own burning indignation at the sight of wrong [and] in his fervid belief in an Unseen Justice" (209). The text suggests that this unrecognized overidentification with suffering may derive from Savonarola's own lowly upbringing. Mill saw popular democracy as part of the rational logic of the extension of the notion of justice to all. Eliot suggests that rationality is often dangerously absent from calls for justice and from the unfolding of its "logic." Savonarola is moved by the widest human sympathies: he desires the regeneration of Florence to move outward to embrace a world order. Yet the text implies a slippage between these universal aspirations for justice and a more egoistic desire for retaliation against detractors. As Savonarola's position becomes increasingly threatened, so his emphasis on God's vengeance pushes aside his claims for divine love.

Baldassarre's identifying belief that Tessa is part of a whole world of suffering that must be avenged indicates how an all-consuming outrage at a personal hurt can project itself into calls for universal sympathy and justice. A recognition that others are also sufferers only intensifies and further justifies the sense of grievances that must be assuaged. Self-interest is masked as disinterest or public interest. Early in the novel, Bardo comments on the way "private grudges" may be disguised under "the name of public zeal" (124). Savonarola threatens Florence with the "sharp razor" of God's justice if reform is not implemented; Baldassarre arms himself with a knife "as the unfailing friend of feeble justice" (272). The text insinuates a negative, underlying political logic in Mill's basing of justice in retaliation; it offers a rhetoric that can incite and condone riot, murder, and plunder —"the Masque of the Furies" in which the mob exacts it own justice. Those citizens whose natures have been brutalized by an existence that is only a struggle with physical necessity may demand punishment and retribution of the hated others, not votes. When Baldassarre finally kills Tito, he believes that "Justice" will send witnesses to seal his act as disinterested, righteous retribution, but nobody comes. "Justice is like the Kingdom of God," concludes the narrator: "it is not without us as a fact, it is within us as a great yearning" (549).

It is no surprise that Eliot takes a far more pessimistic view of democratic justice than Mill. Her fictional representation of the way narcissistic desires project themselves onto even our finest ideals points to the way that Mill, too, has been projecting his own ideal of rational critique onto his not wholly rational belief in the collective impulse for social justice. It is, of course, easy to demonstrate how the plot structure of *Romola* likewise projects Eliot's own more conservative notion of the irrevocable shaping force of small, almost unnoticed, self-interested acts upon the outcome of human lives. Nevertheless, the dramatic showing, in the story, of the complex narcissistic investments of every character in ideals of all kinds is powerfully imagined, and, by extrapolation, it does suggest that there is within Mill's optimism a certain self-willed blindness. Beyond the engagement with Mill, however, there is, within *Romola*, a much more radical critique of what we might see as the imaginary foundation of all social collectivities; namely, the oedipal order based upon sacrifice as the ultimate ideal of disinterestedness. The language of the text looks beyond this oppressive order to suggest a more utopian form of disinterested sympathy upon which to imagine community.

Mill centers his argument for justice and duty around the notion of doing as you have been done by. To emphasize this, he uses the language of indebtedness. A duty, he says, is "a thing which may be *exacted* from a person, as one exacts a debt" (*Utilitarianism*, 246). In *Romola*, Savonarola, speaking to Romola, uses the same language of civic debt: she owes to Florence "the debt of a fellow-citizen" (358). Yet inevitably all children are indebted to their parents for the gift of life, as, in a wider sense, each child owes its existence to the society, race, city, or nation that has nurtured its being. This obligation is understood by society ultimately as the right of a life for a life; the individual is expected to give his life for his society. The fact that it is usually *his* life has provided long-standing

arguments against women's claims to citizenship. The patriotic duty of all citizens is, if necessary, to die for one's country, and Mill identifies military service as
one of the few acts that the state can lawfully compel individuals to accept. The
notion of sacrifice is venerated in the Christian symbol of the cross as the ideal of
total self-renunciation.

Eliot radically suggests that this external or socially sanctioned ideal of sacrifice is another form of narcissistic projection and therefore devoid of any self-
transcending truth. Self-renunciation is the oedipal sacrifice demanded by all the
fathers of their sons in *Romola*. Just as Mill and Arnold can be seen as attempting
to remake the working class in the image of their own ideals of rationality and
culture, so, within the story, Bardo, Baldassarre, and Savonarola demand that
their sons identify totally with the beliefs and values of their fathers, renouncing
any right to self definition. Baldassare, we are told, was "constantly scrutinising
Tito's mind to see whether it answered to his own exaggerated expectations" (99).
Freud tells us that in contemplating their children, parents rediscover their own
narcissistic perfection in a nostalgic misrecognition of self that disavows death,
time, and change. The law of the father demands the obedience of sons upon the
pain of death. Throughout *Romola*, law and justice are persistently linked to
oedipal imagery of knives, swords, and cutting edges. Baldassarre adopts Tito for
the self-avowed egoistic purpose of making Tito "care for *me*" (270), and Tito
does indeed become a mirror image of that self-interest underlying his father's
nurture and teaching. Baldassarre misrecognizes this identity between himself
and Tito as treacherous betrayal, and his possessive love reverses into possessive
loathing that longs to "clutch forever an undying hate" (270). Within the narcissism of hatred, the disavowal of death and change can be maintained.

Bardo also demands that his son Dino sacrifice his own life to guarantee his
father's narcissistic desire for fame that will live beyond death. When Dino, too,
appears to deny these "just" claims, Bardo, like Baldassarre, anathematizes his
son (127). However, Dino's desertion, like that of Tito's, is actually identification
with the law of the father. Dino's rejection of family and the world, his perception
of his fellow beings as only "human souls related to the eternal unseen life" (155),
mirrors his father's contempt for the present world and sense that "the living
often seemed to me mere spectres" (51). Savonarola, as spiritual father to the
people of Florence, tries to shape them according to his ideal of purity, ordering
the symbolic Bonfire of the Vanities to purge away their worldly pleasures. His
attack upon venality is seen by the pope, his spiritual father, as rebellion deserving
death. Savonarola himself grows "more and more severe in his views of resistance

to malcontents" (443). Eventually, his vision excludes all who do not identify totally with his view: "The cause of my party *is* the cause of God's kingdom" (492). Savonarola holds out the willing sacrifice of his own life to vouchsafe his obedience to his divine father. To his earthly sons, he preaches the reviling of flesh, and at his death the people, whom he sought to identify with his other-worldly values, revile his flesh with degradation, gross taunts, and curses. What is exposed by this recurrent pattern of paternal anathemas, directed at only apparently rebellious sons, is the vested interest of any existing power structure in advocating an ideal of disinterestedness expressed ultimately as sacrifice.

The patriarchal order, the narrative suggests, is founded upon the law of sameness, which, of course, paternity can never know as certainty. Unlike maternity, knowledge of fatherhood is not founded upon the intimate proximity of bodily touch. What is apprehended as other, therefore, arouses all the violence of a threatened identity. What is more, rebellion by sons never breaks out of the enclosure of narcissism; change only resituates the father's law. Throughout the text, there is a subtle linking of masculinity with aggression as response to any form of alterity. As Tito is forced into active opposition to Romola, it was "time for all the masculine predominance that was latent in him to show itself" (285). When the moment comes for him to assert "the husband's determination to mastery," his face is altered by muscular tension like that of a man "secretly throttling or stamping out the life of something feeble yet dangerous" (412). As Savonarola faces his opponents, his voice becomes "a masculine cry . . . [that] rang like a trumpet" (507). The call to arms resounds throughout the story of *Romola*. In contrast to the utopian universal order that Savonarola had sought to inaugurate, the historical world represented in the narrative is constituted of the hostile identities of conflicting states and nations. In this it bears considerable resemblance to the aggressive politics of nineteenth-century Europe, in which national identity as sameness was increasingly expressed as aggressive hostility to racial difference.

Almost at the end of the story, with all personal, family, and civic ties broken, Romola asks herself, "What force was there to create for her that supremely hallowed motive which men call duty?" (500). This is the central question resonating through the story, just as, beyond the text, it was resonating through 1860s Britain. For Eliot, the transcendent expansion into disinterested idealism always has its starting point in proximity and particularity. For this reason, the moral principle of putting the welfare of an other before the self must be grounded in material reality, not divine or state dictate. The answer to Romola's impassioned question comes in the form of a child's cry. Although fathers and sons dominate at the level of plot structure, there is within the language and imagery of the novel a persistent network of references to an archaic maternal force "whose life and power were something deeper and more primordial than knowledge" (95). Whereas Mill had based justice on an animal instinct to retaliate a hurt, in *Romola* an impulse for active compassion is associated with the instinct of "the brute mother [who] shields her young" (101). This ancient and hidden maternal impulse of protective and nurturing love is linked throughout the story to a quality of "tenderness," as Romola's "ready maternal instinct" is the "one hidden source of her passionate tenderness" (460). It is the "mysterious hidden Image . . . of the Pitying Mother," whose intercession seems to bring relief to the hard-pressed city of Florence, a relief that appears to the citizens to have come "from that region of trust and resignation which has been in all ages called divine" (382).

What the text is suggesting is that an archaic memory of maternal love and tenderness remains hidden beneath a social order based upon the paternal law of identity and vengeance. This hidden force offers an alternative ethos to that of sacrifice as a foundation for civic disinterestedness. When one of the rough-looking, hungry men in famine-stricken Florence wants to convince Romola he can be trusted not to take the food reserved for the sick, he appeals, "I've got an old mother who eats my porridge for me. There's a heart inside me" (376). In contrast, as Baldassarre commits himself wholly to retaliatory justice against Tito, he symbolically exchanges the hidden sapphire contained within the *brevi* given him as a child by his mother for money to buy a poniard: "All piety now was transmuted into a just revenge" (271). Savonarola's preaching alternates between threatening the punishment of God's sword and offering mercy and love: "O people, over whom my heart yearns, as the heart of a mother over the children she has travailed for!" (229).

Men as much as women retain the hidden memory of maternal love, and, as with Savonarola, this can be projected and expanded into an ideal of social order based upon egalitarian compassion for all suffering humanity. Yet the term *tenderness* evokes a sense of material fragility and vulnerability as well as caring concern. The sense of proximity to the physical particularity of fleshly experience has to be retained within the idealizing movement of imaginative expansion to guard against narcissistic projection that ends in fantasies of desire. A keen sense of the vulnerability of all fleshly creatures ensures that "tender fellow-feeling" does not succumb to an idealism in which "the votary lets his son and daughter pass through fire with a readiness that hardly looks like sacrifice" (501). Savonarola's loss of tenderness for human life in self-interested visions is brought back to fleshly origins in the trial by fire: "When Savonarola . . . imagined a human body entering the fire, his belief recoiled again. It was not an event that his imagination could simply see: he felt it with shuddering vibrations to the extremities of his sensitive fingers" (524).

This is the significance of the Magdalen in the picture of the three masks discussed early in the novel (34). It is not the idealizing mysticism of virgin birth that is evoked but the fleshliness of actual nativity, the "travail" of childbirth. This experience offers a radically different way of understanding identity to that of the one and the same that underlies the intolerance of an oedipal order. The physical process of childbearing offers a material experience and, thus, potentially, an imaginative symbolization of identity that can be understood simultaneously in terms of both oneness and otherness. The process of conception and birth is, in fact, remarkably similar to Eliot's description, in her essay "Form in Art," of the evolution of knowledge as "the conception of wholes composed of parts more and more multiplied and highly differenced, yet more and more absolutely bound together by various conditions of common likeness or mutual dependence" (*Essays*, 433). In the essay, Eliot imagines form as difference within unity, held together through a consensual mutual interdependence. Similarly within maternity, difference is encompassed sympathetically as part of self. This tolerant acceptance of the coexistence of sameness with otherness provides a radically innovative way of imagining social inclusion to that of enforced moral and cultural conformity or of commodified massification. It also offers a utopian alternative for a political world order to that of the competing national interests and racial conflicts that increasingly characterized nineteenth-century international relations. In addition, the symbolism of physical birth, as opposed to that of crucifixion, insists not upon renunciation of bodily life but upon the common proximity of fleshly needs and the vulnerabilities of shared human existence.

It is important, however, not to confuse this symbolism of the subtext with the idealizing identifications of Romola with the Madonna that structure the main plot. As Margaret Homans argues, these function to return women to the role of passive bearers of the male word and law (*Bearing the Word*, 189–222).[25] It is significant, in this context, that the image of the unseen Madonna that is carried through the streets is referred to as the Pitying Mother, rather than a mother of tenderness. Despite the utopian intuition of maternal fleshly compassion inscribed in the language of the text and despite the references to Romola's blushes, suggesting that passionate blood flows through her veins, the narrative shudders away from its own tenderness of vision; it could be said to fail its own trial by fire.[26] The story persistently shrinks from fleshliness.

Like Bardo and Romola, the narrative consciousness exists at a rarefied distance from the common life of Florence. Even when Romola becomes conscious of her particular life as a part of the "great drama of human existence," the awareness is understood only as offering "the motive of self-denying practice," with no counterbalancing joy of participatory fellowship in the common drama (388). The anonymous characters who crowd the streets and marketplaces during the many festivals and public occasions represented in the course of the story remain "common," in the derogatory sense. Carnival would appear to be only fit for a bonfire, constituted almost wholly of "grossness and barbarity" (192). Whenever there is an account of a public gathering, the narrative shows an almost comical obsession with the propensity of the crowd to throw stones; it was stone throwing by working-class demonstrators in London that so enraged Matthew Arnold that he demanded the flogging of the rank and file. At their most good-humored, the Florentine populace are dehumanized as noisy and eager poultry, while at their worst they become a demonic mass of violence and hatred (261, 539).

Eliot's political conservatism is well-known, and it is not surprising perhaps that the impulse of tenderness shrinks back from common life en masse.[27] What is more disturbing is that in those passages relating to the heroine's individual acts of fellowship and compassion, the language eerily dematerializes bodies of all fleshliness. Despite the narrative affirmation that "the warm grasp of living hands," rather than visionary phantoms (323), should guide action, physical suffering and compassionate response are represented throughout the story in language devoid of substance and emotional force. Mass starvation of the city's population is dematerialized as "Pale Famine" (369). Similarly, Romola's "passionate tenderness" (a key term in the novel) is never realized imaginatively; in the cliched language of nineteenth-century journalistic discourse, she is said to visit the "abodes of pestilence and misery" (456). Ideas, the narrator insists, gain effective force only when taken in "a solvent of feeling" (444), but in *Romola* compassionate response to human suffering never moves beyond the realm of ideas.

The text confesses its own utilitarian appropriation of suffering as merely the means to an abstract ideal of altruism. It represents Romola hastening "to her sick people in the courtyard, and by some immediate beneficent action, revive that sense of worth in life which at this moment was unfed by any wider faith"

(445). Proximity to particular fleshly needs, it seems, is required only to excite in the imagination the idealizing energy for transcendence from fleshliness. Death, sickness, plague, and famine abound in the narrative, but there is no imaginative evocation of smell, no corruption, no stomach-wrenching physical revulsion, no sense of the proximity of bodies. In the intensity of Savonarola's passionate aspiration for otherworldly power, "his hands . . . in their exquisite delicacy, seemed transfigured from an animal organ for grasping into vehicles of sensibility too acute to need any gross contact" (507). Sensibility here as exquisite delicacy is sundered from the animality of the physical body. So, too, the language of the novel constructs a sensibility that pulls way from gross contact with living flesh.

Perhaps the most disturbing of the linguistic transformations performed by the text is the changing of children into "things" and animals. Tito is very fond of his children as "wide-eyed human things that clung to him," while Tessa's "brute-like incapacity" for judgment is soothing to his conscience; Romola also sees the childlike Tessa as a "poor, trusting, ignorant thing" (423, 301, 464). The children of the sick women in Florence whom Romola is tending are "little pale things," and the child orphaned in the plague-stricken village is called a "dark bantling" (387, 554). This dehumanizing impulse is literally embodied in the monkey disguised as a baby (172). There are, moreover, several images in the story of babies being stifled at birth.

Moving in the opposite direction to this verbal process of abstracting and dehumanizing acts of fleshly compassion is a linguistic impulse to vivify antipathy in terms of a loathed physical closeness. The language used draws upon the discourse of populousness as an unwholesome proximity, as when Romola is weary of "this stifling crowded life" in which a degraded "common nature" of human kind seems to dull the "finer impulses of the soul" (502). The repellent quality of close contact with brutish sensibilities is felt as a sensory revulsion, particularly as invasive bad breath or smell. The coarse, desecrating stare of Dolfo Spini is "as intolerable as a bad odour or a flaring light" (392). Romola's repugnant shrinking from Tito is expressed as aversion to "the breath of soft hated lips . . . the breath of an odious mind stifling her own" (329). Tito himself complains of being "breathed upon by wool-beaters" in the streets, while suspicion of his double dealing is described as "some odour of the facts" (393, 474). Notably when the narrator wishes to objectify the hidden working of guilt, the imagery resorted to is the language of lurking urban disease and criminality and of a dangerous, pestilential fertility: "Under every guilty secret there is a hidden brood of guilty wishes, whose unwholesome infecting life is cherished by the darkness" (100).

It is the "solvent" effect of this feeling of repugnance for proximate bodily life that in the novel energizes the movement toward an idealizing transcendence and away from fleshliness. As the novel elsewhere shows, ideals are often the hiding places of self-interest, and the ideal of disinterested human sympathy is no exception. The passion of the Magdalen remains hidden or disavowed in the narrative. Ultimately, the daughter cannot accept the mother's fleshliness. Early in the story, Romola looks into the mirror and sees her brother Dino reflected back (319); and the novel ends chillingly with Romola positioning herself, in relation to Tito's children, in the father's place and insisting, to his son, Lillo, upon the ideal of self-sacrifice (582–83).

Eliot's historical novel *Romola* is, of all her fiction, perhaps the one that engages most passionately and ambitiously with the exigencies of its moment of production in the early 1860s — with the need to imaginatively accommodate incipient political, social, and cultural inclusiveness. *Romola* constitutes a rigorous critique of the spots of blindness and narcissism within Arnold's and Mill's proffered "solutions" to the need for civic disinterest as the basis of popular democracy. In its recognition that transcendent ideals of the common good need to retain a vital proximity to material life, the novel also moves toward a self-critical reevaluation of Eliot's own ideal of an extension of human sympathies by means of the hard-won heroism of agonistic self-sincerity. However, an almost palpable horror of fleshliness pulls away from the political utopianism of the subtext. Nevertheless, the glimpse of a possible social order alternative to that of sacrifice and sameness articulates the need to imagine community in radically new ways. In *Romola*, the passionate tolerance — the tenderness — of maternal love is distanced and abstracted into "pity." Human sympathy located in an isolating sensibility of contemplative sincerity reaches only to pity. Pity is evoked by that which seems *pitiful* — a word that can be used to imply contempt. Tenderness is felt for what is *tender* — a word that encompasses within its definition the sensual, tactile, fragility of life. By implication, pity, as opposed to tenderness, denies commonality between the pitying sensibility and the object of that sentiment. It would be a mistake to seek to explain this swerve of imaginative energy away from fleshliness in narrowly biographical terms. Rather, it testifies to the power of visceral fears of engulfing numbers and aggregation. The imagining of social inclusion has to encompass the libidinal implications of bodily proximity and identity. This suggests that the achievement of community, whether of city or nation or of a world order, has to be understood in more complex ways than those of rational social and political ideals. Community has to be imagined as fully embodied. The hygienic modern politics of stylized charm and manipulative sincerity, epitomized in Tito and produced within a commodified public sphere, seem particularly ill-suited for such envisioning.

CHAPTER EIGHT

Our Mutual Friend

Visualizing Distinction

In 1863, a reviewer in *Blackwood's Magazine*, a journal that had remained adamantly opposed to any measure of popular reform for almost half a century, wrote enthusiastically of a new era of national social inclusiveness in terms that foregrounded an ethos of sympathetic sincerity as the medium of community. "Railways and newspapers now bind together all parts and classes of the country," the reviewer wrote; the increased wealth of the nation has been the means of "uniting all classes of our people — classes who have so often warred with one another — in bonds of sympathy and confidence; . . . the British nation has at length perfected its social existence, by growing into a compact and harmonious community, every part of which knows intimately and sympathises heartily with the conditions of the rest."[1] This is a remarkable statement of the distance traveled toward acceptance of an inclusive model of society in just two decades from the divisive 1840s. It is also typical of a congratulatory, idealistic imagining of the nation as a united community that began, in the 1860s, to be somewhat smugly celebrated as a distinctive British achievement, even while its practical implementation, in terms of democratic rights and social relationships, was stubbornly resisted. It is a Podsnappian comment both in its social myopia and its complacent boastfulness. Proclamations of social mutuality veiled over a continuing actuality of mass poverty, with all its attendant problems of disease, overcrowding, dirt, deformity, and criminality. "Community" as an especially British virtue was becoming gratifying to imagine, but massification, sameness, and proximity still evoked visceral fear and revulsion in the respectable.

The article in *Blackwell's Magazine* extolling the bonds of sympathy and confidence uniting the nation characteristically concludes by warning that "we have already gone as far toward democracy as it is safe to go" (248). In this sense, the code of sincerity that had come to dominate the public sphere and especially the discourse of politics has to be seen as manipulative sincerity; it projected an invitation into mutuality that had no practical equivalent in social reality. The manipulative force of the public performance of sincerity is clearly demonstrated in Palmerston's manner and language in speaking to the working class "as confidentially and unreservedly as to the House of Commons, . . . taking them into his counsels as colleagues in the internal government and foreign policy of this empire." Palmerston also uses this code of sincerity to project a complacent national community whose mutual achievements "have made England on the whole so prosperous, so happy and so respected."[2] This linkage of prosperity, wealth, and commerce to a code of sincerity as indicative of confidence and trust is not accidental. The decade of the 1860s was the era in which speculative capitalism came to dominate the commercial world. Somewhat paradoxically, speculative finance depends upon sumptuous outward display to encourage the necessary mass investors with promises of dividends and wealth while, equally, it requires an ideology linked to interiority — to notions of confidence, trust, and integrity.

A performative code of sincerity functioning as a means of projecting a fiction of social mutuality and as a medium of speculative capitalism constitutes a total reversal of what Carlyle was proposing in the 1840s in his passionate advocacy of sincerity as heroic struggle against hypocrisy and cant. By the 1860s, the direct expression of emotions and feelings was no longer associated with a notion of general human interiority. Evolutionists like Darwin and Herbert Spencer claimed that even brutes had the capacity to express feelings involuntarily. In the wake of evolutionary thinking, a fully human, evolved sensibility came to be understood as the capacity to intellectualize and aestheticize feeling. Shaftesbury's aristocratic, class-based aestheticization of moral sensibility was reconstituted by Spencer especially as scientific truth. Within this context, sincerity came to be reconceived as a dispassionate sensibility able to pursue the truth by a disinterested distance from all forms of pushy, excited self-interest. Eliot pro-moted this form of contemplative self-sincerity as the heroic achievement of her most noble-minded characters. At a less-elevated level, *Blackwood's Magazine*, in 1862, published an essay, titled "The Union, in Practical Life, of Sincerity and Conciliation," in which sincerity was directly opposed to passionate feeling and direct, forceful expression of opinion. Urban Frankland, the article suggested, gained his way in public and personal affairs by means of his "conciliatory can-dour." This is characterized by an urbane, patrician manner of disinterestedness, of having no passionate opinion to promote. This aloof appearance and manner, the writer, claimed, constituted an irresistible force over others: "Power is so characteristically calm, that calmness in itself has the aspect of power."[3] What this actually describes, of course, is the publicness of total self-assuredness de-rived from an unquestioned sense of cultural authority. In similar terms, and also in 1862, the *Westminster Review* translated Matthew Arnold's notion of the sim-plicity of the grand style of classical and aristocratic culture as "perfectly calm, perfectly reposed, never unduly identified with excitement or passion."[4]

The much publicized controversy in 1862 over the Revised Education Code provides a dramatic illustration of the effective limits placed upon the realization of a national community of social mutuality based on bonds of sympathy and trust. It also indicates the way that sensibility, as interiority, was becoming an index of cultivation, rather than of humanity in a general sense. Prior to the new education code, teacher training for those who were to educate working-class children entailed a five-year apprenticeship as a pupil-teacher working under a certificated teacher, followed by two years in a training college to become a certificated schoolmaster or schoolmistress. Since 1846, a government grant had financed the scheme, and on qualifying the certificated teacher was guaranteed a specific wage. This provided one of the few established routes whereby bright, working-class children of either sex could enter the ranks of respectability and financial security. By the 1860s, the system of college training was the focus of much criticism. This was ostensibly on account of its cost to the public, and the revised code cut the funding to colleges, insisting on a much more utilitarian and less intellectual syllabus, and substituted payment by results to teachers, instead of the salary previously guaranteed by their certificate. Desire to reduce public expenditure was undoubtedly a factor, but clearly what was of equal concern to many commentators was a perception that the unrevised system was producing teachers full of the "symptoms of turbulence and discontent" due to their not being received "by the world at large as gentlemen."[5]

Indignant articles on the subject invariably quoted the words of an unfortunate teacher, Mr. Snell, who made the mistake of responding too sincerely and confidentially to the enquiries of the education commissioners. Trained teachers, Mr. Snell told them, enjoy their work as honorable, intellectual, and benevolent, but believe that "society has not yet learned how to value them." They were not accepted on equal and familiar terms with the lawyer and the parson; they were "snubbed by the little shop-keeper" and they were expected by the wealthy to walk in through the backdoor like the servants. Mr. Snell, however, does not appeal against this discriminatory treatment on the grounds of egalitarian bonds of sympathy and confidentiality that unite all classes into a mutual community: Mr. Snell declared that teachers felt the snubs and exclusions directed at them "with all the sensitiveness that belongs to educated and professional men."[6] Mr. Snell claimed affinity with those who keep him at a social distance in terms of an evolved sensibility that belongs only to a minority of the population. Mr. Snell is ironically categorized "a representative man" by reviewers, but the claims he makes for his fellow certificated teachers are dismissively projected to readers of journals like the *Quarterly Review* and *Blackwood's* as the unwitting self-importance of those whose upbringing, education, and experience are too narrow to enable them properly to judge their actual social position. Mr. Snell's "sensitivity," by means of which he lay claim to a cultivated interiority, was read by "the cultivated" as the intemperate petulance and pushy self-interest of those who know no better.

The virulence of the response to the hapless Mr. Snell — and that surely has to include Dickens's representation of Bradley Headstone[7] — is indicative of social unease, rather than the unquestioned power that expresses itself as calm authority. Mass politics and mass culture were beginning to undermine the traditional bases of social distinction and authority, especially those founded upon older forms of cultural capital. In a review of "Sensation Novels" in 1863, the *Quarterly Review* commented disdainfully: "A commercial atmosphere floats around works of this class, redolent of the factory and the shop. The public want novels and novels must be made — so many yards of printed stuff, sensation pattern, to be ready by the beginning of the season."[8] The equation of fiction here with a visual medium like fashion points to the increasing domination of the visual over the written within the public sphere. Nancy Armstrong has argued that during the nineteenth century reality was increasingly coded according to an "archive" of visual representations (18). Writing that wanted to be convincing had to accommodate itself to this visual ordering of reality. Armstrong indicates how interiority came to be pictorialized according to certain visual conventions used exclusively for the portraits of the well-to-do, while photography of working-class subjects utilized poses and contexts that assimilated them to "primitive" peoples and "less evolved" cultures (112, 104). Jennifer Green-Lewis also argues that the popularity of photography among the Victorians must have intensified the belief, already established by the many popular editions of Lavater's *Essays on Physiognomy* published during the century, that outward appearance offered reliable testimony of inner state (151). This was the period when cheap mirrors were mass-produced for the first time and the *Quarterly Review* noted that whereas at the time of the Great Exhibition "photography was . . . in its infancy," by the opening of the International Exhibition in 1861 it had become "the livelihood of thousands and the recreation of tens of thousands."[9]

Visual mass culture had arrived, and with it systems of classification and knowledge based upon appearance. At the International Exhibition, the artifacts and commodities on display were evaluated confidently as transparently revealing the essential identity of the nation of origin: "The French style of ornament is capricious and fantastic as the people are fickle . . . The English mode, as we have said, is more sober, more within the limits of propriety." English commodities indicate "a people rich and well to do."[10] In *Our Mutual Friend*, it is precisely this equation of commodities with moral worth that Eugene Wrayburn parodies when he fits out his kitchen with every possible domestic appliance as surety of his respectability. In the Victorian public sphere, newly opened museums and historical exhibitions conveyed a sense of history, more akin to that of geography in being set out spatially as panoramic display. Distance in time and geographical space were erased in the presentness of visual representation. An essay in *Blackwood's Magazine*, "Under the Limes. Pen and Ink Photographs," encapsulates in its title the subordination of writing to the truth-telling authority of visual media, especially photography. The essayist persistently reads interior qualities off from external appearances, but in doing so recognizes no separation whatsoever between the reality status of photographic portraits, "real-life" passers-by, and his own written sketches.[11] All three forms are understood as unmediated visual images of an interior psychological reality to be reliably categorized and evaluated on the basis of physical appearance. In this sense, the essay is a paradigm of naive realism in which signifiers are unproblematically attached to signifieds.

In association with evolutionary theories, which perceived the human species as dispersed along a continuum of organic progress stretching from bestiality to the most cultivated interiority, what this new interpretive code of visuality constituted was a shift of social classification from birth to appearance. Social distinctions were reinscribed and naturalized upon bodies, which were taken as reliable signifiers of worth as moral-aesthetic sensibility. As such, bodies came to function within two classificatory schemes. On the one hand, they became, as it were, exhibition surfaces for commodity display, and those commodities, understood in terms of taste, were the basis for the cultural evaluation and categorization of the bearers. Refined taste and manner became visual signs of an inherent discriminating sensibility — a new form of birthright. On the other hand, the body itself, either as a charismatic vessel of grace, disavowing physical materiality, or, conversely, by betraying signs of its own gross fleshliness, was thereby positioned high or low upon the evolutionary scale. Brutishness was held to be devoid of the sensitivity, sympathies, and sensibility that constituted replete humanness. Both classification systems therefore involved a disavowal of the body in terms of the material needs and functions of physical life. Within these classification systems, visible signs of closeness to origins could be perceived only in terms of personal shame and embarrassment. Origins, as aristocratic birthright, retained value as a form of social capital, but this was disassociated from any sense of history as family chronology; gentility and nobility reassumed publicness as visual presence, often in the form of "taste."

George Eliot's response to the imagined congestion and proximities of an inclusive public order was to project a sanctioned inner spaciousness as location of an agonistic striving for enlightenment available only to the heroic individual. In her fiction, she valorizes interiority by means of redefining sincerity as the inner struggle needed to transcend egoistic self-illusions and attain the comprehensive and illuminating truth of reality in its multiple wholeness. In *Romola*, this ideal of spacious self-sincerity is opposed to the manipulative sincerity of politics in a contentious, restless public sphere and to the mass stupidity, prejudices, and appetites upon which manipulation works. In *Our Mutual Friend*, Dickens's response to the perceived problems of ramifying commercial vulgarity and greed is to reconstitute sincerity as an aesthetic spaciousness that disavows interiority altogether. Sincerity becomes purely stylized performance, a disinterested aloofness of manner that expresses itself by means of parody, playfulness, and irony as opposed to the manipulative and sentimentalized code of sincerity operating in the popular public sphere.

Eliot criticized Dickens for sentimentality in his representation of working-class characters. In the earlier part of the twentieth century, critical accounts of Dickens's characterization and social concern tended to support Eliot's judgment. Dickens's Christmas philosophy, Louis Cazamian claimed, depends, for the desired eradication of social ills, upon a change of heart on the part of the wealthy. In 1970, Barbara Hardy, in *The Moral Art of Dickens*, argued that this happens miraculously in his plots, unprepared for by any meticulous analysis of inner processes of feeling. Eliot's psychological realism of interiority was regarded as the supreme achievement of the great tradition of the novel, and Dickens's fiction, by comparison, was held to be less intelligent, less mature, and even somewhat vulgar.[12] Raymond Williams's powerful political and historicized readings of Dickens's fiction overturned this critical condescension by insisting upon the innovative ways in which Dickens was responding to the new experience of urban popular culture and his shaping of artistic form "to dramatise those social institutions and consequences which are not accessible to ordinary physical observation" (*Culture and Society*, 30). Since then, critical recognition of the imaginative power of Dickens's writing has remained largely unchallenged. New historicist studies, like those of D. A. Miller (1988) and Jeremy Tambling (1990), have built upon Williams's insight into Dickens's representation of invisible structures of inequality and oppression to read his work in terms of carceral regimes. Hillis Miller instituted a postmodern Dickens whose realism was everywhere fissured by an awareness of the fictionality of all representation, although this insight comes at the cost of blindness to Dickens's political radicalism.[13] Studies of Dickens's psychological, as opposed to his political, imagination tend to take their cue from Edmund Wilson's seminal essay "Dickens: The Two Scrooges" and John Carey's *The Violent Effigy* to foreground Dickens's fascination with extreme states of mind, Gothic conventions, sadism, and insanity.[14]

Our Mutual Friend can be read as the culminating point of all these aspects of his fiction. In the story, interiority, as a general attribute of human nature, is not connected with any upward evolutionary scale toward a refined moral sensibility. Instead, inner motivation is associated only with the most aggressive and primal impulses of visual speculation. Social evaluation and classification is imposed by means of a disciplining visual scrutiny that measures the body's distance from physical materiality. Ascending evolution is recognized and evaluated solely as an aesthetic taste, articulated in the common desire for visual beauty. This aesthetic distance from materialism is symbolically figured in the rooftop garden shared by Jenny Wren and Lizzie Hexam high above the fretful world of commercial greed and from which Jenny sings out "Come up and be dead" (280). Since interiority is associated only with the lowest instincts of life, aesthetic taste cannot be articulated as sensibility but only as surface performance and playfulness — as an ascen-

dancy of the signifier. This displacement of aesthetics into an idealized, nonsig-
nifying spaciousness disavows cultural capital as the inheritance of class and
wealth. To recognize the social determinants of taste would involve an acknowledgment of history, whereas the temporality of the novel is only the present plane
of a visual publicness.

Our Mutual Friend (1864), more than any other nineteenth-century novel,
registers the encroaching force of a commodified visual order of reality. In this
novel, Dickens seems presciently to foreground those qualities of one-dimen-
sional presentness, repetition, and banality that have become central to a postmodern critique of consumer capitalism. In particular, he parodies a national
culture constituted and dominated by speculation, in all senses of the word: to spy
out, to watch; to reflect on, to conjecture; to invest in the hope of profit, to enter
into a risky enterprise, to gamble. Speculative energy is shown to drive the
restless activity of the fictional world at every level; speculation is also shown as
the dominant form of public consciousness within that world and, more strikingly, as constitutive of the individual self's conjecturing of interiority. Readers of
Our Mutual Friend are given a swift induction course in chapter 1, "On the Look
Out," into the prevailing speculative practice of the society represented in the
novel. In the opening paragraphs, the appearance of a boat containing two figures
is minutely scrutinized, while the narrative voice speculates and conjectures upon
the boat's occupants' possible means of livelihood so as to categorize and evaluate
them: "He had no net, hook, or line, and he could not be a fisherman; his boat
had no cushion for a sitter, no inscription, no appliance beyond a rusty boathook
and a coil of rope, and he could not be a waterman; his boat was too crazy and too
small to take in cargo for delivery, and he could not be a lighterman or river-
carrier" (15).

In a similar way, throughout the story, characters are constituted by their
appearance, evaluated and categorized by others according to how they look, and
there is a pervasive foregrounding of the act of looking and looking out as speculation. As George Levine notes, "*Our Mutual Friend* seems at times to be one
long sequence of spying" (*Darwin and the Novelists*, 223). References to mirrors
and portraits are recurrent in the text: the surface showiness of the world of the
Veneerings is suggested by the narrative perspective of mirror reflections, and
Georgiana Podsnap, Bella Wilfer, and the Lammles are also perceived and perceive themselves in looking glasses. As if in police custody for an identity mug
shot, Mr. Boffin is forced by Silas Wegg to sit on top of a box "as if he were about
to have his portrait painted," and Mr. Wilfer is so chubby and innocent in ap-

pearance that a cherub "might be photographed as a portrait of Wilfer" (644, 41). Mrs. Lammle seizes the opportunity to speak confidentially to Mr. Twemlow while they look through a book of portraits of public figures, and Mrs. Wilfer, as a disciple of Lavater, prides herself on her knowledge of physiognomy. It is part of Headstone's tragic misunderstanding of the larger world that his arduous ambitions have been focused on the traditional expectation that his inherent worth will be guaranteed by the authority of the written word, by his certificates, only to recognize uneasily and incompletely that evaluation has shifted to appearances. Yet in representing his downfall as a return to bodily origins as inescapable destiny, the text reinscribes those naturalizing mechanisms of social exclusion based upon appearances that it elsewhere excoriates.

The imagined society in *Our Mutual Friend* is a more inclusively national one than that represented in any other novel in this study. Its cultural mode of existence is shown to be generated and sustained by a national public sphere in which commercial, political, professional, and media interests are completely entangled. As such, it is a world typified by heterogeneity, rather than social exclusiveness. It is constituted of characters representing cultural, social, and economic capital — old money and new. *Our Mutual Friend* represents the culminating point of the trend that Gaskell highlighted in *North and South:* the public sphere is now dominated by nonlanded wealth. There has also been a transition from the authority of birthright and letters to the power of visual and manipulative publicness. Those with high family connections, like Lady Tippins and Mr. Twemlow, are cultivated purely as signifiers of aristocratic glamour, but they are marginal to all the transactions of the plot that turn entirely upon money speculation. The characters Lightwood and Wrayburn, of the gentry class, are there to represent the gloss of cultural capital; they are, in effect, licensed entertainers in a milieu in which everyone is playing a theatrical game of some kind. The shift of value from birthright to appearance is most comically parodied in the marriage of Mr. and Mrs. Wilfer. Mrs. Wilfer laments a literal coming down in the world from her origins in a tall family. Her parent's "cherished hopes [were] that I should be united to a tall member of society," and when she turns down "a gentleman measuring six feet four inches in height" her mamma foresees the worst: "This will end in a small man" (451–52). Mrs. Wilfer marries beneath her, and indeed her husband's "appearance was a reason for his being always treated with condescension." This is great fun, but there is an underlying point that the text takes seriously: the only inheritance and origins that matter are those of the physical body. It could be claimed that the text is obsessed by bone structure and skeletons.

Despite the boned substance underlying appearances, the text represents the public sphere as characterized by surface and circulation; the identities of the players (*players*, in its suggestion of gambling and theatricality, is a more accurate term than *characters*) are constituted as wholly commodified identities. Indeed, in *Our Mutual Friend*, Habermas's term *publicness* might be appropriately modified to *presentness* to suggest the way in which characters assume identity only as appearance, as a surface for display, and lack depth either as personal interiority or as history. The novel's own mode of "knowing" these characters eschews the omniscience of conventional realist fiction: the characters that constitute the public sphere are represented as essentially what they look like and what they buy, devoid of interiority. The narrative perspective holds them in a relentless, evaluating appraisal as if they were items on display. In the case of Lady Tippins, the narrator comments, "You could easily buy all you see of her, in Bond Street; or you might scalp her and peel her and scrape her, . . . and yet not penetrate to the genuine article" (122).

Performance and visual appearance are represented as the evaluative currency of this milieu. It is not just Bella Wilfer's looks that are worth money (460). As paper currency and shares are taken as signs of a guaranteed substance of wealth, so, too, in a world dominated by financial speculation, people's appearances are taken to indicate their assets. Lady Tippins calculates to a penny the cost of the Lammle wedding: bride's dress thirty shillings a yard, bridesmaids' twelve and sixpence; Mrs. Veneering "never saw such velvet, say two thousand pounds as she stands" (123). Even the meek Mr. Twemlow is represented as employing "a secret artist who has been doing something to his hair with egg yolks," while the more calculating Fledgby is "sensible of the value of appearances as an invest-ment and liked to dress well" (244, 269). Mr. Wilfer's daydreams are visualized in the commodified terms of an ambition "to wear a complete new suit of clothes, hat and boots included, at one time" (40). His daughter's dreams are for even more luxurious commodities: silks and shawls from China, sweet-smelling woods, Cashmere shawls, an Indian prince with diamonds and emeralds blazing in his turban (315–16).

The narrative pervasively alludes to the commodities of empire. As Mary Poovey suggests, the public sphere of the novel is represented as a microcosmic flux within the circulating macrocosm of speculative world capital (*Making a Social Body*, 155–222). Yet no enlarged public perception of reality emerges from this metropolitanism; the circumscribed chauvinistic vision perpetuated within the public sphere is exemplified by Podsnap's contemptuous dismissal of the rest of the world whence comes his wealth. Mrs. Boffin's promise to Bella that they will "go everywhere and see everything" exemplifies the belief that the world can be encompassed locally and visually (113). It also exemplifies the mode of existence of most characters within the public sphere. Like paper currency, they are represented in continuous circulation. The entire work of bringing in Mr. Veneering as a member of Parliament consists of "going about." The narrator comments, "Whether the business in hand be to get a man in, or to get a man out, or get a man over, or promote a railway, or jockey a railway, or what else, nothing is understood to be so effectual as scouring nowhere in a violent hurry — in short, as taking cabs and going about" (249). The narrative recourse to present tense, in those chapters concerning the public sphere, represents the consciousness of the public sphere itself as constituted by a photographic presentness: a spatial and temporal plane of visuality. People inhabiting this world, like shares, have no antecedents (118). The City, the West End and the East End, and the new suburbs of London, with street names constantly referred to as characters circulate from location to location, are presented as a panoramic plane. Even the interior of the houses seems to lack any sense of depth; the notion of lodgers, indicative of a temporary mode of urban existence, is recurrent. When Mr. Wilfer asks their new lodger for references, Harmon, under the guise of his assumed identity as Rokesmith, declines, saying he is a stranger to London. As such, he disavows personal history and family credentials, and Mr. Wilfer compliantly agrees that money and goods are more than adequate substitutes (46–47).

Far from sustaining a civic ethos of critical reason, the public sphere in *Our Mutual Friend* is represented as the circulating space of sensationalism, financial rumor, and sentimental and repetitive banality. The Buffers at the Veneerings' dinner parties are interchangeable, Alfred Lammle's friends all resemble each other, and Lightwood "is but the double of the friend on whom he has founded himself" (259, 404). Under the Podsnappian regime of moral and cultural conformity, the public sphere has become a force of intolerance and chauvinistic enclosure of vision. The character of Podsnap is represented as the projected publicness of an illiberal national identity. This is represented domestically as a bullying domination, disciplining national culture into a "collective mediocrity." In particular, education and the formation of the young person as future citizen are subjected to a relentless repressive supervision that produces "school-buildings, school-teachers, and school pupils, all according to pattern and all engendered in the light of the latest Gospel according to Monotony" (219). A pervasive hypocritical squeamishness allows the fleshly needs of the poor and the sexual

208 *Embodying Mass Culture*

needs of the population at large to be disavowed as unmentionable vulgarity and bad taste. Within this regulatory puritanism, aesthetic values recognize only a coercive form of realism in which all available ways of understanding the variety of human existence are reduced to a repetitive regimen of getting up, working, and going to bed. Daily close shaving is prescribed to efface all sign of the body's physical vitality.

Dickens's parodic representation of a national public sphere as a visual regime of surface, circulation and repetition is strikingly similar to current critiques of the postmodern culture of developed capitalism.[15] Yet the radical insights of the text go beyond this critique: the language of the novel insists that there is a constitutive interrelationship between speculative finance, fictions of interiority, and the code of sincerity. The social existence of characters within the story is represented as a photographic flatness, yet they are all busy imagining depth and interiority. In a society founded upon speculation, appearance is regarded as a visible sign system indicating the underlying substance of personal worth. What the speculators in *Our Mutual Friend* are seeking below the surface is hidden gold, not moral sensibility or virtuous interiority. Almost every character, like Gaffer in the first chapter, is described as on the look out.

Looking is foregrounded as an instinctive, predatory, speculative act. Characters continually scrutinize and evaluate other characters, and, like Gaffer, they believe surface is to be read, as a photograph or the river, for clues as to what it reveals or suggests is below the surface. Pleasant Riderhood "had an eye for sailors" as eligible prey; Silas Wegg looks over Mr. Boffin speculatively as potential profit; Mr. and Mrs. Lammle make a speculative marriage on the basis of each other's appearance of wealth and subsequently weigh up Georgina Podsnap's worth: "And so, looking about her, she [Mrs. Lammle] saw Miss Podsnap," and, catching her husband's eyes, they embark on their speculation (347, 54, 139). In the world of the text, only the dead, like Mr. Dolls, have no speculation in their eyes (712). When Fledgby wants to persuade Jenny Wren to profit by her knowledge of Lizzie Hexam's whereabouts, he encourages her to "look alive" (698). The juxtaposition, in that phrase, of looking with being alive and with speculating on another for self-gain is not fortuitous. To be alive, the novel suggests, is necessarily to be on the look out, to speculate, and in the conjectural, predatory gaze at an other as possible source of profit, a sense of self as interiority comes into consciousness: self-interest, not sensibility or sympathy, is understood in the text as the instinctual basis of self.

Depth and subjectivity are closely associated in the novel with the primal ooze of the riverbed and with a primitive survival impulse of speculation in the form of watchfulness, greedy designs, and secret plotting. "We judge others by ourselves," the narrator says (495). Those who speculate for financial gain are represented as quick to conjecture hidden designs and motivations in others. Secret calculations produce a sense of inner self in the speculator that is simultaneously projected, in a mirror or specular logic, onto the person who is the object of the speculative gaze. To that extent, many characters in *Our Mutual Friend* are like realist fictionalists: they read faces as testimony of interiority and motivation. Mrs. Wilfer provides a comic parody of this pervasive speculation on the designs of others in her physiognomist's readings of Mrs. Boffin's face: "Of the disinterestedness of their intentions toward Bella, I say nothing. But the craft, the secrecy, the dark deep underhand plotting, written on Mrs. Boffin's countenance, make me shudder" (117). Bella projects her own mercenary design of "looking out for money to captivate" onto John Harmon's intentions toward her (317). A scheming Wegg also reads in Harmon's face the unmistakable signs of "an underhand-mind," and Fledgby speculates suspiciously on Riah's hidden motives (303, 700). The hidden, "dark, deep" origin of these fictions of interiority, the text implies, is an instinctual, almost Darwinian competitive impulse, a desire to gain at the expense of an other and an uneasy suspicion that the other is the site of similar self-interested speculation. Speculative capitalism, as the derivations of the word *speculation* indicates, must bring into being, must envision, or at least elaborate and develop those desires and motivations for acquisition of wealth upon which its continued profitability depends. We might say that speculative capitalism has a heavy investment in notions of interiority.

It is also largely dependent upon a code of sincerity. As Marx pointed out in *Capital*, a visual appearance of immense wealth becomes a crucial requirement for attracting speculative interest and investment: sumptuous display is "capitalism's cost of representation" (1:741). Yet gaining public confidence in the honesty and transparency of the promises and proceedings is equally paramount. In *Our Mutual Friend*, the code of sincerity is represented as complicit with speculative activity in two ways: it perpetuates a sentimentalized, flattering fiction of interiority as "sympathy," "reciprocity," and "sensibility," and it performatively elicits a corresponding trust and confidence. The word *confidence*, with its double meaning of assurance and security and of intimate personal revelation, is a central term within the public code of sincerity. It is also a key term in the world of finance. The code of sincerity is preeminently the interpellative discourse of interiority, conjuring a mutuality in which each participant recognizes the other as a like subjectivity. Most nineteenth-century novels participate in the ideological code of sincerity, especially in terms of the psychological realism with which the interiority of the central characters is represented most intensely at those moments when confidences are finally exchanged. By contrast, *Our Mutual Friend* satirizes the pretensions of the code and reveals its manipulative, ideological functioning.

Mr. Veneering is identified in the text as the "representative" political man of a wholly speculative culture (243). To this role he brings the two main requisites: the appearance of sumptuous wealth and a mastery of the performative code of sincerity, welcoming all newcomers in terms of confidence and trust as dearest friends and intimates. He is ably supported by his wife's discourse, which interpellates every passing acquaintance into a banal, popularized sensibility of domestic confession and womanly intimacies. Veneering does not quite kiss babies as part of his election campaign, but the representation of Mrs. Veneering trailing their brand-new baby around assorted guests for synthetic pathos provides a comic premonition of the modern popular politics of sincerity. "Sincerity" is circulated as the discursive currency of the public sphere at all social levels, promoting a cultural idealization of sensibility, sympathy, and trust that masks a speculating interiority of calculating greed. Riderhood and Wegg persistently insinuate their honesty, hailing projected victims as "pardner," "brother in arms," "comrade," and "fellow man."

The text provides plenty of fictional demonstrations of the psychological effectiveness of sincerity as the manipulative code of "bonds of sympathy and confidence." Bella is instantly won over to Mrs. Boffin by the latter's directness and honest transparency: "You mustn't feel a dislike to us to begin with, because we couldn't help it, you know, my dear." Bella is "so touched by the simplicity of this address that she frankly returned Mrs. Boffin's kiss" (113). Expressions of sincerity almost irresistibly elicit trust as a response; hence, the utility of the code for those who want to gain privileged information. Mr. Boffin also regulates his relations with others upon an ideal of transparency and trust: he feels "in his frankness . . . that it did not become him to have a gentleman in his employment five minutes, without reposing some confidence in him" (182). Speculative characters in the story are represented as acutely aware of the power of sincerity as an insinuating and manipulative mode of address. Mr. Wegg convinces Mr. Boffin of his honesty by the air of "melancholy candour" with which he seems reluctantly to admit to the latter that he does not like the name Boffin (56). Mr. Lammle attempts to disarm the suspicious Mr. Fledgby "with a flourish of frankness," and his wife much more successfully ensnares Georgiana Podsnap with protestations of desired intimacy: "You make me ten times more desirous, now I talk to you, to know you well than I was when I sat over yonder looking at you. How I wish we could be real friends!" (268, 140). Such is the bond of sympathy generated by confidence that Georgiana's genuine sincerity threatens to undermine Mrs. Lammle's speculative intent (259). John Harmon recognizes with hindsight that when he and George Radfoot "got to be confidential together," Radfoot was cynically exploiting the relationship of mutual trust to gain information that would enable him to murder Harmon for his fortune (361).

The mutual regard implied by the code of sincerity is represented in the public world of the novel as filming over the watchfulness of speculative conjecture. Visual appearance as commodified display presents an inviting surface to be read for underlying worth, hidden substance. Looking and desire are intimately related in the language of the text, understood as the driving energies of the survival impulse of life—the instinct to "look alive." Both Gillian Beer and George Levine point out that what was "revolutionary" in Darwin's account of evolution was the emphasis upon selection as a force of physical attraction (Beer, *Darwin's Plots*, 22, 157; Levine, *Darwin and the Novelists*, 84–118). More recently, commentators have pointed to the analogies between the blind, competitive market forces at the center of nineteenth-century economic theory and Darwin's notion of competitive selection.[16]

Dickens is undoubtedly associating a speculative visual instinct with the restless, acquisitive energies of capitalism. As such, visual desire is located as the evolutionary impulse that drives commodity appeal. The linkage of looking with evolutionary forces in the text, however, is much more complex and contradictory than I have thus far suggested. The primitive requirement to look and evaluate is also connected to the possibility of evolutionary ascent—what the narrative calls "the vital force of all the noblest and prettiest things" (171). It is by this means that the narrative's ideological structure rehabilitates origins and appearances as testifying signifiers—signifiers that function as naturalized mechanisms of social exclusion inscribed upon the body. Within this evolutionary ideology, taste, understood as an inherent aesthetic impulse, is located in a noncultural space, disassociated from class, education, and tradition.

A responsiveness to, or desire for, beauty is shared by a socially heterogeneous group of characters in the story: the Boffins, Jenny Wren, and Bella, among others. Mr. and Mrs. Boffin, having worked all their lives in "one dull enclosure," take an untaught delight in "the variety and fancy and beauty" on display in shop windows (386). In contrast, Mrs. Milvey has been forced to repress "many pretty tastes and bright fancies" due to her husband's meager salary despite his "expensive education" (109, 107).[17] The two words *pretty* and *taste* are recurrent within this concern of the text with specular delight. It is not just commodity goods that attract by their prettiness: bonds of sympathy and confidence are shown to be more readily forthcoming for those characters who are fortunate enough to have pleasing faces. Miss Abbey Potterson excuses her sentimental concern for Lizzie Hexam as the influence of Lizzie's beauty: "I don't believe I should do it if you were not good-looking. Why ain't you ugly?" (73). Charlie Hexam relies upon the same visual appeal when he responds to Headstone's doubts about his sister: "I wish you'd come and see her, Mr. Headstone, . . . and judge her for yourself" (217). The text explicitly emphasizes that the basis of Lizzie's and Bella's mutual sympathy and trust derives from the pleasing appearance each has for the other:

> "It's quite new to me," said Lizzie, "to be visited by a lady so nearly of my own age, and so pretty, as you. It's a pleasure to me to look at you."
> "I have nothing left to begin with," returned Bella, blushing, "because I was going to say that it was a pleasure to me to look at you, Lizzie." (514–15)

Evolutionary selection is dominated by sight. The delicate, blue-eyed, curly-haired orphan, Johnny, whom Mrs. Boffin selects to adopt, is constantly referred to by his grandmother, Betty Higgins, as "my pretty," and Mrs. Higgins recognizes that Mrs. Boffin's plan will be the making of him in terms of social evolution: "He'll be a gentleman when I'm dead" (201). Mrs. Higgins's faithful helper, Sloppy, on the other hand, is all bone and no delicacy; he is, the narrator claims, with no satiric intonation, "Full-Private Number One in the Awkward Squad of the rank and file of life" (201). After Johnny's death, Mrs. Boffin is represented as recognizing that concern with physical attractiveness predominated her imagining of the orphan: "Why did I seek out so much for a pretty child, and one quite to my own liking? Wanting to do good, why not do it for its own sake, and put my tastes and likings by?" (330). Mrs. Boffin seems here to reject inequalities based upon physical appearance. Social bonds of sympathy and confidence ought to be founded upon an egalitarian respect for all fellow beings. With this new insight, Sloppy is perceived as an obviously deserving candidate for patronage. Already, he has been provided with a new suit of clothes aimed at smoothing over the angularities of his bodily form, but the utmost cunning of the tailor's art has been to no avail. Sloppy's unfortunate skeleton cannot be concealed; in all his physical ungainliness, "Sloppy stood confessed" (332). Interiority as depth is parodied here; interiority is only skeleton beneath the skin.

Mr. Inspector tells Lightwood and Wrayburn that "you never got a sign out of bodies"; but he is wrong (35). Throughout the text, bodies may be said to speak louder than words; they are the "genuine article" beneath commodified surfaces. In *Our Mutual Friend,* characters that perform within the public sphere are persistently represented within a dual perspective. Textual attention appears to focus upon a dazzling reflective surface. Yet narrative scrutiny intersperses descriptions of commodified appearance with reminders of the materiality of the underlying body.[18] These comments articulate a barely disguised physical disgust. Mrs. Podsnap has a "quantity of bone" that would be of interest to Professor Owen's evolutionary theories; there is a "certain yellow play in Lady Tippin's throat, like the legs of scratching poultry"; and Mr. Lammle's savagery is indicated by white dints that appear upon his nose (21, 23, 128). Hidden skeletons confess origins. Although Pleasant Riderhood, the object of Mr. Venus's affections, does not wish to be regarded "in that boney light" (90), bodies cannot be disavowed. Bodies are social destiny in the story. Sloppy is adopted by the Boffins in place of pretty little Johnny with his auburn curls, but there are no plans to elevate Sloppy into gentlemanly identity. Sloppy is apprenticed to become a carpenter, always on condition that he promises to be "industrious and deserving" (332). In a similar way, Headstone's body cannot adapt itself to the trappings of respectability. In his decent coat and shirt and tie he conveys an impression of "mechanics in their holiday clothes," whereas when he imitates the dress of Rogue Riderhood it seems as if it were his own (218, 619). Headstone's bodily form not only ensures that Lizzie feels no sexual attraction to him, it ties him irrevocably to his social origins. Education, the text suggests, is powerless against the resistance of the body's materiality. Mr. Venus is unable to accommodate Mr. Wegg's leg to any other skeleton because the bone seems to have a twist in it.

The plot structure indicates only two ways of rising in the scale of a society structured by speculative capitalism. One is by wealth, as illustrated by the Boffins's easy access to the public sphere. The other is by being talent-spotted as of exceptionally pleasing physical appearance, as old Mr. Harmon spots Bella as a very promising girl (50). Pretty Johnny was similarly picked out from the competitive, overstocked orphan market and would have become a gentleman. Lizzie is perceived through the window in painterly terms by Wrayburn as "a deep rich piece of colour," and thus singled out she becomes a lady. The collapse of human value into aesthetic value is articulated by Wrayburn's claim that Lizzie won his love "by her beauty and her worth," in that order (679). Her acceptance by society is guaranteed when Wrayburn's father, "a professed admirer of beauty," having condescended to meet Lizzie, bestows upon her the highest accolade of a cultural regime of visuality: he recommends that she have her portrait painted (790).

Despite the satiric treatment of Wrayburn's father, it needs to be noted that, in the value system of the text, the naturalizing identification of Lizzie's social worth with her looks is placed in sharp contrast to the worldly speculation of most characters, who judge people's appearances only to discover profitable hidden depths of money. Within this logic, Wrayburn's recognition of Lizzie's beauty has to be read as a disinterested, aesthetic appraisal. The Boffins gain entry into the public sphere by means of their financial value, Lizzie by means of her aesthetic value: Lizzie's worth coalesces with her physical appearance. Her brother says of Lizzie, "What she is, she is, and shows herself to be. There's no pretending about my sister" (217). Lizzie, then, is sincere because, insofar as she has no hidden depths, her surface constitutes her identity and value. The absence of interiority within this logic constitutes sincerity as aesthetic integrity.

The novel continually plays upon images of surface and depth, and it does so to call into question the conventional notion of interiority as depth that is at the center of a realist model of subjectivity. Notions of sincerity would normally be associated with a character's inner feelings and intentions. *Our Mutual Friend* relentlessly overturns such realist values and assumptions. Confidences and confessions are shown to constitute only manipulative fictions of sensibility and sensitivity, as when Bella "confides" in Mrs. Lammle as to John Harmon's indelicate advances and Mrs. Lammle feels scrupulously bound to "confess" this knowledge to Mr. Boffin. Sloppy can only "confess" his sin of having an ungainly body. When Lightwood asks Wrayburn "do you design to capture and desert this girl?" Wrayburn replies, "I don't design anything. I have no designs whatever. I am incapable of designs" (292). This incapacity for plotting is meant to be read literally. Wrayburn's attractiveness for Lizzie lies in his lack of any hidden depths to invite speculation as to underlying worth: "There was an appearance of openness, trustfulness, unsuspecting generosity, in his words and manner, that won the poor girl over" (237). *Manner* is a repeated word in the text, foregrounding the whole embodied, physical presence and bearing of a character.

Wrayburn rejects any self-knowledge of an inner subjectivity. He terms himself an "embodied conundrum," implying that any source of self beyond the physical materiality of flesh and bone is unknowable (283). His claim that "I

mean so much that I—that I don't mean" could be read as a radical reversal of
Eliot's critique of Dickens—as an assertion that the rich meanings attached to
notions of subjectivity in realist novels are meaningless fictions: *I* as a signifier
connotes so much that has no actually substance. Wrayburn implicitly denies any
origin of self-identity in interiority, even though he makes this nonconfession
with an engaging air of openness and sincerity (281). Harmon's account of near
death similarly implies the absence of any essential, nonsocial core of self: "I
cannot express it to myself without using the word I. But it was not I. There was
no such thing as I, within my knowledge" (363). Wrayburn's charismatic appeal is
represented as his manner of replete aestheticized self-possession. Like Lizzie,
what he is, he is; his surface constitutes his self. He is his graceful embodied
manner. And, as with Lizzie, this bodily self-plenitude is identified with disinterested sincerity. Wrayburn is self-possessed, disinterested, and sincere, the narrative implies, because he has no intentionality and pursues no inner motivation.

Yet there is a contradiction or paradox in this figuring of Wrayburn as wholly
his embodied manner. Any cultural, class, or educational origin of his style or of
his aesthetic discrimination is disavowed: this would entail a sense of depth or
subjectivity as personal history. Wrayburn insists that he is an embodied riddle
to himself. Yet despite this emphasis upon embodiment, manner, and surface,
Wrayburn is never represented visually in the text. He refuses to accommodate
his father by appearing as "Eligible on View" and he declines to "come out" at
Veneering dinners. Wrayburn and Lightwood are the only guests at the Veneering dinner party in chapter 2 whose faces are not imaged in the mirror. The
narrative perspective, so relentless in its appraisal of other characters' commodified surfaces and bony substance, offers no description of Wrayburn's physical
appearance whatsoever, apart from the repeated emphasis upon his almost disembodied lightness of being. This is surely because, once represented as a physical appearance, Wrayburn could not escape social classification. In a novel that
everywhere insists upon the dominance of visual image over word and the judgment and categorization of people by appearance, Wrayburn is represented in
the text only by means of his disclaiming and playful discourse that eschews all
meaning. His words operate at the surface as riddles, parody, and explicit fictions,
refusing origin in an underlying intention or subjective truth.

As potential lover of Lizzie Hexam, Wrayburn is asexual; his gaze at Lizzie has
to be understood as an aesthetic impulse; hence, its painterly terms of appreciation. All the threatening force of physicality is displaced onto his rival, a man of
low and obscure origins. The text polarizes them in terms of oppositional values:

Wrayburn is persistently associated with qualities of lightness, nondimentional-ity, spaciousness, playfulness, and freedom. When Lizzie bumps into Wrayburn after her final, stormy meeting with Headstone, "his lightest touch, his lightest look, his very presence beside her in the dark common street, were like glimpses of an enchanted world" (399). Wrayburn's character is not represented as in classic realism as an interiority shaped by personal history or as a finely evolved moral sensibility, but as a charismatic gift of social ease and grace. Headstone is associated with darkness, confinement, and passionate earnestness. To the extent that he has interiority, as opposed to instinctive energy, it is constituted as the enclosed mental laboriousness imposed by a utilitarian education. What the rep-resentation of Wrayburn figures is the ability of cultural capital to dissociate itself from the gross materiality of money, class, and the body and to assume the sanctioned spaciousness of aesthetic disinterestedness. This aestheticism is not represented in *Our Mutual Friend* in terms of Shaftesbury's moral sensibility and refined sympathies: the novel wholly disclaims interiority. Discrimination and disinterestedness are located neither in bodily nature nor in culture and can be signified only as entirely performative, as pure style and "publicness."

Expression of strong feeling is not associated with sincerity in the narrative. Spencer and Darwin had linked passions with animality and dangerous instinctual forces. In *Our Mutual Friend,* emotions are expressed in close conjunction with bodily articulations. Passionate feelings are represented almost exclusively as predatory aggression, envy, or retaliation. When Wegg vents his barely controlled desire to harm Mr. Boffin, the narrator comments: "All this was quite familiar knowledge down in the depths of the slime, ages ago" (570). The Lammles express a similar venomous impulse of retaliation toward Veneering. The disgust that informs the narrative voice as it persistently points to the ugly bodily substance underlying the sumptuous surfaces of characters in the public sphere indicates the prevalence of an instinctive aggression as the dominant force propelling specula-tive activity. Yet despite the persistent identification of the national public sphere of politics and finance with the "dismal swamp" of predatory behavior,[19] it is the working-class poor that the narrative most frequently associates with the phys-ically repulsive imagery of primal slime and ooze — an otherness that obliterates visual distinctions and identity. Gaffer Hexam's boat is "allied to the bottom of the river rather than the surface, by reason of the slime and ooze with which it was covered"; the poor and often criminal population of Rotherhide is so much "accumulated scum of humanity," the "moral sewage" of the city; Riderhood's footsteps are "shapeless holes" in the "fast melting slush," lacking even the "fash-ion of humanity"; his common death with Headstone returns them both to "the

ooze and scum" of the riverbed (13, 30, 158, 781). Any ideal of national community held together by bonds of sympathy deriving from recognition of a common
human interiority is unthinkable from the perspective of such loathsome, shared
physical origins.

Headstone is held in a textual gaze compounded of an intense ambivalence of
compassion and repulsion. It is difficult to account adequately for the disturbing
power of the representation. In contrast to Wrayburn's openness of manner,
Headstone is represented as having "a suspicious manner, or a manner that would
be better described as one lying in wait" (218). Headstone's dark inwardness,
therefore, is constituted of self-interested designs and conjectures. In that sense,
even though he claims to be "in dreadful earnest" in his passionate declarations to
Lizzie, he is not, within the novel's system of values, perceived to be sincere.
Sincerity is identified in the text with a disembodied, aesthetic disinterestedness.
When Headstone meets with Lizzie to reveal the "whole case," he says "I love
you. What other men may mean when they use that expression, I cannot tell"
(389). In most novels, such moments constitute the supreme validation of "sincerity" as the interchange of intimate confidentiality. The only "depth" that
Headstone can reveal, however, is not interiority or sensibility; it is represented
as an unmediated physical force of desire that "overmasters" him and terrifies
and repels Lizzie (389). Headstone's words constantly fail him: only his body
language, the text implies, is eloquent of his primitive being.

Headstone continually asks to be judged not by his appearance but rather by
his certificates as proof of his higher worth. Yet narrative perspective insists on
positioning him within a cruel spotlight of visuality. In the passage representing
his interview with Wrayburn, the reader is forced to regard him as if within the
gaze of Wrayburn's semblance of dispassionate, aesthetic curiosity. A sense of
almost physical proximity is constituted by the intimate closeness with which
Headstone's involuntary bodily responses are noted: the pale quivering lips, the
clutching right hand, the starting perspiration, the stab of blood to the face, and
the shaking frame. In contrast, Wrayburn's appearance is unspecified throughout
the episode, apart from the reiterated stress upon his manner of aloof disdain and
repeated references to his delicate play with his cigar. What is evoked is a sense of
sexualized horror and fascination at the physicalness of the uncultured male
body. Despite the disavowal of all fleshliness in the representation of Wrayburn,
there are, as Eve Kosofsky Sedgwick suggests, intimations of sadomasochism in
this class interchange between the two men (*Between Men*, 162–63).[20]

The representation also suggests that a complex visual transaction takes place
between them. It is a transaction that symbolizes the shift of authority and legit-

imation from letters to visual testimony. Headstone wants to impose upon Wrayburn the substance of his personal worth as guaranteed by his certificated learning. Wrayburn dismissively responds to every attempt Headstone makes to impress his meaning with "Is that all?" (290). The import of Headstone's worth and words are imputed as nothing; only his appearance is subjected to a relentless, evaluating appraisal. Thus subjected to the categorizing order of visuality, Headstone himself becomes the horrified spectator of his self through the eyes of another. This is not a panopticon gaze constituting the inwardness of a confessional subject: only bodies confess. The disciplinary mechanism works in exactly the opposite direction: it denies subjectivity. Caught up in visuality, Headstone tries, like poor Mr. Snell, to lay claim to sensitivity as indicative of inner value and cultivation, but he appears to himself only as a wretched creature unable to command the vicissitudes of his body: " 'Oh, what a misfortune is mine,' cried Bradley, breaking off to wipe the starting perspiration from his face as he shook from head to foot, 'that I cannot so control myself as to appear a stronger creature than this, when a man who has not felt in all his life what I have felt in a day can so command himself!' "

Like his sweat, all that Headstone's passionate feeling conveys is his proximity to animal origins. In effecting the transaction of visual evaluation, Wrayburn reverses realist ordering that privileges signifieds over signifiers. While Headstone's worth is reduced to his physical bodily appearance, Wrayburn's style of replete calmness assumes the substance of power. It is the power of cultural capital to disavow encumbering or shaming bodily origins. One of the many strange things about this unnerving chapter is the way the writing simultaneously lays bare these mechanisms of exclusion and naturalizes them.

Jonathan Arac argues that *Our Mutual Friend* approaches modernist form in its fragmentation of plot and discontinuous narrative overview (164–85).[21] Dickens certainly appears to abandon most of the ideology of realism in his last completed novel: the language of subjectivity, sincerity, meaning, and truth is deprived of its anchoring authenticity in interiority. Within the literary realm of the fictional public sphere, popular forms of realist art are represented as peddling a sentimental and banal version of social existence, thereby normalizing a repressive regime of puritanical mediocrity. The code of manipulative sincerity is shown to construct a cultural fiction of mutual confidence and regard that hides from view subjectivities always on the look out, constituted by aggressive conjecture and speculative greed.

Within the world of the novel, there is a pervasive sense of meaning in crisis.

Characters obsessively ask each other and themselves what they mean. Speculation as a mode of social and individual existence is represented as precluding any fixed point of authenticity or origin. Most characters live beyond their means, speak what they do not mean, assume identities that belie intentionality. The language of the novel plays continually across the complicit slippage of "living beyond one's means" in terms of financial substance, "meaning to" as intentional interiority, and "meaning" as semantic truth. In its ramifying circles within circles of duplicity, the chapter entitled "Meaning Mischief" constitutes an almost surreal dislocation of any grounding of truth. Within the regime of commodified visuality that constitutes the fictional world of *Our Mutual Friend*, meaning appears to exist only at the surface level of signifiers. Truth and knowledge derive from performance and visuality, not from words, still less from depth or substance.

One of the most striking examples is of the Lammles's reflections in a mirror on the wall of their dining room. Their imaged faces in the glass express disdain and dislike, but in the nonmirror world they continue to talk quietly to each other "as if they, the principals, had had no part in that expressive transaction" (259). The reality of their relations appears externalized in the visual image. A similar displacement of substance by sign takes place when Mrs. Lammle shows Mr. Twemlow a book of portraits while confessing to him the money-speculation of marrying Georgiana Podsnap to Fledgby. Astounded and shocked by what he hears, Mr. Twemlow does not know what to believe. He looks distractedly from the portrait of Alfred Lammle in the book to the original in the room, but belief in what he has heard is confirmed as he continues to look at the portrait while the other guests take their leave (411). Bella asks her image in the looking glass, "What do you mean by this, you inconsistent little Beast?" (460). As with Eugene Wrayburn, no answer is forthcoming to the riddle of what self means. Indeed, echoing Wrayburn's "embodied conundrum," Bella's "inconsistent little Beast" encapsulates the nonrealist view of human identity put forward by the text: consciousness as riddle attached to a material bodily basis. Bella is taught to recognize the sordid nature of greed by the external theater of avarice performed by Mr. Boffin for her benefit. Signifiers, that have no substance in Mr. Boffin's actual generosity, convey to Bella the economic and personal reality of her ambitions, whereas her subjective soul-searching elicits only silence in place of the inner voice of conscience. Riah rejects Fledgby's misrepresentation of Jews when he perceives in externalized form how his compliance is used, "seeing the thing visibly presented as upon a theatre" (708). Knowledge, perceptions of reality, and evaluation in all these cases are shown to depend upon visuality.

Wrayburn is the character who is represented as most skeptically aware of the force of the visual and the predominance of signifiers over signifieds. For the chambers he shares with Lightwood, he purchases a complete range of kitchen commodities. These are not acquired for the substance of their use-value as tools of work but for their second order of signification: they are visual signifiers of those inner "vagaries" called moral virtues (281). This parodic and performative gesturing to the absence or vagary of any empirical substance behind signs is usually associated with a modernist and postmodernist perception of reality — with the consciousness produced by the world of late capitalism. Within this perspective, the only means of articulating sincerity is that practiced by the narrative and by Wrayburn: parody and skepticism.

The novel concludes with those who had constituted the heterogeneous public sphere at the beginning of the story dividing into two distinct groups. The Veneerings disappear in bankruptcy, but the public sphere of commodified visuality, manipulative sincerity, and popularized sentimentality, as perpetuated in coercive realist literary forms, has been shown to have the capacity to repeat its mediocrity endlessly. Lightwood and Wrayburn as members of the gentry grow weary of marketing their cultural capital to the vulgar materialism of this world. Their pose of cynical disaffection is exchanged for the distinctive fellowship offered by the small, select group who are accommodated in the palace of good taste furnished by the Harmon money. The materiality of waste is transformed into taste.[22] What this narrative structure intimates is a second reconfiguration of the public sphere that occurred in the actual world of the latter half of the nineteenth century. This reconfiguration constituted the public sphere as two distinct realms: the realm of popular mass culture and an aesthetic realm that perceived itself in terms of social and cultural distinction and discrimination.

Yet despite their mutually defining opposition, these two cultural realms shared from their inception a common basis in the materiality of money. This puts into sharp question any claims to radicalism made for the aesthetic realm of discrimination. The dominance of visuality was an inevitable consequence of the growth of speculative finance, as luxurious display became central to "capitalism's cost of representation." Increasingly, this cost of representation came to include the purchase of prestigious products of "high" art and patronage of the "high" culture industry. From the mid-nineteenth century onward, social evaluation by appearance and taste began to drive the financial speculation in "quality" goods. The result is the modern consumer-market demand for "fashion," design, and discrimination, which, by definition, must be always new. Popular culture is also wholly part of the capitalist enterprise. The general shift to embodied appearance as naturalizing site of social classification is profitably productive of continuous anxiety about looks and looking better (when did this suggestive meaning of the word *looks* come into play?), providing the motor force of much commodity circulation. The desire to "look good" and to be "good-looking" requires and constitutes the self as a disciplinary site of what old Harmon recognized as a "promising" (and always only promising) appearance. The cultural products of the popular public sphere, especially the visual media of television, cinema, and magazines, sustain that system of classified identities and classifying commodities as well as actively producing and expanding the ideology of visuality. The ideal, endlessly varied and perpetuated, of the charismatic body as vessel of grace functions to naturalize inequality. The mechanisms of narcissistic identification with specular ideals produce subjects who emulate, rather than criticize, privileged lifestyles. In this marketed desire for the charismatic body, the real physical body and its material needs are disavowed. The sweat of labor and the disfigurements of hunger, poverty, and its diseases disappear under the dazzling face of commodities, rather as Darwin saw that the bright surface of the natural world distracted attention from the destructive underside.

The performative code of sincerity remains all-forceful as an ideological value within the culture and politics of the popular realm. Manipulative sincerity, with its interpellative insinuation of shared confidence and mutual regard, is especially powerful when directed by the charismatic personality at the ordinary masses; it seems, in its offer of intimacy, to bridge the distance between desiring self and the narcissistic ideal. Cultural commodities within the popular realm tend to adhere to forms of romance and realism that perpetuate a notion of sincerity based upon interiority and the uniqueness of individual feelings. In the realm of discrimination, sincerity does not really disappear. It is reconfigured as skepticism, irony, and cynicism. As such, it retains its interpellative effectiveness, projecting a knowing invitation to the shared sensibility of intellectual superiority and distinctive taste, disdaining or aestheticizing popular culture and the realist forms of truth entertained by the masses. Fear of proximity and loss of identity in a proliferating, engulfing sameness have been deflected by belief in the charismatic gift of inherent aesthetic disinterestedness.

Conclusion

This study has aimed to map what Mary Poovey calls "a process of forming": the collective, ongoing work of imagining society as an inclusive formation rather than one structured by naturalized divisions and hierarchies (*Making a Social Body*, 1). While I have attempted to look at a reasonably wide range of nonfictional writing that envisions, in various ways, the problems of and possible solutions to the contentious issue of social inclusiveness, my primary focus has been upon literary fiction. If the general outlines of change that I suggest here have reference beyond the texts I discuss, then doubtless there would be other means of mapping the transformations I locate around leadership, the interpersonal discourse of the public sphere, and the inscription of social distinctions upon bodies. One gain of my approach, unexpected when I began exploring this topic, has been to perceive the novels in this study as forming an impressive and coherent body of political fiction that has not previously been critically recognized. The six novels I discuss explore issues of political leadership within mass culture, the shifting locations of power, the obligations and potential of citizenship and community, and the discursive and visual mechanisms of social inclusion and exclusion. They do so often consciously, always intelligently, and at times with prescient imaginative insight into future developments.

Signifying practices always exceed their own explicit intentions and limits. Clearly, no writer fully comprehends the range of meanings inherent in narrative language and structures, but to understand the fiction in this study as wholly determined by and complicit with disciplinary strategies and dominant ideologies would seem to me a massive act of condescension. Brontë, Thackeray, Dickens, Gaskell, and Eliot deliberately directed their voices to the contested public sphere, helping to shape, and in turn receiving the impress of, the conflicting interests struggling for dominance in that discursive space. Doubtless, as participants in this multivoiced, dialogic activity, their writing became saturated with more voices and perspectives than they always quite recognized.

Read together, these novels tell a remarkable story of the social transformations of the two decades from the mid-1840s to the mid-1860s. It is a story articulated through a range of novelistic structures, and it is also a story in which novels are active participants in a variety of ways. At the level of realist or mimetic representation, contemporary readers of *Shirley* and *Henry Esmond* would encounter fictional worlds structured, like their own, by social exclusions, whose characters also understand reality as divided and conflictual. Unlike the world of Jane Austen's fiction, in which most social exclusions are barely visible, these divisions are represented by Brontë and Thackeray as urgent problems needing attention and resolution. *North and South* and *Bleak House* are both structured, although quite differently, upon the meeting of previously divided social worlds. *Romola* and *Our Mutual Friend* represent a social reality that is fully heterogeneous, with public spheres open to all sections of the nation or state.

These fictional worlds are represented as in process of forming: narrative transformations in each text figuratively stage significant transitions from one kind of social and political reality to another, differently structured, one. These structural transformations largely center upon the public sphere of the represented world of the story. The bildungsroman structure of *Henry Esmond* maps the transition of status and influence from the traditional locations of power in the court, the church, and the military to the public sphere of letters. *North and South* is structured upon the decline of the public sphere of civil society and its replacement by a heterogeneous public forum of all the nation's voices. In *Romola*, the public sphere is many-voiced, and the shift here is mediated by the representation of public opinion as a negative force. This new conception of power is imagined as producing a transformation in popular leadership, figured in the substitution of Tito for Savonarola. In *Our Mutual Friend*, the narrative stages the division of a national public sphere into a realm of distinction and a popular realm. These transformations of the public sphere, tracked in the narratives, from civility to inclusiveness to division, also figure the loss of authority of the written word in a commodified culture increasingly dominated by manipulative publicness and visuality. *Our Mutual Friend* represents a culture entirely determined by speculative activity.

In *Henry Esmond, Bleak House, North and South*, and *Our Mutual Friend*, characters representative of the gentry class are represented taking central roles in the public sphere and in the public domain of the state. This provides a suggestive illustration of the way fictional texts can keep in sight aspects of social reality that get lost in history. Until very recently, historiography has tended to submerge the gentry in the more amorphous term *middle class* in a way that has effaced their distinctive identity and values. The novels suggest that their particular role within the transformations of the public sphere and in the formation of a culture industry would be worth investigation.

The novels and the novelists have also an extrinsic relationship to the public sphere. In *Shirley* and *Henry Esmond*, the narrative voice aligns itself with intrinsic thematic advocacy of sincerity as an interpellative code of community, based upon recognition of difference within sameness: the differing individual interests and perspectives of an interiority shared by all as a defining aspect of humanness. Yet the narrative voices also speak within the actual nonfictional public sphere and thereby contribute to the popularization of the code of sincerity as discursive mode of an inclusive society, replacing the class-specific urbanity of the code of civility. A review of Thackeray's published lectures, *The English Humourists*, indicates the essential force of a stylistic performance of sincerity. The reviewer clearly disapproves of Thackeray's disrespectful attitude, but admits that "the style is so captivating, so *insinuating* in its deceiving plainness."[1] This also indicates the influential public personae adopted by writers like Carlyle, Thackeray, and Dickens and the unstable boundaries between their voices as letter writers, lecturers, speech makers, journalists, essayists, and novelists in the public sphere. In addition to voice, *North and South* and *Romola*, especially, structure their narratives in the form of debates that address the same issues that were currently being contested in the national public sphere during the 1850s and 1860s. In this way, these texts explicitly offer themselves in the traditional role of novels in the public sphere: to stimulate rational critique. *Romola* in particular is a paradigm of this intellectual function of literature in its rigorous and detailed challenge to the political writing of John Stuart Mill. Paradoxically, part of that challenge is to dismiss the possibility of informed, collective critique. In *Our Mutual Friend* the rejection of the tenets of realism and a shift toward a foregrounding of signifiers over signifieds and to parodic representation marks the beginnings of a stylistic removal of literary writing from an inclusive public sphere to an aesthetic realm divided from the popular.

By means of narrative voice and thematic structures, the novels in this study can be seen as complicit with the ideological popularization of a code of sincerity as an interpersonal communicative mode. At the same time, they conjointly constitute a sustained, many-angled critique of the decidedly non-utopian functioning of public sincerity. They also indicate a further ideological transformation in the perceived location of sincerity from interiority, as an attribute of human kind generally, to sensibility, as the distinctive capacity of a finely evolved humanness. In *Shirley, Henry Esmond*, and *North and South*, an interpersonal code of sincerity is put forward as an imagined solution to the divisive conflicts of class and gender. In *North and South*, though, in the charismatic persons of the three main protagonists, Gaskell suggests there is an easy, less utopian transition from sincerity, as an interpellative code based upon a mutual recognition of differing personal interiorities, to a mode of manipulative publicness. In *Romola*, Mill's ideal of interpersonal sincerity as the basis of community is rejected. Sincerity, as understood by Eliot, becomes the lonely heroism of a rarefied individual sensibility, struggling to attain a truth purified of narcissistic self-interest. The egoistic immediacy of desires that constitute the public sphere facilitates a popularly acclaimed leadership of duplicitous, manipulative sincerity. In *Our Mutual Friend*, manipulative sincerity is shown to constitute the public discourse of politics, but also, and more sinisterly, it is closely linked to the psychology necessary for a culture dominated by speculative finance. Its opposition is represented as aesthetic sincerity — a performance of self that disavows hidden meaning located in an interiority. Eliot's and Dickens's perceptions of sincerity derive from starkly different evaluations of sensibility, but both associate "genuine" sincerity, as opposed to duplicitous sincerity, with an imaginary spaciousness and freedom that escapes the crowding and engulfing embodied mass. Nevertheless, I have argued, despite the reconfiguring, sincerity retains its manipulative or insinuating force as an interpellative code proffering an invitation to community. The significant difference is that this is an invitation into an election of the distinctive few as opposed to the anonymous aggregate.

During the nineteenth century, the revisioning of leadership, to meet the demands of an inclusive social formation, and the consequent reimagining of power was relocated in the public sphere of representation. In most of the novels

I discuss, this shift of leadership into the public arena is associated with the insinuating or manipulative utility of the code of sincerity. The import of leadership in democracies has been a neglected object of investigation, but it is of central concern to all the novels in this study and a recurrent theme in journalism and political writing of the period. The term *revisioning* is deliberately chosen to draw attention to the way in which most of the texts recognize visual force as an essential component of acclaimed leadership. In *Shirley*, there is an exploration of the problem that came into visibility in the 1840s: what ethos of domestic leadership could replace the aristocratic military hero of the sword? Subsequent novels locate leadership in the public sphere and, like Hazlitt, foreground it as a problem of representation. *Shirley, Henry Esmond, North and South*, taking a cue from Carlyle, all suggest that a domestic charisma can be fashioned by a projection of sincerity. Unlike Carlyle, they all explore various contradictions inherent to the functioning of sincerity as a public performance and sincerity as transparent interiority. The imaginative association of leadership with power entails that charismatic popular leaders can rarely afford the luxury of confessional sincerity. In inclusive societies, legitimacy is formally vested in the people. The complex narcissistic transaction of power from the many to the one demands a projection of replete humanness that reflects back a promised plenitude of the ordinary upon the mass of the population. As in Eliot's representation of Tito's substitution of popular leadership for that of Savonarola, this deflection of power back as a gift onto those who confer it is most easily achieved by means of manipulative sincerity.

The first four texts discussed all structure their narratives upon a shift of visible power from a landed aristocratic class. They also explore a general fascination with and attraction to power as the spectacle of might with the capacity to conquer and dominate. With the establishment of a bureaucratic state, the visible publicness of authority and power traditionally associated with an aristocratic class was displaced. Power as intervention in the lives of most of the population became invisible. *Bleak House* uniquely suggests that this vacuum tends to be filled by a new imagining of power as an omnipotence even more mighty in its omnipresent invisibility.

Novels are relentlessly concerned with the visual, but this is rarely just in the interest of mimetic representation. Nineteenth-century novels undoubtedly helped propagate the ideology that bodies and appearances provide testimony of interior values. Yet, against this, they also testify to the intense power of what Brontë calls the "desire of the eye." In this sense, they were illustrating Darwin's notion of natural selection before it was published. In *Shirley, Henry Esmond, Romola,* and *Our Mutual Friend,* sexual desire is recognized explicitly as an intense visual impulse of attraction. Yet beyond this, these texts indicate that visual appearance also mediates a much wider range of interpersonal relationships. *Shirley* links the "desire of the eye" to structuring inequalities of class, gender, and age; in *Henry Esmond* and *Romola,* popularity and trust are shown to be generated by charming appearance. In *Our Mutual Friend,* sympathy and compassion, it is suggested, are more readily extended to deprivation and want that is pleasing to the eye: "Why ain't you ugly?" Miss Potterson complains to Lizzie Hexham, when she feels constrained to befriend her. *North and South,* as well as *Our Mutual Friend,* points to the mass commodification of "taste" as furthering this domination of the visual as a system of personal and social categorization. In this context, bodies, rather than interiority, become confessional, disciplined into testimony of hygienic grace or, as Dickens represents Bradley Headstone, encumbered with a repellent physicality.

The language of *Shirley* testifies, at the level of subtext, to a powerful general yearning to belong: a desire for community. This utopian impulse is shared by all six novels. In *Shirley, Henry Esmond,* and *North and South,* communities existing across the traditional divides of class and gender are brought into existence through the mediation of interpersonal sincerity as confidence and trust. In addition, in *North and South* and particularly in *Bleak House,* differing practices of knowledge, based in experiential interests and perspectives, are conceived as an oppositional way of understanding an inclusive society in place of the totalizing rationality of aggregation. Perhaps most radically of all, the conservative text of *Romola* explores the imaginative potential of a nonsacrificial foundation of community. An understanding of maternity as comprehending sameness and difference within unity, an intuition close to Eliot's ideal of knowledge, allows for the configuration of a social order founded upon tolerance and tenderness. I have argued that the retreat to aesthetic spaciousness at the conclusion of *Our Mutual Friend* is largely a negative response that stems from Dickens's horrified Darwinian perception of rapacious consumerism and avaricious speculation as manifestations of a primal competitive instinct for survival. Yet the utopian community — comprising a former dustman and his wife with an instinct for fashion, a dolls' dressmaker, a skilled carpenter, and a seamstress, headed by those endowed with cultural as well as financial capital — materializes in fictional form the aspirations of John Ruskin and William Morris for a creative regeneration of culture through the mediation of a classless fellowship of arts and crafts. In *Our Mutual*

Friend, the debilitating condescension directed toward Sloppy, and even Jenny Wren, as well as the loss of imaginative power of the writing at the conclusion of the story are indicative of the disassociation of the utopian ideal from the experiential perspectives of those who are meant to be its main cultural beneficiaries. What remains striking and impressive, though, is that even in this most horrified and repelled imagining of the pushing and striving heterogeneity that constitutes the mass societies of mature capitalism, there remains the same need to articulate community as belonging — the yearning that Brontë expressed in *Shirley*. It is this need that a manipulative use of the code of sincerity exploits as a means of insinuating confidence and trust in politics, social relations, and financial speculation. Nevertheless, these narratives suggest it is also the felt absence of social connection that energizes the imaginative quest for inclusiveness as a new, progressive way of ordering human existence.

Notes

ONE: Imagining Inclusive Society, 1846–1867

1. See also François Bédarida, *A Social History of England, 1851–1990* (London, 1991), who insists: "We must now once and for all refute . . . the cleverly fostered legend of a bourgeois England in 1832 usurping the position of the old aristocratic England" (41); Dror Wahrman, *Imagining the Middle Class: The Political Representation of Class, c. 1780–1840* (Cambridge, UK, 1995) also challenges the myth that the bourgeoisie usurped power in 1832.

2. Mary Poovey, *Uneven Developments: The Ideological Work of Gender in Mid-Victorian England* (Chicago, 1988), *Making a Social Body: British Cultural Formation, 1830–1864* (Chicago, 1995), and *A History of the Modern Fact: Problems of Knowledge in the Sciences of Wealth and Society* (Chicago, 1998); Catherine Gallagher, *The Industrial Reformation of English Fiction* (Chicago, 1985); Nancy Armstrong, *Desire and Domestic Fiction: A Political History of the Novel* (Oxford, UK, 1987), *Fiction in the Age of Photography* (Cambridge, MA, 1999).

3. Mary Poovey, *The Proper Lady and the Woman Writer: Ideology as Style in the Works of Mary Wollstonecraft, Mary Shelley, and Jane Austen* (Chicago, 1984) and Nancy Armstrong, *Desire and Domestic Fiction* were the groundbreaking initiators of this tradition. Also highly influential in consolidating the notion of separate spheres has been Leonore Davidoff and Catherine Hall, *Family Fortunes: Men and Women of the English Middle Class, 1780–1850* (London, 1987).

4. Mark Bevir, "The Long Nineteenth Century in Intellectual History," *Journal of Victorian Culture* 6, no. 2 (2001) provides a very helpful overview of this revisionist way of seeing continuities across traditional century divisions, 313–35.

5. Jürgen Habermas, *The Philosophical Discourse of Modernity: Twelve Lectures*, trans. Frederick Lawrence (Oxford, 1987) contains Habermas's main critique of the Frankfurt School and his own conception of the possibility of communicative reason.

6. Leo Braudy, *The Frenzy of Renown: Fame and Its History* (Oxford, UK, 1986), 434, cited in P. David Marshall, *Celebrity and Power: Fame in Contemporary Culture* (Minneapolis, 1997), 7.

7. Peter Mandler, *Aristocratic Government in the Age of Reform: Whigs and Liberals, 1830–1852* (Oxford, UK, 1990), argues convincingly that after 1832 the aristocratic grandees of the Whig party made a successful bid for national leadership in terms that combined popularism with aristocratic glamour and theatricality.

8. See, for example, Joan Landes, *Women and the Public Sphere in the Age of the French Revolution* (Ithaca, NY, 1988); Mary P. Ryan, "Gender and Public Access: Women's Politics

in Nineteenth-Century America," in *Habermas and the Public Sphere*, 259–88; Amanda Vickery, *The Gentleman's Daughter: Women's Lives in Georgian England* (New Haven, CN, 1998), and Amanda Vickery, ed., *Women, Privilege, and Power: British Politics, 1750 to the Present* (Stanford, CA, 2001); Geoff Eley, "Nations, Publics, and Political Cultures: Placing Habermas in the Nineteenth Century," in *Habermas and the Public Sphere*, 289–339; Nicholas Rogers, *Crowds, Culture, and Politics in Georgian Britain* (Oxford, UK, 1998).

9. Leon Guilhamet, *The Sincere Ideal: Studies on Sincerity in Eighteenth-Century English Literature* (Montreal, 1974), provides a scholarly summary of the development of an ideal of sincerity from sixteenth- and seventeenth-century puritan concern with the sincerity of individual religious conviction. He argues that while sincerity became important as a poetic theme in the eighteenth century and as a virtue in Richardson's fiction, there is little explicit concern with the idea in public critical discourse (4, 297). See also David Perkins, *Wordsworth and the Poetry of Sincerity* (Cambridge, MA, 1964).

TWO: Producing Inclusive Society, 1846–1867

1. W. Eyton Tooke, "Third Emigration Report," *Westminster Review* 9 (1828): 117.

2. William Ellis, "State of the Nation: Neglect of Industrial Science," *Westminster Review* 52 (1849): 92.

3. See, for example, Helen Rogers, *Women and the People: Authority, Authorship, and the English Radical Tradition* (London, 2000); Kathryn Gleadle, *The Early Feminists: Radical Unitarians and the Emergence of the Women's Rights Movement, 1831–51* (Houndmills, Basingstoke, UK, 1995).

4. William Henry Smith, "Voltaire at the Crystal Palace," *Blackwood's Magazine* 70 (1851): 145.

5. William Ellis, "State of the Nation: Neglect of Industrial Science," *Westminster Review* 52 (1849): 95.

6. Margaret Homans, "Victoria's Sovereign Obedience: Portraits of the Queen as Wife and Mother," in Carol T. Christ and John O. Jordan, eds., *Victorian Literature and the Victorian Visual Imagination* (Berkeley, CA, 1995), discusses the double role required of nineteenth-century monarchy. She argues that Victoria consciously transformed monarchy into a "spectacle of royal domestic privacy," 171.

7. *Times*, 15 Sept. 1852, 4.

8. *Times*, 16 Sept. 1852, 4.

9. G. H. Francis, *Orators of the Age, Comprising Portraits, Critical, Biographical, and Descriptive* (London, 1847), 69, 73. Significantly, Sir Robert Peel is presumed "insincere" due to his need, coming from nonpatrician origins, to court popular support (26–27).

10. Alexander Bain, "Cromwell's Letters and Speeches," *Westminster Review* 46 (1847): 473.

11. *Parliamentary Papers* (1868), 28, *Report of the Schools Inquiry Commission* 1:17–18.

12. *Christian Observer*, 1842, 588.

13. Frederick Meyrick, "Popular Education—the New Code," *Quarterly Review* 111 (1862): 111.

THREE: *Shirley*

1. See, for example, W. E. Hickson, "The French Republic," *Westminster Review* 50 (1848): 90; W. E. Hickson, "Lessons of Revolution," *Westminster Review* 50 (1849): 516;

W. E. Ayton, "Review of *Essays: Political, Historical, & Miscellaneous* by Archibald Alison," *Blackwood's Edinburgh Magazine* 68 (1850): 605–21; George Croly, "The Times of George II," *Blackwood's Edinburgh Magazine* 62 (1847): 444; T. B. Macauley, "Review of *The Life of Joseph Addison* by Lucy Aikin," *Edinburgh Review* (July 1843): 193–260.

2. W. E. Hickson, "Address to the Queen," *Westminster Review* 49 (1848): 486.

3. Ayton, "Review of Essays by Alison," 607.

4. "Ministerial Crisis," unattributed, *Westminster Review* 55 (1851): 204.

5. John Wade, "The Session of 1849," *Westminster Review* 52 (1850): 479.

6. "Ministerial Crisis," 205–6.

7. *Times*, 15 Sept. 1852, 4.

8. See, for example, *Times*, 11 Apr. 1848, 4; 22 Apr. 1848, 4.

9. W. E. Hickson, "Of February 1848," *Westminster Review* 49 (1848): 195.

10. Ann Monsarrat, *The Uneasy Victorian: Thackeray the Man, 1811–1863* (London, 1980) describes the novel as "a brilliant piece of historical reconstruction" (179); K. C. Phillips, *The Language of Thackeray* (London, 1978) claims that Thackeray's use of eighteenth-century style is "subtle," "serious," and "sustained" (149); in contrast, Catherine Peters, *Thackeray's Universe: Shifting Worlds of Imagination and Reality* (London, 1987) sees the novel as damaged by "the suffocating blanket of Victorian respectability" (201); Donald Hawes, in his introduction to the Oxford edition (1991), also points to an "early Victorian ethos" (ix).

11. Albany Fonblanque, unsigned review, *Examiner*, 3 Nov. 1849, 692–94, reprinted in Mirriam Allott, *The Brontës: The Critical Heritage* (London, 1995), 129; Eugene Forcade, from an article in *Revue des deux mondes*, 15 Nov. 1849, vol. 4, 714–35, reprinted in Allott, 144.

12. Unsigned review, *Spectator*, 3 Nov. 1849, 1043–45, reprinted in Miriam Allott, *The Brontës: The Critical Heritage*, 130; unsigned review, *Atlas*, 3 Nov. 1849, 696–97, reprinted ibid., 121.

13. Terry Eagleton, *Myths of Power: A Marxist Study of the Brontës*, 2nd ed. (Houndmills, Basingstoke, UK, 1988), argues persuasively that the text is concerned "to protect conservative pieties against . . . Whiggism," 52; Nancy Armstrong, *Desire and Domestic Fiction: A Political History of the Novel* (Oxford, UK, 1987), provides a powerful reading of the domestic plot of *Shirley* as functioning to underpin bourgeois hegemony, 213–24.

14. Asa Briggs, "Private and Social Themes in *Shirley*," *Brontë Society Transactions*, 1959, discusses the novel's historical accuracy of detail, 203–19.

15. "Occupations of the People," unattributed, *Westminster Review* 48 (1848): 395–96.

16. H. Longueville Jones, "Feudalism in the Nineteenth Century," *Blackwood's Edinburgh Magazine* 65 (1849): 715. The association of virile leadership with patriotism and empire predates the nineteenth century. For a discussion of this traditional linkage in the eighteenth century, see Kathleen Wilson, *The Sense of the People: Politics, Culture, and Imperialism in England, 1715–1785* (Cambridge, UK, 1995), 185–205.

17. Archibald Alison, "Eugene, Marlborough, Napoleon, and Wellington," *Blackwood's Edinburgh Magazine* 61 (1847): 48.

18. Terry Eagleton, *Myths of Power*, 45–49; also critical of Brontë's class sympathies are Rosemarie Bodenheimer, *The Politics of Story in Victorian Social Fiction* (Ithaca, NY, 1988), 43–47; Penny Boumelha, *Charlotte Bronte* (London, 1990), 93–99.

19. Alexander Bain, "Review of *Oliver Cromwell's Letters and Speeches*, Second Edition, by Thomas Carlyle," *Westminster Review* 46 (1847): 433.

20. Elliot Vanskike, "Consistent Inconsistencies: The Transvestite Actress Madame

Vestris and Charlotte Brontë's *Shirley*," *Nineteenth-Century Literature* 50 (1996), 464–88, offers a detailed account of negative criticism of the capitulation of the protagonist, Shirley, to Louis Moore; Vanskike argues that this criticism fails to recognize that Brontë's representation is satirical.

21. Unsigned review, *Fraser's Magazine* 11 (Dec. 1849): 691–94, reprinted in Allott, 155. Recent critics who have stressed the importance of Yorkshire in the story include Tim Dolan, "Fictional Territory and a Woman's Place: Regional and Sexual Difference in *Shirley*," *ELH* 62 (1995), 197–215, and Susan Belasco Smith, " 'A Yorkshire Burr': Language in *Shirley*," *Studies in English Literature, 1500–1900* 27 (1987): 637–45, Dolan discusses the novel in terms of a woman writer's affirmation of a radicalizing provincial perspective. Belasco gives Hiram Yorke a prominent position in the novel's regional and class politics, but strangely ignores his republicanism.

22. Rose Yorke expresses this ambition (399); Robert and Louis Moore have similar plans (538).

23. I am aware that my reading of the narrative voice of *Shirley* as a projection of "sincerity" cuts across some of the most perceptive and groundbreaking feminist studies of Brontë's fiction, most notably Eve Sedgwick's classic essay "Immediacy, Doubleness, and the Unspeakable: *Wuthering Heights* and *Villette*," where she points out the "gratuitousness" of the narrator's deception of the reader in *Villette* (London, 1988), 97–133. No reader could subsequently ignore the artful duplicities of the female narrative voice in that text. On the contrary, I think it is illuminating to connect that switch to a more personal woman's voice, as it articulates a need for circumspection and veiling, to the rebuff Brontë received from the public sphere following the publication of the earlier, more politically ambitious *Shirley*.

FOUR: *The History of Henry Esmond, Esq.*

1. J. A. Roebuck, "Organic Reform," *Westminster Review* 55 (1851): 476–77.

2. Henri-A. Talon, "Time and Memory in Thackeray's *Henry Esmond*," in *Review of English Studies* 13 (1962): 147–56, compares *Henry Esmond* with *Le Temps Retrouve*, 152; George Levine, *The Realistic Imagination: English Fiction from Frankenstein to Lady Chatterley* (Chicago, 1981) also argues convincingly that Thackeray's fiction generally provides strong evidence that mid-Victorian novels contain "elements of a fragmentary, unstable, and self-conscious art" (140).

3. See also John Loofbourow, *Thackeray and the Form of Fiction* (Princeton, NJ, 1964), who sees the novel as combining history, biography, and epic, 107; Catherine Peters, *Thackeray's Universe: Shifting Worlds of Imagination and Reality* (London, 1987) sees the book as unbalanced by Thackeray's unmediated emotions for Jane Brookfield.

4. Thackeray drew extensively on the writing of Thomas Babington Macauley (1800–59) while researching for *Henry Esmond*. The first two volumes of *History of England*, giving an account of the end of the Stuart dynasty, were published in 1849; in particular, chapter 10 of vol. 2 magisterially sums up the lasting political benefits to the nation of the Act of Settlement. In addition, Thackeray read and used Macauley's review of *The Life of Joseph Addison* by Lucy Aikin that appeared in the *Edinburgh Review* (July 1843): 193–260. The review draws attention to the many parallels between the eras of the Hanoverian succession and the Reform Bill of 1832.

5. For an account of the political struggles over Roman Catholic emancipation, see R. K. Webb, *Modern England: From the Eighteenth Century to the Present* (London, 1969), 187–

90; Robert Blake, *Disraeli* (London, 1966) provides a full political context to the Corn Law debates.

6. In *The Four Georges*, Thackeray makes a devastating contrast between George Washington and George IV (7:709). However, after his second reading tour of America, Thackeray was less impressed with the country and its culture of "rabble supremacy"; see Ray, *Thackeray: The Age of Wisdom*, 264.

7. As the reference above to "rabble" indicates, Thackeray was an ambivalent advocate of inclusivity. In this he is typical of the 1840s: utopian in vision, but in practice finding popularism alarming and often offensive. When Thackeray's *Punch* series *The Snobs of England* was first brought out in book form, he subtitled it *By One of Themselves;* in his editor's introduction to *The Book of Snobs*, John Sutherland gives an account of the accusations of snobbery leveled at Thackeray by his contemporaries (13–18).

8. See *Book of Snobs*, 221 n. 1; Deborah A. Thomas, *Thackeray and Slavery* (Athens, OH, 1993), 76–78.

9. For other moments when Henry Esmond recognizes hypocrisy, see 30, 41, 119.

10. John E. Tilford Jr. gives an account of contemporary and critical reception of "The 'Unsavoury Plot' of *Henry Esmond*" in *Nineteenth-Century Fiction* 6 (1951): 121–30.

11. In this respect, it is interesting that in both *Henry Esmond* and *The English Humourists*, Thackeray claims that Addison's sincere impartiality, his lack of all party interest, is the basis of his genius and derives from Addison's self-sufficiency — the absence of narrow personal desires and ambitions; see *Henry Esmond*, 258–59, *The English Humourists*, 472–73.

FIVE: *Bleak House*

1. F. M. L. Thompson, *English Landed Society in the Nineteenth Century* notes that the gentry were "less favourably placed than the aristocracy in the struggle for economic survival" (23).

2. For detailed discussions of the complex social interrelations of the gentry and upper classes, see Lewis Namier, *The Structure of Politics at the Accession of George III*, 2nd ed. (Houndmills, Basingstoke, UK, 1957), 1–61; F. M. L. Thompson, *English Landed Society in the Nineteenth Century* (London, 1963), 1–25; Paul Langford, *Public Life and the Propertied Englishman, 1689–1798* (Oxford, UK, 1991), 1–58.

3. Essays in *Blackwood's Edinburgh Magazine* during the second half of the 1840s and into the early 1850s return continually to this theme; see, for example, Archibald Alison, "How to Disarm the Chartists," 63 (1848): 653–73; H. Longueville Jones, "Feudalism in the Nineteenth Century," 65 (1849): 713–26; J. S. Hogan, "Civil Revolution in the Canadas," 67 (1850): 249–68.

4. "Ministerial Crisis," unattributed, *Westminster Review* 55 (1851): 199.

5. See, for example, *Times*, 1 May 1848, 4; *Christian Observer*, 1848, 15; *Westminster Review* 49 (1848): 137.

6. W. E. Hickson, "Review of Works on the French Revolution," *Westminster Review* 49 (1848): 137.

7. On 11 Apr. 1948, the *Times*, for example, conceded that the six points of the charter were "honest and allowable doctrines" and admitted that "the main body of the Chartists [were not] compromised" by the violence of a minority; see also leading articles in the *Times*, 22 Apr. 1848, 2 June 1848.

8. Harriet Martineau, "The Crystal Palace," *Westminster Review*, n.s. 6 (1854): 534.

9. Typical of this pervasive discourse is a leading article in the *Times*, 27 Jan. 1848, on the rapid increase of pauperism in London: "The great thoroughfares 'are alive' with beggars"; William Ellis, "Relief Measures," *Westminster Review* 53 (1850), in a lengthy response to the "terror" of cholera, claims that "every tenth person among us is a pauper," so that in the midst of "the surrounding civilization" are dwellings and habits of life "such as to cause the humane to shudder and the timid to tremble" (145).

10. See Eileen Janes Yeo, "The Professional Ideal and Community Service," *The Contest for Social Science: Relations and Representations of Gender and Class* (London, 1996), 102–8. I am indebted to the scholarly detail offered in this work. See also P. Corrigan and D. Sayer, *The Great Arch: State Formation as Cultural Revolution* (Houndmills, Basingstoke, UK, 1985), 114–65, for discussion of the coming into being of the state as machinery of government.

11. Yeo discusses the claims put forward by women as justification for their increasing role in the social domain of the state (120–47).

12. *Christian Observer*, 1849, 82.

13. Sydney Turner, "Review of Works on Prison and Juvenile Delinquency," *Edinburgh Review* 94 (1851): 404–5.

14. W. E. Hickson, "The French Republic," *Westminster Review* 50 (1848): 191.

15. D. A. Miller, *The Novel and the Police* (Berkeley, CA, 1988) provides a powerful reading of the novel in which he assimilates Chancery in this way to a pervasive carceral regime (64). Other Foucauldian approaches to the novel include Martin A. Danahay, "Housekeeping and Hegemony in *Bleak House*," *Studies in the Novel* 23 (1991): 416–31; Jasmine Yong Hall, "What's Troubling Esther? Narrating, Policing and Resisting Arrest in *Bleak House*," *Dickens Studies Annual* 22 (1993): 171–94; Laura Fasick, "Dickens and the Diseased Body in *Bleak House*," *Dickens Studies Annual* 24 (1996): 135–51. Kathleen Blake, "*Bleak House*, Political Economy, Victorian Studies," *Victorian Literature and Culture* 25 (1997) usefully argues for the need to distinguish historical Benthamism from Foucault's construction of a panopticon state, 1–21.

16. J. A. Roebuck, "Organic Reform," *Westminster Review* 55 (1851) compared Lord John Russell to a gamester: "Playing as he does with the fortunes of the state, he is like a gambler with another man's money. . . . To him it appears a part of the necessary and natural order of things that certain great families should supply ministers of state" (487).

17. *Times*, 17 May 1848.

18. Yeo, *Contest for Social Science*, makes a similar point about Edwin Chadwick, 78, 94.

19. John Chapman, "The Civil Service," *Westminster Review*, n.s. 6 (1854): 89.

20. By 21 Jan. 1852, Dickens was writing critically to Henry Austen about Chadwick's obsessive "harking" on unimportant matters: *The Letters of Charles Dickens*, Pilgrim ed. (Oxford, UK, 1965–2002), 21 Jan. 1852.

21. It seems less than coincidental that George Eliot, in *Romola*, figures a rather similar insight, using the character Baldassarre to represent just such a desire to imagine power as omnipresent and irrevocable.

SIX: *North and South*

1. Early criticism followed Louis Cazamian, *The Social Novel in England, 1830–1850: Dickens, Disraeli, Mrs Gaskell, Kingsley*, trans. Martin Fido (London, 1973) in focusing upon *North and South* as a social-problem novel in which Gaskell is unable to engage wholly with the more radical insights of her story. Critics who argue for this view include Raymond

Williams, *Culture and Society, 1780–1950* (London, 1958); Coral Landsbury, *Elizabeth Gaskell: The Novel of Social Crisis* (New York, 1975); John Lucas, *The Literature of Change: Studies in the Nineteenth-Century Provincial Novel* (New York, 1980); Joseph Kestner, *Protest and Reform: The British Social Narrative by Women, 1827–1857* (Madison, WI, 1985); Sally Minogue, "Gender and Class in *Villette* and *North and South,*" in *Problems for Feminist Criticism,* ed. Sally Minogue (London, 1990).

2. Patricia Ingham, *The Language of Gender and Class: Transformation in the Victorian Novel* (London, 1996) also claims that the class and gender politics of the text are more radical than those of *Shirley.* For other readings of the novel that discuss the heroine's positioning within the public and private spheres, see: Hilary Schor, *Scheherezade in the Market Place: Elizabeth Gaskell and the Victorian Novel* (Oxford, UK, 1992), Dorice Williams Elliott, "The Female Visitor and the Marriage of Classes in Gaskell's *North and South,*" *Nineteenth-Century Literature* 49 (1994): 21–49.

3. Harriet Martineau, "The Crystal Palace," *Westminster Review,* n.s. 6 (1854): 541.

4. Alan Kidd and David Nicholls, eds., *Gender, Civic Culture, and Consumerism: Middle-Class Identity in Britain, 1800–1940* (Manchester, UK, 1999), contains useful essays on the spread of commodified culture to the provincial cities of Britain.

5. John Eagles, "The Fine Arts and the Public Taste in 1853," *Blackwood's Magazine* 74 (1853): 90–91.

6. W. E. Aytoun, "Minor Morals," *Blackwood's Magazine* 73 (1853): 753.

7. Herbert Spencer, "Manners and Fashion," *Westminster Review,* n.s. 5 (1854): 387.

8. James Hannay, "Pedigree and Heraldry," *Westminster Review,* n.s. 4 (1853): 111.

9. W. Lucas Collins, "A Few More Words on University Reform," *Blackwood's Magazine* 74 (1853): 583.

10. John Chapman, "The Civil Service," *Westminster Review* n.s. 6 (1854): 79.

11. A. C. Tait, "Government Education Measures for Poor and Rich," *Edinburgh Review* 99 (1854): 167.

12. John Eagles, "Civilization — the Census," *Blackwood's Magazine* 76 (1854): 524, 451.

13. John Chapman, "The Spheres and Duties of Government," *Westminster Review,* n.s. 6 (1854): 486, 487.

14. John Chapman, "Constitutional Reform," *Westminster Review,* n.s. 5 (1854): 3.

15. W. R. Greg, "Parliamentary Purification," *Edinburgh Review* 98 (1853): 568, 599, 569.

16. W. E. Forster, " 'Strikes' and 'Lock-Outs,' " *Westminster Review,* n.s. 5 (1854): 127, 122.

17. Deidre David, *Fictions of Resolution in Three Victorian Novels: "North and South," "Our Mutual Friend," "Daniel Deronda"* (Houndmills, Basingstoke, UK, 1981) reads the act of the heroine in throwing herself between master and men as a metaphor of Margaret Hale's function within the class conflicts of the plot; Jane Spencer, *Elizabeth Gaskell* (Houndmills, Basingstoke, UK, 1993), 94, argues that the heroine achieves class reconciliation by bringing out the womanliness within men.

18. Spencer sees the ending as typifying the compensating promise of moral influence in exchange for women's loss of economic power and independence.

19. Mary Poovey, *Uneven Developments: The Ideological Work of Gender in Mid-Victorian England* (London, 1989), 164–98, analyzes the ambivalent influence of the public idealization of Florence Nightingale upon perceptions of women's professional capacities and opportunities.

20. Eileen Janes Yeo, *The Contest for Social Science: Relations and Representations of Gender*

and Class (London, 1996) provides a comprehensive discussion of women's political and professional activities in the 1850s. I am indebted to Yeo's discussion in what follows.

21. Kathryn Gleadle, *The Early Feminists: Radical Unitarians and the Emergence of the Women's Rights Movement, 1831–51* (Houndmills, Basingstoke, UK,1998) offers a detailed account of Unitarian women's feminist thinking and campaigns for greater equality.

22. Yeo discusses women's use of the metaphor "social motherhood" to mitigate opposition to their activities (120–47).

23. P. N. Furbank, "Mendacity in Mrs. Gaskell," *Encounter* 40 (1973): 51. Rosemarie Bodenheimer reads the melodramatic and idealizing language used of the heroine in relation to Thornton as imaginatively ambiguous, suggesting at once the culturally approved, self-sacrificing, womanly ideal and undercurrents of unconscious sexual drives (67).

SEVEN: *Romola*

1. Robert Chambers's popular, if inaccurate, evolutionary text was *Vestiges of the Natural History of Creation* (1844). And see Charles Lyell, *Principle of Geology* (1830–33) and *The Geological Evidences of the Antiquity of Man* (1863).

2. E. S. Dallas, "The Reform Bill and the Tory Party," *Blackwood's Magazine* 88 (1860): 129.

3. John Eagles, "Civilization — the Census," *Blackwood's Magazine* 76 (1854): 445.

4. *Times*, 28 Oct. 1863, 8.

5. *Times*, 16 July 1863, 10.

6. A. J. Beresford-Hope, "South Kensington Museum and Loan Exhibition," *Quarterly Review* 113 (1863): 198. *All the Year Round*, 10 (1863) also printed an article, "Paint and Varnish," that spoke of covering over hidden faults and blemishes (352–56).

7. R. H. Patterson, "The Opening of the Session," *Blackwood's Magazine* 93 (1863): 386.

8. *Times*, 2 Apr. 1863, 8.

9. "Parties and Prospects in Parliament," unattributed, *Westminster Review*, n.s. 25 (1864): 121.

10. F. R. Leavis, *The Great Tradition: George Eliot, Henry James, Joseph Conrad* (London, 1948) was the most significant and earliest study to establish Eliot's reputation; his claims received support in Barbara Hardy, *The Novels of George Eliot: A Study in Form* (London, 1959); W. J. Harvey, *The Art of George Eliot* (London, 1961).

11. W. B. Adams, "Review of *Lectures on Races of Men* by Robert Knox," *Westminster Review* 52 (1849): 2.

12. George Croly, "Political and Literary Biography," *Blackwood's Magazine* 68 (1850): 210.

13. Jane Frances Teleki von Szék, "The Organization of Italy," *Westminster Review* n.s. 18 (1860): 409.

14. Frederic Harrison, "Cavour and Garibaldi," *Westminster Review* n.s. 19 (1861): 190–91, 194.

15. I am not suggesting Eliot was simply a passive recipient of their ideas. The influence between herself and Lewes was undoubtedly mutual and interactive, and Eliot actively took hold of ideas that interested her and molded them to her own artistic and intellectual perceptions. For discussions of the influences that inform Eliot's writing, I am indebted to David Carroll, *George Eliot and the Conflict of Interpretations: A Reading of the Novels* (Cam-

bridge, UK, 1992); Valerie A. Dodd, *George Eliot: An Intellectual Life* (Houndmills, Basing-stoke, UK, 1990); William Myers, *The Teaching of George Eliot* (Leicester, UK, 1984); K. M. Newton, *George Eliot, Romantic Humanist: A Study of the Philosophical Structure of Her Novels* (Houndmills, Basingstoke, UK, 1981).

16. The quotation is from the famous passage in *Middlemarch* (bk. 1, ch. 16) that describes Lydgate's scientific aspirations by means of "the imagination that reveals subtle actions inaccessible by any sort of lens, but tracked in that outer darkness through long pathways of necessary sequence by the inward light which is the last refinement of Energy, capable of bathing even the ethereal atoms in its ideally illuminated space." Gilliam Beer points out the closeness of this passage to scientific ideas in John Tyndall and G. H. Lewes (*Darwin's Plots*, 151).

17. Forest Pyle, "A Novel Sympathy: The Imagination of Community in George Eliot," *Novel* 27 (1993): 5–23, argues that within Eliot's fiction there is an inherent contra-diction between her sense that the achievement of "community" requires an imaginative expansion of sympathies and her distrust of imagination as location of the self's nonaltruis-tic desires.

18. America was the frequent point of reference in discussions of democratic societies, both from negative and optimistic viewpoints; see, for example, Arnold, "Democracy," 2:18, 2:25, and Mill, *Representative Government*, 300.

19. It seems very likely that Eliot was also using this episode in the novel to make gentle fun of the scholarly quarrel Matthew Arnold had become embroiled in with Francis W. Newman, among others, over the correct language for translating Homer; for an account of this "learned squabble," see *Complete Prose Works*, 1:248–50.

20. Similar to Dowling's argument in *The Vulgarization of Art*, Mary Poovey, *A History of the Modern Fact: Problems of Knowledge in the Sciences of Wealth and Society* (Chicago, 1998), 178, traces this individualistic tradition of moral-political sensibility back to the eigh-teenth-century idealist philosophy of Shaftesbury.

21. Eliot recorded in her journal on 12 May 1863 that she "Killed Tito in great excitement"; quoted by Gordon S. Haight, *George Eliot: A Biography* (Oxford, UK, 1968), 365.

22. I am indebted to Felicia Bonaparte, *The Triptych and the Cross: The Central Myths of George Eliot's Poetic Imagination* (Brighton, UK, 1979) for her comprehensive elucidation of Eliot's pervasive use of classical myth in the novel. See also David Carroll, *George Eliot and the Conflict of Interpretations: A Reading of the Novels* for an account of Eliot's reworking of the history of European civilization in *Romola*, 167–200.

23. In *Utilitarianism*, Mill identifies Epicurian philosophy with Utilitarianism (209–11).

24. Janet K. Gezari, "*Romola* and the Myth of the Apocalypse," in Anne Smith, ed., *George Eliot: Centenary Essays and an Unpublished Fragment* (London, 1980), 77–102, dis-cusses Savonarola within a tradition of charismatic religious leaders.

25. For other critical discussions of Eliot's interest in the figure of the Madonna and the Virgin, see Gillian Beer, *George Eliot* (Brighton, UK, 1986), 110–25; Bonnie Zimmerman, "'The Mother's History' in George Eliot's Life and Political Ideology," in *The Last Tradi-tion: Mothers and Daughters in Literature*, ed. Cathy N. Davidson and E. M. Broner (New York, 1980), 81–94.

26. The language Eliot uses to describe her anguished process of writing the book recalls the language of the text itself: "I could swear by every sentence as having been

written with my best blood," she says, while in the novel the poet and scholar Angelo Poliziano is praised for a writing "whose phrases had blood in them and are alive still" (339). However, Eliot also agreed that "Romola is ideal"; both comments are quoted by Gordon S. Haight, *George Eliot: A Biography*, 361, 362.

27. Some of Eliot's most explicit political and social comments are to be found in her two essays "The Natural History of German Life," *Westminster Review* 66 (1856): 51–79, and "Address to Working Men, by Felix Holt," *Blackwood's Magazine* 103 (1868): 1–11. Both essays are reprinted in Thomas Pinney, ed., *Essays of George Eliot*, 266–99, 415–30.

E I G H T : *Our Mutual Friend*

1. R. H. Patterson, "Politics at Home and Abroad," *Blackwood's Edinburgh Magazine* 93 (1863): 247. Further references are given in the text.

2. *Times*, 2 Apr. 1863, 8.

3. Edward G. Bulwer-Lytton, "Caxtonia: A Series of Essays on Life, Literature, and Manners," no. 17, "Faith and Charity; or, The Union, in Practical Life, of Sincerity and Conciliation," *Blackwood's Edinburgh Magazine* 92 (1862): 664, 662.

4. S. H. Reynolds, "On Translating Homer," *Westminster Review* 21 (1862): 161.

5. Frederick Meyrick, "Popular Education — the New Code," *Quarterly Review* 111 (1862): 98.

6. Quoted in W. Lucas Collins, "The Poor and Their Public Schools: The New Minute," *Blackwood's Edinburgh Magazine* 91 (1862): 98.

7. *All the Year Round* 2 (1860): 315–17, also published an article on the subject. Its title, "The Schoolmaster All Abroad," is strikingly similar to Eugene Wrayburn's designation of Headstone in the novel.

8. H. L. Mansel, "Sensation Novels," *Quarterly Review* 113 (1863), 483.

9. A. J. Beresford-Hope, "The International Exhibition," *Quarterly Review* 112 (1862): 200.

10. J. B. Atkinson, "The International Exhibition. Its Purpose and Prospects," *Blackwood's Edinburgh Magazine* 91 (1862): 482.

11. Frederick Hardman, "Under the Limes. Pen and Ink Photographs from Berlin," *Blackwood's Edinburgh Magazine* 94 (1863): 89.

12. F. R. Leavis, *The Great Tradition: George Eliot, Henry James, Joseph Conrad* omitted Dickens from the roll call of great novelists; while the subsequent reevaluation of his work in F. R. and Q. D. Leavis, *Dickens the Novelist* (London, 1970) gives due emphasis to the complexity of Dickens's response to his age, critical judgments still tend to discuss artistic achievement in terms of moral seriousness.

13. I here refer to Hillis Miller's introduction to Dickens's *Bleak House* (Penguin, 1971) and Miller's essay "The Fiction of Realism: *Sketches by Boz, Oliver Twist*, and Cruikshank's Illustrations," in *Dickens Centennial Essays*, ed. Ada Nisbet and Blake Nevius (Berkeley, CA, 1971), 85–126, rather than to his earlier *Charles Dickens: The World of His Novels* (Cambridge, MA, 1958).

14. John Carey, *The Violent Effigy: A Study of Dickens's Imagination* (London, 1973) was undoubtedly influential in revising the "sentimental" reading of Dickens, but his book suffers from a pervasive superiority of tone toward its subject.

15. John Crary, *Techniques of the Observer: On Vision and Modernity in the Nineteenth Century* (Cambridge, MA, 1992) provides the most detailed discussion of changes in ways of looking that heralded a shift to modernist perceptions of reality.

16. Catherine Gallagher, "The Bioeconomics of *Our Mutual Friend*," in *Subject to History: Ideology, Class, Gender,* ed. David Simpson (Ithaca, NY, 1991), 47–64, explores the relationship of commodities to economic and bodily health in the novel.

17. The reference to Milvey's expensive education seems to be an allusion to the debates over the revised code: teachers outraged cultivated opinion by claiming that their training put them intellectually on a par with men educated at public school and university, like clergymen. Wrayburn's sarcastic comment that he hopes the trouble Headstone has taken to see him "may prove remunerative" also seems to be a reference to the anger of teachers at the introduction of payment by results (287).

18. This dual perspective suggests Darwin's well-known contrast of the bright face of nature that deflects notice from the destructive forces that are equally part of evolutionary life cycles. George Levine suggests that this Darwinian image underlies many similarly dualistic pictures in Victorian fiction (104). Levine also provides a detailed overview, "Dickens and Darwin," 119–52.

19. Howard W. Fulweiler, " 'A Dismal Swamp': Darwin, Design, and Evolution in *Our Mutual Friend*," *Nineteenth-Century Literature* 49 (1994): 50–74, discusses the plotting of the novel in relation to Darwin and notions of design and teleology.

20. See also Jeremy Tambling, *Dickens, Violence, and the Modern State* (Houndmills, Basingstoke, UK, 1995), 208.

21. See also Audrey Jaffe, *Vanishing Points: Dickens, Narrative, and the Subject of Omni-science* (Berkeley, CA, 1991), 157, which discusses the lack of knowledge on the part of the narrator as well as the characters.

22. *Times,* 20 July 1863, carried a leading article on "drainage as the great problem of civilization." The article ridiculed cheap solutions that promise "to deodorise our material sewage, and turn it into gold" (8).

Conclusion

1. John Eagles, "Thackeray's Lectures: Swift," *Blackwood's Edinburgh Magazine* 74 (1853): 494.

Works Cited

NINETEENTH-CENTURY JOURNALS

The Times
The Morning Chronicle
Blackwood's Edinburgh Magazine
The Edinburgh Review
Quarterly Review
The Westminster Review

GENERAL

Adorno, Theodor W., and Max Horkeimer. *Dialectic of Enlightenment.* Translated by John Cumming. London: Verso, 1997.

Allot, Miriam. *The Brontës: The Critical Heritage.* London: Routledge, 1995.

Anderson, Benedict. *Imagined Communities: Reflections on the Origin and Spread of Nationalism.* Revised edition. London: Verso, 1991.

Anderson, Patricia. *The Printed Image and the Transformation of Popular Culture, 1790–1860.* Oxford, UK: Clarendon Press, 1991.

Arac, Jonathan. *Commissioned Spirits: The Shaping of Social Motion in Dickens, Carlyle, Melville, and Hawthorne.* New Brunswick, NJ: Rutgers University Press, 1979.

Armstrong, Nancy. *Desire and Domestic Fiction: A Political History of the Novel.* Oxford: Oxford University Press, 1987.

———. *Fiction in the Age of Photography: The Legacy of British Realism.* Cambridge: Harvard University Press, 1999.

Arnold, Matthew. *The Complete Prose Works.* 8 vols. Edited by R. H. Super. Ann Arbor: University of Michigan Press, 1960.

———. *Culture and Anarchy.* Edited by J. Dover Wilson. Cambridge: Cambridge University Press, 1971.

Auerbach, Nina. *Woman and the Demon: The Life of a Victorian Myth.* Cambridge: Harvard University Press, 1982.

Bagehot, Walter. *Collected Works.* Edited by Norman St. John-Stevens. London: The Economist, 1974.

Balibar, Etienne, and Immanuel Wallerstein. *Race, Nation, Class: Ambiguous Identities.* Translation of Etienne Balibar by Chris Turner. London: Verso, 1991.

Bédarida, François. *A Social History of England, 1851–1990.* Translated by A. S. Forster and Jeffrey Hodgkinson. 2nd edition. London: Routledge, 1991.

Beer, Gillian. *Darwin's Plots: Evolutionary Narrative in Darwin, George Eliot, and Nineteenth-Century Fiction*. London: Routledge & Kegan Paul, 1983.

———. *George Eliot*. Brighton: Harvester, 1986.

Bentley, Eric. *A Century of Hero Worship*. 2nd edition. Beacon Hill, Boston, MA: Beacon Press, 1957.

Bevir, Mark. "The Long Nineteenth Century in Intellectual History." *Journal of Victorian Cultural Studies* 6, no. 2, (2001): 313–35.

Blake, Kathleen. "*Bleak House*, Political Economy, Victorian Studies." *Victorian Literature and Culture* 25 (1997): 1–21.

Blake, Robert. *Disraeli*. London: Methuen, 1966.

Bodenheimer, Rosemarie. *The Politics of Story in Victorian Social Fiction*. Ithaca, NY: Cornell University Press, 1988.

Bolingbroke, Viscount St. John Henry. *The Idea of a Patriot King*. 1749. Reprint, Menston, Yorkshire, UK: Scolar Press, 1971.

Bonaparte, Felicia. *The Triptych and the Cross: The Central Myths of George Eliot's Poetic Imagination*. Brighton, UK: Harvester, 1979.

Bond, Donald F., ed. *The Spectator*. 5 vols. Oxford, UK: Clarendon Press, 1965.

Boumelha, Penny. *Charlotte Bronte*. London: Harvester Wheatsheaf, 1990.

Bourdieu, Pierre. *Distinction: A Social Critique of the Judgement of Taste*. Translated by Richard Nice. London: Routledge, 1986.

Boyte, Harry C. "The Pragmatic Ends of Popular Politics." In Calhoun, ed., *Habermas and the Public Sphere*.

Braudy, Leo. *The Frenzy of Renown: Fame and Its History*. Oxford: Oxford University Press, 1986.

Briggs, Asa. "Private and Social Themes in *Shirley*." *Brontë Society Transactions* (1959): 203–19.

Brontë, Charlotte. *Shirley*. Edited by Herbert Rosengarten and Margaret Smith. Oxford: Oxford University Press, 1981.

Brooks, Peter. *Body Work: Objects of Desire in Modern Narrative*. Cambridge: Harvard University Press, 1993.

Burchell, G., C. Gordon, and P. Miller, eds. *The Foucault Effect: Studies in Governmentality*. Chicago: Chicago University of Chicago Press, 1991.

Burke, Edmund. *Reflections on the Revolution in France*. Harmondsworth, UK: Penguin, 1969.

Calhoun, Craig, ed. *Habermas and the Public Sphere*. Cambridge: MIT Press, 1992.

Calleo, David P. *Coleridge and the Idea of the Modern State*. New Haven, CN: Yale University Press, 1966.

Carey, John. *The Violent Effigy: A Study of Dickens's Imagination*. London: Faber, 1973.

Carlyle, Thomas. *History of the French Revolution*. 3 vols. Centenary edition. London: Chapman & Hall, 1896.

———. *On Heroes, Hero-Worship, and the Heroic in History*. Centenary edition. London: Chapman & Hall, 1897.

———. *Sartor Resartus*. Oxford: Oxford University Press, 1987.

Carroll, David. *George Eliot and Conflicts of Interpretations: A Reading of the Novels*. Cambridge: Cambridge University Press, 1992.

Castoriades, Cornelius. *The Imaginary Institution of Society*. Translated by Kathleen Blamey. Oxford, UK: Polity Press, 1987.

Cazamian, Louis. *The Social Novel in England, 1830–1850: Dickens, Disraeli, Mrs. Gaskell, Kingsley.* Translated by Martin Fido. London: Routledge & Kegan Paul, 1973.

Chadwick, Edwin. *Report on the Sanitary Conditions of the Labouring Population of Great Britain of 1842.* Edited by M. Flinn. Edinburgh: Edinburgh University Press, 1965.

Chapple, J. A. V., and Arthur Pollard, eds. *The Letters of Mrs. Gaskell.* Manchester, UK: Manchester University Press, 1966.

Christie, John, and Sally Shuttleworth. *Nature Transfigured: Science and Literature, 1700–1900.* Manchester, UK: Manchester University Press, 1989.

Coleridge, Samuel Taylor. *On the Constitution of the Church and State.* Edited by John Barrell. London: J. M. Dent, 1972.

Colley, Linda. *Britains Forging the Nation, 1707–1837.* London: Vintage, 1996.

Collins, Philip. *Charles Dickens: The Critical Heritage.* London: Routledge, 1995.

Colquhoun, Patrick. *A Treatise on Indigence.* London: J. Mawman, 1806.

Corrigan, Philip, and Derek Sayer. *The Great Arch: English State Formation as Cultural Revolution.* Oxford, UK: Blackwell, 1985.

Crary, Johnathan. *Techniques of the Observer: On Vision and Modernity in the Nineteenth Century.* Cambridge: MIT Press, 1992.

Danahay, Martin A. "Housekeeping and Hegemony in *Bleak House*." *Studies in the Novel* 23 (1991): 416–31.

Darwin, Charles. *The Expression of the Emotions in Man and Animals.* New York: Greenwood Press, 1969.

David, Deidre. *Fictions of Resolution in Three Victorian Novels: "North and South," "Our Mutual Friend," "Daniel Deronda."* Basingstoke, UK: Macmillan, 1981.

———. *Intellectual Women and Victorian Patriarchy: Harriet Martineau, Elizabeth Barrett Browning, George Eliot.* Basingstoke, UK: Macmillan, 1987.

Davidoff, Leonore, and Catherine Hall. *Family Fortunes: Men and Women of the English Middle Class, 1780–1850.* London: Hutchinson, 1987.

Dean, Mitchell. *The Constitution of Poverty: Towards a Geneology of Liberal Governance.* London: Routledge, 1991.

Dickens, Charles. *Bleak House.* Harmondsworth, UK: Penguin, 1971.

———. *Oliver Twist.* Harmondsworth, UK: Penguin, 1975

———. *Our Mutual Friend.* Harmondsworth, UK: Penguin, 1997.

Dodd, Valerie A. *George Eliot: An Intellectual Life.* Basingstoke, UK: Macmillan, 1990.

Dolan, Tim. "Fictional Territory and a Woman's Place: Regional and Sexual Difference in *Shirley*." *ELH* 62 (1995): 197–215.

Dowling, Linda. *The Vulgarization of Art: The Victorians and Aesthetic Democracy.* Charlottesville: University Press of Virginia, 1996.

Eagleton, Terry. *Myths of Power: A Marxist Study of the Brontës.* 2nd edition. Basingstoke, UK: Macmillan, 1988.

Eisenstadt, S. N., ed. *Max Weber on Charisma and Institution Building.* Chicago: University of Chicago Press, 1968.

Eley, Geoff. "Nations, Publics, and Political Cultures: Placing Habermas in the Nineteenth Century." In Calhoun, ed., *Habermas and the Public Sphere.*

Eliot, George. "Address to Working Men, by Felix Holt." *Blackwood's Magazine* 103 (1868).

———. *Essays of George Eliot.* Edited by Thomas Pinney. London: Kegan Paul, 1963.

———. *Felix Holt.* 1866. Reprint, Harmondsworth, UK: Penguin, 1972.

———. "The Natural History of German Life." *Westminster Review* 66 (1856).

———. *Romola*. Harmondsworth, UK: Penguin, 1996.

Elliott, Dorice Williams. "The Female Visitor and Marriage of Classes in Gaskell's *North and South*." *Nineteenth-Century Literature* 49 (1994): 21–49.

Ermath, Elizabeth Deeds. *The English Novel in History, 1840–1895*. London: Routledge, 1997.

Fasik, Laura. "Dickens and the Diseased Body in *Bleak House*." *Dickens Studies Annual* 24 (1996): 135–51.

Finer, S. E. *The Life and Times of Sir Edwin Chadwick*. New York: Barnes & Noble, 1952.

Foucault, Michel. "Governmentality." In Burchell, Gordon, and Miller, eds., *The Foucault Effect*.

Francis, G. H. *Orators of the Age, Comprising Portraits, Critical, Biographical, and Descriptive*. London: G. W. Nickisson, 1847.

Freud, Sigmund. "On Narcissism: An Introduction." In *On Metapsychology: The Theory of Psychoanalysis*. Penguin Freud Library, vol. 11. Harmondsworth, UK: Penguin, 1984.

Fulweiler, Howard W. " 'A Dismal Swamp': Darwin, Design, and Evolution in *Our Mutual Friend*." *Nineteenth-Century Literature* 49 (1994): 50–74.

Furbank, P. N. "Mendacity in Mrs. Gaskell." *Encounter* 40 (1973): 46–54.

Gagnier, Regenia. *The Insatiability of Human Wants: Economics and Aesthetics in the Market Place*. Chicago: University of Chicago Press, 2000

Gallagher, Catherine. "The Bioeconomics of *Our Mutual Friend*." In David Simpson, ed., *Subject to History: Ideology, Class, Gender*. Ithaca, NY: Cornell University Press, 1991.

———. "The Body versus the Social Body in the Works of Thomas Malthus and Henry Mayhew." In Gallagher and Laqueur, eds., *The Making of the Modern Body*.

———. *The Industrial Reformation of English Fiction: Social Discourse and Narrative Form, 1832–1867*. Chicago: University of Chicago Press, 1985.

Gallagher, C., and T. Laqueur, eds. *The Making of the Modern Body: Sexuality and Society in the Nineteenth Century*. Berkeley: University of California Press, 1987.

Gaskell, Elizabeth. *North and South*. Harmondsworth, UK: Penguin, 1970.

Gezari, Janet K. "*Romola* and the Myth of the Apocalypse." In Anne Smith, ed., *George Eliot: Centenary Essays and an Unpublished Fragment*. London: Vision Press, 1980.

Gleadle, Kathryn. *The Early Feminists: Radical Unitarians and the Emergence of the Women's Rights Movement, 1831–51*. Basingstoke, UK: Macmillan, 1995.

Gould, Stephen J. *Ever since Darwin: Reflections in Natural History*. New York: W. W. Norton, 1977.

Green-Lewis, Jennifer. *Framing the Victorians: Photography and the Culture of Realism*. Ithaca, NY: Cornell University Press, 1996.

Guilhamet, Leon. *The Sincere Ideal: Studies on Sincerity in Eighteenth-Century English Literature*. Montreal: McGill-Queen's University Press, 1974.

Habermas, Jürgen. *The Philosophical Discourse of Modernity: Twelve Lectures*. Translated by Kathleen Blamey. Oxford, UK: Polity Press, 1987.

———. *The Structural Transformation of the Public Sphere: An Inquiry into a Category of Bourgeois Society*. Translated by Thomas Burger, with Frederick Lawrence. Oxford, UK: Polity Press, 1992.

Haight, Gordon S. *George Eliot: A Biography*. Oxford, UK: Clarendon Press, 1968.

Hall, Catherine. *White, Male, and Middle Class: Explorations in Feminism and History*. Oxford, UK: Polity Press, 1992.

Hall, Jasmine Yong. "What's Troubling Esther? Narrating, Policing, and Resisting Arrest in *Bleak House*." *Dickens Studies Annual* 22 (1993): 171–94.

Hardy, Barbara. *The Moral Art of Dickens*. London: Athlone, 1970.

———. *The Novels of George: A Study in Form*. London: Athlone, 1959.

Harvey, W. J. *The Art of George Eliot*. London: Chatto & Windus, 1961.

Hazlitt, William. "Capital Punishment." *Edinburgh Review*, July 1821. In *Collected Works*, vol. 19.

———. *Collected Works*. 21 vols. Centenary edition. Edited by P. P. Howe. London: J. M. Dent, 1930.

———. "Coriolanus." In *Collected Works*, vol. 5.

Hobsbawm, Eric J. *Nations and Nationalism since 1780: Programme, Myth, Reality*. Cambridge: Cambridge University Press, 1990.

Homans, Margaret. *Bearing the Word: Language and Female Experience in Nineteenth-Century Women's Writing*. Chicago: University of Chicago Press, 1986.

———. "Victoria's Sovereign Obedience: Portraits of the Queen as Wife and Mother." In Carol T. Christ and John O. Jordan, eds., *Victorian Literature and the Victorian Visual Imagination*. Berkeley: University of California Press, 1995.

Horton, Susan. "Were They Having Fun Yet? Victorian Optical Gadgetry, Modernist Selves." In Carol T. Christ and John O. Jordan, eds., *Victorian Literature and the Victorian Visual Imagination*. Berkeley: University of California Press, 1995.

Hume, David. *Treatise on Human Nature*. 2nd edition. Edited by P. N. Nidditch. Oxford: Oxford University Press, 1978.

Ingham, Patricia. *The Language of Gender and Class: Transformation in the Victorian Novel*. London: Routledge, 1996.

Jaffe, Audrey. *Vanishing Points: Dickens, Narrative, and the Subject of Omniscience*. Berkeley: University of California Press, 1991.

Jephson, Henry. *The Platform: Its Rise and Progress*. 2nd edition. London: Macmillan, 1892.

Jones, Gareth Stedman. *Languages of Class: Studies in English Working-Class History, 1832–1982*. Cambridge: Cambridge University Press, 1983.

Joyce, Patrick. *Visions of the People: Industrial England and the Question of Class, 1848–1914*. Cambridge: Cambridge University Press, 1999.

Judd, Denis. *Palmerston*. London: Weidenfeld & Nicholson, 1975.

Kestner, Joseph. *Protest and Reform: The British Social Narratives by Women, 1827–1857*. Madison: University of Wisconsin Press, 1985.

Kidd, Alan, and David Nicholls, eds. *Gender, Civic Culture, and Consumerism: Middle-Class Identity in Britain, 1800–1940*. Manchester, UK: Manchester University Press, 1999.

Kingsley, Charles. *The Water-Babies*. 1862–63. Reprint, London: Hamlyn, 1986.

Landes, Joan. *Women and the Public Sphere in the Age of the French Revolution*. Ithaca, NY: Cornell University Press, 1988.

Landsbury, Coral. *Elizabeth Gaskell: The Novel of Social Crisis*. New York: Barnes & Noble, 1975.

Langford, Paul. *English Identified: Manners and Character, 1650–1850*. Oxford: Oxford University Press, 2000.

———. *Public Life and the Propertied Englishman, 1689–1798*. Oxford, UK: Clarendon Press, 1991.

Lavater, Johann Casper. *Essays on Physiognomy*. 19th edition. Translated by Thomas Holcroft. London: Ward, Lock & Bowden, 1840.

Leavis, F. R. *The Great Tradition: George Eliot, Henry James, Joseph Conrad.* London: Chatto & Windus, 1948.

Leavis, F. R., and Q. D. Leavis. *Dickens the Novelist.* London: Chatto & Windus, 1970.

Levine, George. *Darwin and the Novelists: Patterns of Science in Victorian Fiction.* Cambridge: Harvard University Press, 1988.

―――. "George Eliot's Hypothesis of Reality." *Nineteenth-Century Fiction* 35 (1980): 1–28.

―――. *The Realistic Imagination: English Fiction from Frankenstein to Lady Chatterley.* Chicago: University of Chicago Press, 1981.

Loofbourow, John. *Thackeray and the Form of Fiction.* Princeton: Princeton University Press, 1964.

Lucas, John. *The Literature of Change: Studies in the Nineteenth-Century Provincial Novel.* New York: Barnes & Noble, 1980.

Lukács, Georg. *The Historical Novel.* Translated by Hannah and Stanley Mitchell. Harmondsworth, UK: Penguin, 1962.

Macauley, T. B. *History of England.* 1849. Reprint, London: Everyman, 1953.

―――. "Review of *The Life of Joseph Addison* by Lucy Aikin." *Edinburgh Review,* July 1843.

Magnus, Philip. *Gladstone.* 2nd edition. London: John Murray, 1963.

Mandler, Peter. *Aristocratic Government in the Age of Reform: Whigs and Liberals, 1830–1852.* Oxford, UK: Clarendon Press, 1990.

Marshall, P. David. *Celebrity and Power: Fame in Contemporary Culture.* Minneapolis: University of Minnesota Press, 1997.

Marx, Karl. *Capital.* 3 vols. Translated by Ben Fowkes. Harmondsworth, UK: Penguin, 1976.

Matthew, H. C. G. *Gladstone, 1875–1898.* Oxford, UK: Clarendon Press, 1995.

Mayhew, Henry. *London Labour and London Poor.* 4 vols. New York: Dover, 1968.

Mill, John Stuart. *Autobiography.* 1873. Reprint, Harmondsworth, UK: Penguin, 1989.

―――. *Collected Works.* 33 vols. Edited by John M. Robson and Jack Stillinger. London: Routledge & Kegan Paul, 1981.

―――. *Considerations on Representative Government.* In *Collected Works,* vol. 19.

―――. "Miss Martineau's Summary of Political Economy." *Monthly Repository* n.s. 8 (1934): 319–25.

―――. *On Liberty.* In *Collected Works,* vol. 18.

―――. *Utilitarianism.* In *Collected Works,* vol. 10.

Miller, D. A. *The Novel and the Police.* Berkeley: University of California Press, 1988.

Miller, Hillis J. *Charles Dickens: The World of His Novels.* Cambridge: Harvard University Press, 1958.

―――. "The Fiction of Realism: *Sketches by Boz, Oliver Twist,* and Cruikshank's Illustrations." In Ada Nisbet and Blake Nevius, eds., *Dickens Centennial Essays.* Berkeley: University of California Press, 1971.

Minogue, Sally. "Gender and Class in *Villette* and *North and South.*" In Sally Minogue, ed., *Problems for Feminist Criticism.* London: Routledge, 1990.

Monsarrat, Ann. *The Uneasy Victorian: Thackeray the Man, 1811–1863.* London: Cassell, 1980.

Mullan, John. *Sentiment and Sociability: The Language of Feeling in the Eighteenth Century.* Oxford, UK: Clarendon Press, 1988.

Myers, William. *The Teaching of George Eliot.* Leicester, UK: Leicester University Press, 1984.

Namier, Lewis. *The Structure of Politics at the Accession of George III.* 2nd edition. Basingstoke, UK: Macmillan, 1957.

Newton, K. M. *George Eliot, Romantic Humanist: A Study of the Philosophical Structure of Her Novels.* Basingstoke, UK: Macmillan, 1981.

Perkin, Harold. *The Rise of Professional Society: England since 1880.* London: Routledge, 1989.

Perkins, David. *Wordsworth and the Poetry of Sincerity.* Cambridge: Harvard University Press, 1964.

Peters, Catherine. *Thackeray's Universe: Shifting Worlds of Imagination and Reality.* London: Faber & Faber, 1987.

Philips, K. C. *The Language of Thackeray.* London: Andre Deutsch, 1978.

Pinch, Adela. *Strange Fits of Passion: Epistemology of Emotion, Hume to Austen.* Stanford, CA: Stanford University Press, 1996.

Plotz, John. *The Crowd: British Literature and Public Politics.* Berkeley: University of California Press, 2000.

Poovey, Mary. *A History of the Modern Fact: Problems of Knowledge in the Sciences of Wealth and Society.* Chicago: University of Chicago Press, 1998.

———. *Making a Social Body: British Cultural Formation, 1830–1864.* Chicago: University of Chicago Press, 1995.

———. *The Proper Lady and the Woman Writer: Ideology as Style in the Works of Mary Wollstonecraft, Mary Shelley, and Jane Austen.* Chicago: University of Chicago Press, 1984.

———. *Uneven Developments: The Ideological Work of Gender in Mid-Victorian England.* London: Virago, 1989.

Porter, Roy. *Enlightenment: Britain and the Creation of the Modern World.* Harmondsworth, UK: Penguin, 2000.

Price, Richard. *British Society, 1680–1880: Dynamism, Containment, and Change.* Cambridge: Cambridge University Press, 1999.

Procacci, Giovanna. "Social Economy and the Government of Poverty." In Burchell, Gordon, and Miller, eds., *The Foucault Effect.*

Pyle, Forest. "A Novel Sympathy: The Imagination of Community in George Eliot." *Novel* 27 (1997): 5–23.

Ray, Gordon. *Thackeray: The Age of Wisdom, 1847–1863.* Oxford: Oxford University Press, 1958.

Renan, Ernest. "What Is a Nation?" In Homi K. Bhabha, ed., *Nation and Narration.* London: Routledge, 1990.

Richards, Thomas. *The Commodity Culture of Victorian England: Advertising and Spectacle, 1851–1914.* Stanford, CA: Stanford University Press, 1990.

Rogers, Helen. *Women and the People: Authority, Authorship, and the English Radical Tradition.* London: Ashgate, 2000.

Rogers, Nicholas. *Crowds, Culture, and Politics in Georgian Britain.* Oxford: Oxford University Press, 1998.

Ryan, Mary P. "Gender and Public Access: Women's Politics in Nineteenth-Century America." In Calhoun, ed., *Habermas and the Public Sphere.*

Schor, Hilary. *Scheherazade in the Market Place: Elizabeth Gaskell and the Victorian Novel.* Oxford: Oxford University Press, 1992.

Sedgwick, Eve Kosofsky. *Between Men: English Literature and Male Homosocial Desire.* New York: Columbia University Press, 1985.

————. "Immediacy, Doubleness, and the Unspeakable: *Wuthering Heights and Villette.*" In Eve Kosofsky Sedgwick, *The Coherence of Gothic Conventions.* London: Methuen, 1988.

Sennett, Richard. *The Fall of Public Man.* Cambridge: Cambridge University Press, 1974.

Shaftesbury, Anthony Ashley Cooper, 3rd earl of. *Characteristics of Men, Manners, Opinions, Times, Etc.* Edited by John M. Robinson. London: Macmillan, 1900.

Shannon, Richard. *Gladstone, 1809–1865.* London: Methuen, 1982.

Smith, Adam. *Theory of Moral Sentiments.* Edited by D. D. Raphael and A. L. Macfie. Oxford, UK: Clarendon Press, 1998.

Smith, Susan Belasco. "'A Yorkshire Burr': Language in *Shirley.*" *Studies in English Literature, 1500–1900* 27 (1987): 637–45.

Spencer, Herbert. *Essays: Scientific, Political, and Speculative.* 3 vols. London: Williams & Norgate, 1883.

Spencer, Jane. *Elizabeth Gaskell.* Basingstoke, UK: Macmillan, 1993.

Talon, Henri-A. "Time and Memory in Thackeray's *Henry Esmond.*" *Review of English Studies* 13 (1962): 147–56.

Tambling, Jeremy. *Confession: Sexuality, Sin, the Subject.* Manchester, UK: Manchester University Press, 1990.

————. *Dickens, Violence, and the Modern State.* Basingstoke, UK: Macmillan, 1995.

Thackeray, William Makepeace. *The Book of Snobs.* 1848. Reprint, St. Lucia, Queensland: University of Queensland Press, 1973.

————. *The English Humourists of the Eighteenth Century.* In *Works.*

————. *The Four Georges.* In *Works.*

————. *The History of Henry Esmond, Esq.* Oxford: Oxford University Press, 1991.

————. *The Works of William Makepeace Thackeray.* 13 vols. London: Smith, Elder, 1898.

Thomas, Deborah A. *Thackeray and Slavery.* Athens: Ohio University Press, 1993.

Thompson, E. P. *The Making of the English Working Class.* Harmondsworth, UK: Penguin, 1963.

————. *Whigs and Hunters: The Origin of the Black Act.* Harmondsworth, UK: Penguin, 1977.

Thompson, F. M. L. *English Landed Society in the Nineteenth Century.* London: Routledge & Kegan Paul, 1963.

Tilford, John E. "The 'Unsavoury Plot' of *Henry Esmond.*" *Nineteenth-Century Fiction* 6 (1951): 121–30.

Tilly, Charles. *Popular Contention in Britain, 1758–1834.* Cambridge: Harvard University Press, 1995.

Trilling, Lionel. *Sincerity and Authenticity.* Cambridge: Harvard University Press, 1972.

Uglo, Jenny. *Elizabeth Gaskell: A Habit of Stories.* London: Faber & Faber, 1993.

Vanskike, Elliot. "Consistent Inconsistencies: The Transvestite Actress Madame Vetris and Charlotte Brontë's *Shirley.*" *Nineteenth-Century Literature* 50 (1996): 464–88.

Vernon, James. *Politics and the People.* Cambridge: Cambridge University Press, 1993.

Vickery, Amanda. *The Gentleman's Daughter: Women's Lives in Georgian England.* New Haven, CN: Yale University Press, 1998.

————, ed. *Women, Privilege, and Power: British Politics, 1750 to the Present.* Stanford, CA: Stanford University Press, 2001.

Wahrman, Dror. *Imagining the Middle Class: The Political Representation of Class, c. 1780–1840.* Cambridge: Cambridge University Press, 1995.

Warner, Michael. "The Mass Public and the Mass Subject." In Calhoun, ed., *Habermas and the Public Sphere.*

Webb, R. K. *Modern England: From the Eighteenth Century to the Present.* London: Routledge & Kegan Paul, 1963.

Williams, Raymond. *The Country and the City.* Frogmore, St. Albans, UK: Paladin, 1975.

———. *Culture and Society.* Harmondsworth, UK: Penguin, 1961.

———. *The English Novel from Dickens to Lawrence.* Frogmore, St. Albans, UK: Paladin, 1970.

Wilson, Edmund. "Dickens: The Two Scrooges." In *The Wound and the Bow.* Oxford: Oxford University Press, 1941.

Wilson, Kathleen. *The Sense of the People: Politics, Culture, and Imperialism in England, 1715–1785.* Cambridge: Cambridge University Press, 1995.

Wise, Thomas James, and John Alexander, eds. *The Brontës: Their Lives, Friendships, and Correspondence, in Four Volumes.* Vols. 12–15 of *The Shakespeare Head Brontë.* Oxford, UK: Shakespeare Head Press, 1931–38.

Yeo, Eileen Janes. *The Contest for Social Science: Relations and Representations of Gender and Class.* London: Rivers Oram, 1996.

Zimmerman, Bonnie. " 'The Mother's History' in George Eliot's Life and Political Ideology." In Cathy N. Davidson and E. M. Broner, eds., *The Last Tradition: Mothers and Daughters in Literature.* New York: Frederick Ungar, 1980.

Index

absolutism: struggles against, 5

Act of Settlement (1701), 58, 89, 111

Addison, 96, 99, 100

Adorno, Theodor W., 8, 37

aggregate/aggregation, 6, 7, 111, 116, 124, 135, 139, 142–43, 147, 158, 161, 165, 169, 172, 174, 195, 228. *See also* mass culture

Anderson, Benedict, 30, 96; *Imagined Communities*, 7

Anderson, Patricia: *The Printed Image and the Transformation of Popular Culture*, 50

appearance: as naturalizing site of social classification, 25, 29, 49, 50, 68, 169, 201, 202, 206, 220–21, 228. *See also* beauty; visual

Arac, Jonathan, 218

aristocracy: aligning of leadership to use of force and masculine virility, 63–64; critique of in *Bleak House*, 118–20; and cult of heroism, 90, 94; defense of Corn Laws, 90; hold on to power, 14–15; landed property as justifying right to power, 90; loss of authority, 89; rejection of birthright as the prerogative to rule, 14, 58, 88–89, 90. *See also* nobility

Armstrong, Nancy, 5, 51, 200–201

Arnold, Matthew, 169, 170–71, 177, 184, 193, 199; *Culture and Anarchy*, 47–48, 171; "Democracy," 166, 171; essays on Homer, 48; "My Countrymen," 49

Auerbach, Nina, 107

Austen, Jane, 20, 224; compared with Brontë, 64; narrative tone of novels, 61

authenticity: movement from value of sincerity to value of, 18

Bagehot, Walter, 38–39

beauty, 14, 46, 50, 78; responsiveness and desire for in *Our Mutual Friend*, 211–14; Spencer on, 49. *See also* appearance; visual

Beer, Gillian, 165, 166, 211

Bentley, Eric, 37

birthright: rejection of as prerogative to rule, 14, 58, 88–89, 90

Blackwood's Magazine, 34, 58, 140, 141, 168, 197; "Civilization — The Census" article, 142–43; "Feudalism in the Nineteenth Century," 63–64; "Under the Limes. Pen and Ink Photographs," 201; "The Union, in Practical Life, of Sincerity and Conciliation," 199; view of movement toward more heterogeneous society, 166

Blake, Robert, 89, 90

Bleak House (Dickens), 64, 91, 111–36, 224, 225–29; characterization of Esther, 131–33, 134; characterization of Tulkinghorn, 125–27, 128–30, 131; construction of power as impersonal and unlocated, 130–31; critique of aristocratic government, 118–20; dual perspective of the poor, 119; elaboration of new practice of knowledge, 132–35; portrayal of poverty and destitution, 123–24, 126; professional practice of knowledge as opposition to aristocratic self-interest, 120–21; references to revolutionary struggles, 114–15; representation of industrious working-class poor, 124–25; representation of professions, 121–23; shift of power from nobility to a professional authority, 126; transfer of

Henry Esmond (*continued*)

temporality, 87; historicism of, 60, 86, 87–88; identification of Henry Esmond with national community as opposed to nation as territory, 96–97; and inclusiveness, 88, 97–98; paralleling of Beatrix and Henry, 106; and principle of affinity, 97–99; and problem of language, 95; rejection of traditional fields of leadership, 95; relationship between narrator and reader, 103–4; representation of heroes, 100–102; representation of women, 105–7; representation of worship of nobility as charismatic figures with divine grace, 92–94; and sincerity, 16, 21, 88, 100, 101–2, 104–5, 105, 106, 225, 226; study of political dimensions of transition toward inclusivity, 88; sustaining of myth of birthright by means of publicness, 91–92

heroes/hero-worship, 39–40, 74, 78, 226; and aristocracy, 90, 94; Brontë's reservations about, 71–72; Carlyle on, 39–40, 44, 58–59, 60, 71, 77, 88; representation of in *Henry Esmond*, 100–102; representation of in *Shirley*, 60, 62, 71, 72–78, 83; and sincerity, 40

hierarchy: movement away from, 3, 8

Hill, Rowland, 44

Hobbes, 37

Hobsbawm, Eric, 10

Homer, 48

homogenization, 6

Horkheimer, 8, 37

Horton, Susan, 50–51

House of Lords: partial abolition of hereditary, 89

humanity, 47

Hume, David, 18, 19; *Treatise on Human Nature*, 18

Hyde Park riots (1866), 48

"inclusive society," use of term, 8

individualism, 23, 33, 38, 47, 174

insincerity, 168

interiority, 24, 27, 28, 44, 50, 51, 53; and code of sincerity, 15, 21, 22, 23, 27–28, 45, 88, 113, 198, 199, 209–10, 226; and

Eliot, 169–70, 202, 203; in *Our Mutual Friend*, 203, 204, 210, 213, 214–15, 216; perception as location of an evolved distinction from the mass, 169. *See also* sensibility

International Exhibition (1861), 167, 201

Italy, 173; national movement to unite, 171–72

Jephson, Henry: *The Platform*, 42

Jones, Gareth Stedman, 35

Joyce, Patrick, 35, 36

Judd, Denis, 41

Juvenile Offenders Act (1854), 144

Kant, 47

kingship, 39

Kingsley, Charles: *The Water Babies*, 51–52

knowledge, 139, 141; elaboration of new practice of in *Bleak House*, 132–35; professionals and disinterested, 115–16; unease at new forms of empirical and statistical, 142–43

laboring class. *See* working class

landed property: shift to population from, 10–11; sources of wealth vested in, 112

language: evolution of, 49–50

Lavater, Johann Casper: *Essays on Physiognomy*, 50, 201

leadership, 4, 8, 9, 10–16, 88; aristocracy and aligning of with use of force and masculine virility, 63–64; Bagehot on, 38–39; Carlyle on, 39–40; challenging of popular by Eliot in *Romola*, 171, 172, 181, 183, 186, 224, 227; and charisma, 10, 12, 13, 37; Coleridge on, 38; concern with after challenge to aristocratic prerogatives, 58–59; debates on constitutional in 1840s, 58–60; duality of glamour and ordinariness, 39; and Gladstone, 42–44; intellectual, 77; as location of representation, 12; and manipulative sincerity, 227; and mass meetings, 42; producing of own legitimacy in inclusive society, 11; requirement of conflict and conquest to constitute traditional model of, 11, 115; revisioning of,